C0-GJW-344

A Guide to Capital Expenditure Analysis

A Guide to Capital Expenditure Analysis

Moustafa H. Abdelsamad

amacom
A DIVISION OF AMERICAN MANAGEMENT ASSOCIATION

© 1973 AMACOM
A division of American Management Association, Inc., New York

All rights reserved. Printed in the United States of America.

This publication may not be reproduced, stored in a retrieval system, or transmitted in whole or in part, in any form or by any means, electronic, mechanical, photocopying, recording, or otherwise, without the prior written permission of the Association.

International standard book number: 0-8144-5301-5
Library of Congress catalog card number: 72-78298

First printing

To my father

Acknowledgments

OBVIOUSLY, this report on capital expenditure analysis as actually practiced by business firms would not have been possible without the help of business executives. Several executives, in particular, went out of their way to provide information and answers to my questions. They were kind and generous enough to grant me personal interviews and to provide copies of their capital expenditure analysis policies and procedures. To those individuals I am very grateful and deeply indebted. Unfortunately, because of the confidential nature of the material provided, they must remain anonymous.

A Guide to Capital Expenditure Analysis is based in part upon my doctoral dissertation* at The George Washington University. My thanks go to Dr. Edward J. Mock for his guidance as the chairman of my dissertation committee and for his help in cultivating the idea for this book.

I am grateful to George Terborgh, the developer of the MAPI method, who was, until his recent retirement, Research Director of the Machinery and Allied Products Institute. He permitted me a lengthy interview, answered many questions, read drafts of the MAPI chapter, and granted me permission to reproduce some of the MAPI charts and forms.

I wish to express my appreciation to the staff and executives of the Robertshaw Controls Company—and especially to H. N. Robinson, Controller—for allowing me several interviews and for reviewing parts of this book. I would also like to thank the Westinghouse Electric Corporation, the American Can Company, and TRW Inc. for granting permission to reprint excerpts from their manuals.

I am indebted to several of my colleagues at Virginia Commonwealth University: my close friend D. Robley Wood, Jr., for acting as a sounding board

*"Evaluating Capital Expenditure Proposals in Large Industrial Corporations" (completed in June 1970).

by reading drafts of the book and offering many helpful suggestions; Dr. Russell A. Johnston, Chairman of the Department of Business Administration and Management, for reducing my teaching load during the past year; Dr. A. M. Sharshar, for reviewing Chapter 4; Dr. Collin Bushway and Dr. Lawrence K. Finley, for reviewing the systems part of Chapter 1; and Ann R. Coates, my student assistant, for helping with miscellaneous duties.

My wife, Peggy, deserves special thanks for her help and encouragement and for doing miscellaneous research chores that helped to make my life easier. Also, I would like to thank Dorothy Couture for an excellent job of preparing the final draft of the book.

Moustafa H. Abdelsamad

Contents

About This Book

THIS book is designed to serve as a practical guide to capital expenditure analysis for financial and nonfinancial managers at all levels. More and more operating personnel are becoming involved in such analysis. However, careful review of the current literature reveals that many of the most valuable writings on this subject are directed to the ideal manager—one who is an expert on management theory and practice, up to date in accounting and finance, an economics expert, and, above all, a mastermind in mathematics. This approach, while enlightening and academically sound, does not serve the needs of the majority of operating managers.

This book will be different in that only a limited familiarity with mathematics will be required to understand and apply the material presented. The book is practical and progressive. The individual seeking more advanced material is referred to other works.

To be useful, a practical guide should combine theory and practice. With regard to theory, the popular methods of evaluating capital expenditures are discussed. This discussion is followed by an introduction to modern techniques, an examination of some of the key aspects of a good capital expenditure analysis system, and, finally, suggested applications of analysis to other capital expenditures. Methods and techniques are presented with an emphasis, not on their routine application, but on their conceptual framework and the assumptions upon which they are founded.

Five chapters are devoted to the commonly used methods of payback, accountant rate of return (ARR), discounted cash flow rate of return (DCFR), net present value (NPV), and MAPI. Since these methods are often explained in the literature, it may be asked why it is necessary to devote so much attention to them. Unfortunately, while these methods are commonly known (with the exception of MAPI) and commonly used, they are not always understood, and in practice a method is often employed to measure something it was not designed to measure.

The payback method, for instance, is used by approximately 80 percent of the largest industrial corporations in the United States. Some of those using the method treat it as a measure of profitability or as a measure of risk. Yet, payback does not measure profitability, but rather how fast an investment would be recovered. Likewise, it measures not risk, but how long capital would be invested with risk.

Research Procedure

The data on practices of business firms were collected by using a number of research methods to reduce the possible flaws of a single approach. In addition to a survey of the literature, two mail questionnaires were used, one related to methods used in the evaluation of capital expenditures and the other to the cost of capital. These were supplemented by personal interviews and by examination of more than 125 capital expenditure manuals, copies of company policies and procedures, and pieces of written correspondence.

Personal interviews were conducted with executives of 27 corporations. Ten of these were among the 1,000 largest industrial corporations, 9 were subsidiaries of large corporations, 2 were medium-size corporations, 5 were small corporations, and 1 was a railroad corporation. These companies were selected on a convenience basis from firms located in Virginia, Washington, D.C., and New York. In the 27 firms selected, interviews were conducted with 37 individuals involved in capital expenditure analysis.

Evaluation Questionnaire

After careful study of the problem, a tentative questionnaire was developed and pretested. The questions were so phrased that each part could be considered independently; a respondent could ignore some parts and still give a useful answer. The pretest responses were thoroughly studied for possible modifications of format.

This first questionnaire (hereafter referred to as the evaluation questionnaire) was sent to senior financial officers of 460 large industrial corporations in the United States, as listed in the June 15, 1968, *Fortune* directory. Positive replies were received from 200. (Negative replies refer to those replies in which the recipients indicated they were unable to answer the questionnaire because of company policy or lack of time.) The responding firms were classified by major industrial activity, according to the Standard Industrial Classification (S.I.C.) Code, obtained from *Poor's Register of Corporations, Directors and Executives.*

By virtue of their size, these companies are leaders in their fields. Their investment decisions have a significant effect on the level of economic activity, and the magnitude of capital expenditures they incur makes them an ideal population for research. Such companies are also more likely to respond to questionnaires, because of their interest in the topic and their desire to encourage research and maintain good public relations.

The tabulation of the positive and negative replies (see page 4) indicates how responses vary from industry to industry. The overall positive reply rate was 43.5 percent; however, the reply rates vary from 0 percent in the shipbuilding and railroad industries to 78.6 percent in the petroleum refining industry.

A 25 percent or higher positive response was achieved in 20 out of the 24 classifications; 15 of these showed a positive response greater than 40 percent. The replies therefore represent an adequate cross-section of the various industries. Coupled with the fact that a total of 200 firms participated in the study, this justifies generalizations about large corporations. For analysis purposes, it was decided that any industry with fewer than five completed questionnaires would not warrant a separate listing.

Current Usage of the Methods

Each respondent was asked to check, in order of importance, the method or methods currently used by his firm for evaluating capital expenditure proposals, once with respect to major projects (such as new facilities, major replacements, and overhauling) and again with respect to "all other projects" (such as routine projects, regular replacements, cost-saving projects, and other minor capital expenditures).

Advantages and Weaknesses of the Methods

Each respondent was asked to appraise the advantages of the method or methods used by his firm by grading them according to the following code: "2" for great advantage, "1" for slight advantage, and "0" for no advantage. The 13 suggested advantages were: (1) low in cost, (2) simple in use, (3) accurate, (4) well known, (5) easy to understand, (6) requires few assumptions, (7) analyzes future data–not historical, (8) uses market value, (9) can be used for evaluating different types of investment proposals, (10) considers the time value of money, (11) easy to postaudit, (12) easy to sell to top management, (13) easy to sell to operating personnel.

Questionnaires sent and positive and negative replies received, classified by industry

Industry	*No. of Questionnaires Sent*	*Positive Replies*		*Negative Replies*	
		No.	*%*	*No.*	*%*
1. Mining	7	5	71.4	0	0
2. Crude petroleum and Natural gas	16	9	56.3	1	6.3
3. Food and beverage	68	21	30.9	5	7.4
4. Tobacco	6	2	33.3	1	16.7
5. Textiles	18	5	27.8	0	0
6. Apparel	7	1	14.3	2	28.6
7. Paper and allied products	18	9	50.0	4	22.2
8. Publishing and printing	10	2	20.0	2	20.0
9. Chemicals	31	15	48.4	2	6.5
10. Pharmaceuticals	13	3	23.1	4	30.8
11. Soap and cosmetics	7	3	42.9	1	14.3
12. Petroleum refining	14	11	78.6	1	7.1
13. Rubber	12	7	58.3	2	16.7
14. Stone, clay, glass, and concrete products	13	7	53.8	1	7.7
15. Metal manufacturing	37	16	43.2	3	8.1
16. Metal products	22	10	45.5	1	4.5
17. Farm and industrial machinery	40	18	45.0	4	10.0
18. Office machines and other miscellaneous machines	16	8	50.0	1	6.3
19. Appliances, electronics	45	19	42.2	4	8.9
20. Motor vehicles and trucks	15	8	53.3	1	6.7
21. Aircraft	20	13	65.0	2	10.0
22. Shipbuilding and railroad	4	0	0	0	0
23. Measuring, scientific and photographic	13	5	38.5	3	23.1
24. Miscellaneous	8	3	37.5	2	25.0
Total	460	200	43.5	47	10.2

A similar approach was utilized in determining the weaknesses of evaluation methods, the code being: "2" for major weakness, "1" for minor weakness, and "0" for no weakness. The 12 suggested weaknesses were: (1) unnecessarily complicated, (2) too expensive, (3) imposes heavy demands on analysis staff personnel, (4) makes it difficult to delegate the decision-making process, (5) difficult to compare with accounting data, (6) places too much emphasis on estimates, (7) assumes that the company is resource-restricted, (8) overemphasizes profit as a goal, (9) does not allow for variation in depreciation rates, (10) places too much emphasis on quantitative aspects, (11) difficult to sell to top management, (12) difficult to sell to operating personnel.

Respondents were also asked whether the analysts, reviewers, and decision makers in their companies were familiar with the various methods.

Evaluation of Performance of the Methods

Each respondent was asked to check the phrase that best described the results achieved by the method or methods used. Four alternatives were offered: very satisfactory, fairly satisfactory, unsatisfactory, and no opinion. Each respondent was also asked to indicate whether his company had used any of the listed methods within the last five years and subsequently discontinued its use because of unsatisfactory results.

Appraisal of Problem Areas

Each respondent was given a list of sixteen problem areas and asked to rate each as no problem, minor problem, or major problem. (A complete list of the problem areas is given in Chapter 10.) He was asked to do the appraisal twice, once with reference to major projects in his corporation and again with respect to "all other projects."

Current Usage of Techniques

Respondents were also asked to check which techniques (sensitivity analysis, risk analysis, simulation and models, linear programming, PERT/CPM, and computer) are currently used by their companies. Additional questions dealt with postaudits, written policies, minimum amounts, and definition and classification of capital expenditures.

Cost-of- Capital Questionnaire

There is very little literature on the actual practices of business firms with respect to cost of capital. To obtain such information, a written questionnaire was prepared, pretested, and revised. The final version was a simple, two-page questionnaire. Each respondent was asked whether his firm computes the cost of capital, what the cost-of-capital figure is used for, whether his firm uses a single value or a range of values, whether one cost of capital is computed for the firm as a whole, how often his firm updates computations of cost of capital, what is meant by capital, whether the figure before or after taxes is used, how the cost of each type of capital (long-term borrowed capital, common-stock capital, preferred-stock capital, and retained earnings) is determined, whether retained earnings are treated as cost-free, whether the overall cost of capital is determined by a weighted average, and the range within which the firm's after-tax cost of capital falls.

This questionnaire was sent to top financial officers of 673 large industrial corporations in the United States, as listed in the May 1970 *Fortune* directory of the top 1,000 corporations. Completed questionnaires were received from 229 corporations (34 percent).

1 / Introduction

CAPITAL expenditure analysis is an activity of allocating limited resources to unlimited demands. A capital expenditure may be defined as any expenditure other than operating expenditures that represents a large sum of money, the benefits of which extend over a period of time exceeding one year. The key characteristic of a capital expenditure is that at least a major part of the expenditure is made at one point in time and the benefits are realized at different points in time (in the years to come).

The benefits expected are basically inflows of income or advantage resulting from the investment. Benefits may take the form of cost-saving, additional revenue, or profit. The method of computing benefits may depend upon the method of evaluation used. For example, benefits are defined as cash flows when the discounted rate of return method is used and as accounting income when the accountant rate of return method is used.

To appreciate the role played by capital expenditure analysis, let us start by reference to the broader idea of resource allocation.

Resource Allocation: Key to Profitability

While governments have the power to levy taxes to help finance their operations, business firms must earn a profit if they are to survive and grow. Top management in a business firm is entrusted with the challenging task of allocating the firm's limited resources to a variety of uses with the objective of making a profit, though not necessarily a maximum profit. Resource allocation is a challenging assignment. It is the key to profitability. The effectiveness with which this allocation process is performed may determine the growth or decline, survival or death, of a firm.

The allocation process is neither simple nor easy. A manager may be faced with a decision to expand operations by building a new factory or operating the old factory with more than one shift, by increasing the advertising budget or increasing door-to-door selling activities, or by assigning his best engineers to research on new products or improving current products. He may spend the greater part of his time in planning or on current operations.

Key Resources

Identifying the resources available to a business enterprise is a controversial issue. Peter Drucker, a well-known writer and management consultant, suggests that the two key resources are trained people and money.[1]

Alternatively, resources for a going concern may be viewed as equipment and facilities, personnel, money, and time. Trained personnel represent an important asset that does not usually appear on the balance sheet, yet the efficient allocation of this resource to different parts of the organization or to different uses within the organization is one of the keys to profitability.

Present equipment and facilities should be regarded as a resource. They must be allocated in such a way as to assure their most effective use.

Money is the most flexible resource since it can be used for a variety of needed activities. In addition, *money is the common denominator for the comparison of alternative courses of action.*

Time is not a readily apparent resource. Yet, business firms have only a limited number of hours available each working day, and it is as important to spend this time effectively as it is to spend money effectively. This applies to all segments and individuals in the organization.

Capital Budgeting: Sources and Uses

The sources of money for a corporation are shown on the right-hand side of a balance sheet. They may be divided into short-term sources (such as current liabilities and short-term loans), and long-term sources (such as long-term debt, preferred stock, common stock, and retained earnings).

The term capital budgeting is often used when referring to capital expenditure analysis. However, it is preferable to use capital budgeting, as is done in this book, to refer to the process of finding both the best sources and the best uses of long-term capital, with capital expenditure analysis comprising only the latter component.

Because of the large dollar amounts involved and its long-term nature, finding the best sources and uses of long-term capital is a key financial activity that usually plays a significant role in the success or failure of a firm.

Capital Expenditure Analysis

The nature and impact of capital expenditures on the firm's well-being were aptly cited in this summary statement by a large auto manufacturer:

> Capital expenditures involve long-term commitment of resources to realize future benefits. Hence, capital expenditures reflect basic company objectives and have a long-term and significant effect on the economic well-being of the firm.
>
> Effective planning and controlling of such expenditures are particularly important because (1) the long-term commitment increases financial risk, (2) the magnitude of expenditures is substantial and the penalties for unwise decisions are usually severe and (3) the decisions made in this area provide the structure that supports the operating activities of the firm.

Capital expenditures have attracted the attention of top management for quite some time. This attention is properly placed since capital expenditure decisions affect the whole firm and its direction, and they can be evaluated properly only at the highest managerial level in the organization. Even when some of these decisions are delegated, top management usually makes it mandatory to subject capital expenditure proposals to sufficient tests to assure that investments are made in the best interests of the company.

Many business failures can be traced to inadequate capital expenditures. The controller of a manufacturer of trade and custom design machinery recalled the dramatic effect of inadequate capital expenditures on his firm. The firm was unable to bid for jobs at a competitive level. Top management had tried the cost-cutting approach, with no success. Profits continued to decline until someone suggested talking to one of the firm's competitors to see how he could afford such low bids. The suggestion was followed, and the competitor indicated that he was operating at an advantage because of the use of modern electronic equipment that could do the same work at a much lower cost than his old equipment. It was immediately realized that the reason for the firm's high costs was its policy of replacing equipment when completely worn out, thus running an antiquated factory that could not operate at a competitive cost. The lessons learned were that the proper time for replacing equipment is often much earlier than when it is completely worn out, and that companies may fail because they have not made enough capital expenditures.

The large dollar amount of the usual capital expenditure may be regarded as both an evil and a blessing. It is an evil in that mistakes made here are very expensive and can result in the failure of an enterprise. It is a blessing in that a very small percentage improvement can result in a large dollar saving. By the same token, the small percentage saving gained through improvement in capital expenditure evaluation can justify a large expenditure to modify the system.

In evaluating a capital expenditure proposal, a comparison is usually made between costs and benefits to be derived. Since investments are usually made at points in time that do not necessarily coincide with the times when the benefits are received, difficulty arises. This difficulty is partially related to trying to find a common basis for comparing dollars incurred and dollars received at different points in time.

Methods of evaluating capital expenditures vary from the extremely simple to the extremely complicated. A proposed capital expenditure could be evaluated by merely inspecting the data, without further computation. A rule of thumb could be adhered to, such as replacement every six or seven years, or investment of an amount equal to depreciation. In addition, expenditures may be delayed until they can no longer be postponed.

On the other hand, more progressively advanced and efficient methods could be used, such as the Machinery and Allied Products Institute or MAPI formula, net present value, and discounted cash flow rate of return.

By its very nature, capital expenditure evaluation or analysis most often depends on estimates of the far distant future. And in some cases, benefits from an investment cannot be expressed quantitatively. Therefore, one can readily see that there are major problems associated with capital expenditure analysis.

The cumulative effect of investment decisions by individual firms involves employment, economic activity, and economic growth. Thus, a progressive program of capital expenditure analysis in a business firm may not only shape the future of the individual firm but also affect the economy as a whole. It may determine whether the facilities and equipment of a country are new and progressive or old and obsolete.

Capital Expenditure Analysis as a System

Capital expenditure analysis may be regarded as a system because it has a specific purpose, is part of a larger system, and is interdependent with other systems.[2]

Capital expenditure analysis may be viewed as a subsystem of the financial management system, which in turn is a subsystem of the firm, which again in turn is a part of the industry system. The scope of the discussion will be limited to the firm.

Purpose

Like other systems, the capital expenditure analysis system should have a specific purpose. Its objective is to provide information necessary for the effective management of capital expenditures. This objective should, of course, be consistent with the firm's objective. If the capital expenditure analysis system does not provide useful information, or if it functions in conflict with the objectives of the firm, its utility is of negative value.

Relationships

A system is essentially a set of relationships. The absolute essentials of a basic system model consist of an input, a process, and an output. A feedback and control component should be included. A simplified example of a manufacturing firm illustrates this: Raw materials, labor, and machines (inputs) are used together in a certain way (process) to get a product (output). Further, in terms of systems relationships, the inputs into the manufacturing firm are outputs of suppliers (other systems), and the product (output) of the firm will be inputs into other customers' systems.

To a flour mill, for example, wheat is an input, whereas this same wheat is an output of a farming system. The output of a flour mill (flour) is an input to the food manufacturer that uses flour as an ingredient. This, of course, is simple logic, and is not necessarily derived from general systems theory. What the general systems theory does suggest, however, is that things are not as simple as they seem, and it is possible to find some less obvious relationships. For example, assume that the flour is to be processed by a foods manufacturer into cereal. This cereal is inexpensive and used widely by low-income families.

At this point there arises the question of the nutritional adequacy of this food for these families if the processing of the wheat affects its nutritional value. The point in this hypothetical example is that a systematic set of relationships not evident in the original model may exist. An essential feature of general systems theory, therefore, is to analyze all possible sets of relationships, and not to be limited to those that are easily predictable and desirable. This is especially important in evaluating major capital expenditure proposals.

Capital expenditure analysis may be explained in terms of relationships–input, process, output. In considering any capital expenditure proposal, such as the proposal to build a new factory, inputs would include such information as the cost of building the factory, cost of the land, cost of trial runs, capacity of the factory, expected cash inflows (benefits), timing of cash flows, and information about alternatives and the accuracy of estimates. This information would be provided by different departments, such as marketing (market potential and price), engineering (feasibility of the project in terms of engineering, and maintenance problems), production (how many items can be produced at what rate and what cost), personnel (availability of different types of people, time required for training, required incentives), finance (availability of funds), and top management (long-range company plans and objectives). The inputs may also include computer time and other machine needs and outside consultants who may be hired to help with some aspects of the evaluation.

The process represents what is done with the input until it becomes an output. It includes all administrative and economic evaluation aspects of capital expenditure analysis. It includes ways of establishing priorities for the order in which proposals (or self-contained investment requests) are to be analyzed; the forms used; the method or combination of methods, and techniques of evaluating capital expenditures used; and evaluation reports and their distribution.

The output of the capital expenditure analysis system is a report that contains information about the proposal. This information may include a summary regarding the profitability of the proposed investment, recommendations for its approval or rejection, the best timing for its implementation, and some indication of the type of risk involved.

For capital expenditure analysis to be an effective subsystem, its output must be received by someone, for example, the executive committee. This committee may approve or reject the proposal. If it is approved, the proposal will be an input to the capital budget and the cash budget, as well as a host of other areas. If no one reviews the output, and the report is shelved, the capital expenditure analysis system will have failed and become an end unto itself rather than part of a larger system.

To be useful, a capital expenditure analysis report cannot be an end unto itself. Accordingly, such a report should be made with its users in mind. When several individuals with different training, backgrounds, and needs are to receive the report, it may be necessary to prepare several versions, varying in length and technical detail according to the users' needs. The persons preparing capital expenditure analysis reports should ask themselves, How can we make the report more useful to those who will receive it? If a report is sent to an individual with engineering training who is not expected to be familiar with highly specialized financial terms, these terms should be either avoided or explained, or a special summary report should be supplied.

Viewing capital expenditure analysis as a system has several implications. First, to improve the system, changes in the inputs or in the process are needed. This means also that lack of perfection in the estimates (inputs) does not justify using inefficient methods of evaluation (process). Second, the output is dependent upon the inputs. Wrong estimates of cash flows will result in the wrong measure of the economic worth of the proposed investment. Third, the value of the output should exceed the value of the inputs. The cost of evaluating capital expenditures should not exceed the value of the resulting information regarding the economic worth of the proposed capital expenditure.

The capital expenditure analysis needs to be examined, not only in its obvious relationships, but also in terms of relationships that exist but have not as yet been identified, defined, or discovered. A company that, ten years ago, thought of the effects of its factory on the environment would be ready to meet the ecology issue today or would have located in an area where air pollution was not and would not become a problem. Because of the long-term nature of any capital expenditure, it is necessary to try to uncover and study some of the less obvious relationships of these investments.

Feedback and Control

Another important component of the capital expenditure analysis system is that of feedback and control. In addition to the inputs, process, and output, feedback is required so that inputs can be adjusted to assure that the output is an effective input to the next related system. A concept of control is needed to assure that the necessary adjustments are made in the input side of the model. Useless or excessively costly inputs need to be eliminated, while better ones should be sought. In addition, feedback can help in determining the value and utility of the reports (output). Postaudits of capital expenditures and advice from users of the report are ways of getting feedback information necessary to improve the future output of the capital expenditure analysis system.

The components of a capital expenditure analysis system and their relationships are diagrammed in Figure 1.

Figure 1. Basic capital expenditure analysis model.

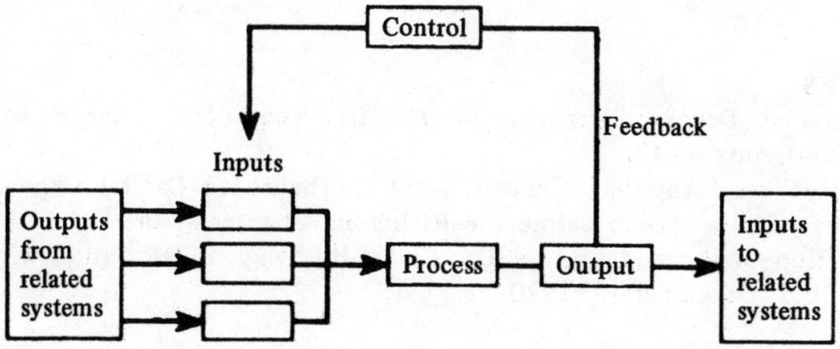

Maintaining a Dynamic System

The capital expenditure analysis system should accomplish its objective within the constraints placed upon it by top management in terms of manpower, operating expenses, and time limits. A progressive system is a dynamic one. A control element should be incorporated to sense changes in economic conditions, organizational objectives, information needs of key operating executives, and location of source data, and to "reprogram" itself internally to adapt to a constantly changing environment.

If a capital expenditure analysis system does not adapt to a changing environment, but continues to produce outputs in a constant and unchanging format that is not responsive to the needs of the larger system, it can be correctly judged a "closed" system. Major organizational changes might have to be made to prevent its eventual deterioration and adverse effects on other parts of the organization.

Some of the reasons why it is beneficial to view capital expenditure analysis as a system are these:

1. It is a way by which individuals involved in capital expenditure analysis can explain to others the purpose and the contribution of this part or subsystem to other parts of the organization.
2. By emphasizing relationships—that each system is dependent upon other supporting systems and is in itself a supporting system—it encourages all individuals involved in capital expenditure analysis to be aware of and sensitive to other people's problems. It encourages a spirit of teamwork.
3. This approach suggests looking for unseen and undiscovered relationships. This more realistic, more long-term and future-oriented look helps to avoid problems, to prepare for facing problems, and to discover and benefit from the work and ideas developed by other individuals in related fields.

In the following chapter, selected general capital expenditure evaluation guidelines are presented, and the more specific methods are discussed in later chapters.

NOTES

1. Peter F. Drucker, *Managing for Results* (New York: Harper & Row, 1964), pp. 46–47.
2. Based on "Applying General Systems Theory to Capital Expenditure Analysis," a speech before the Richmond Chapter of the National Association of Accountants by Dr. Collin Bushway in association with the author, December 17, 1970.

2 / Capital Expenditure Analysis: Rules of the Game

THE topic of capital expenditure analysis or evaluation has been under study for many years. Although many problems are not yet resolved, writers seem to have succeeded in the last few years in reaching what may be considered overall agreement on some broad, general rules or guidelines. Although it is possible to debate the value of steadfastly adhering to a given rule in a specific situation, these rules may be treated as generally acceptable.

This chapter presents briefly some of these general rules and points out some common fallacies with respect to capital expenditure analysis. Although this is not intended to be a complete list, it is hoped that the guidelines necessary for providing a common ground for discussion are included.

Rule 1: Capital Expenditures Include More Than Fixed Assets

A capital expenditure may be defined as any large expenditure from which the benefits are expected to be realized over a long period of time (more than one year). So defined, a capital expenditure has two main features: size and duration.

In terms of size, the expenditure must be large. The exact minimum dollar amount for an expenditure to qualify as a capital expenditure differs from one firm to another and possibly from one time to another in the same firm. All that is required is that the firm clearly state that minimum.

The minimum dollar amount for qualification as a capital expenditure should not be set too low or too high. A very low minimum results in unnecessary and costly analysis of small investments. By the same token, a very high minimum permits many expenditures to escape the rigorous analysis needed.

In terms of duration, a capital expenditure affects years to come—more than one year. The one-year minimum is an arbitrary but useful simplification of the definition. The basic idea is that, unlike operating expenditures, for which the benefits extend over a short period of time, the benefits from a capital expenditure extend over a number of years. As a corollary to this, a capital expenditure is distinguished by being irreversible in the sense that, once a decision is made, it cannot be reversed, or it can be reversed only at very high cost. For example, a decision is made to build an $8 million plant; it would be very expensive to reverse the decision and liquidate the investment after construction had started.

So defined, a capital expenditure does not have to result in an increase in a fixed-asset account. Accounting and tax considerations do not have relevance here. The emphasis for analysis purposes is on internal use. This means that an expenditure for a major advertising campaign should be treated as a capital expenditure as long as it is above the established minimum amount and the benefits are expected to be realized over a period longer than a year.

Other examples include research and development programs, long-term training and development programs, and early retirement of long-term debt.

It is true that some capital expenditures, as defined above, are hard to analyze quantitatively. However, it is important to recognize them as capital expenditures for at least two reasons. First, such recognition justifies a careful study of the expenditures. In terms of economic behavior, an expenditure for a research and development program (or for a long-term employee training and development program) is no different from an expenditure for buying a building or a piece of equipment; in both cases, the expenditure is incurred now and the benefits are expected later. The fact that the benefits from a research and development program are difficult to measure in quantitative terms does not change its definition as a capital expenditure; nor does it justify a less careful evaluation. Second, recognizing capital expenditures as such may encourage further research to find better ways of evaluating them. It is conceivable that in the near future it will be possible to measure the worthwhileness of advertising and similar expenditures in more quantitative terms. The recognition of such expenditures as capital expenditures is a first step in the right direction.

Rule 2: Capital Expenditure Analysis Includes Administrative and Economic Aspects

Capital expenditure analysis may conveniently be divided into two parts: administrative procedures and economic evaluation.[1] This classification is one of the best ways of conveniently dividing and studying the subject.

Administrative Procedures

Administrative procedures include all administrative aspects, from the search and initiation of a capital expenditure proposal to its approval and follow-up. They include written policies and procedures, authorization and approval levels, establishment of minimum amounts for considering an item as a capital expenditure, forms and flow of paperwork, capital expenditure classification, postaudits, preparation of capital budgets, and training in capital expenditure analysis.

Administrative procedures usually differ from one company to another. The ideal procedures are those that are tailored to the needs of a particular firm, its types of people, and its stage of growth.

A good administrative setup is prerequisite to an effective capital expenditure evaluation system.

Economic Evaluation

Economic evaluation, the second component of capital expenditure analysis activity, refers to the technical aspects of the evaluation. These involve all studies of available opportunities and selection of those worthy of further study, all related cost and market studies, and measurement of the profitability of the proposed capital expenditure. A good administrative setup cannot produce effective management of capital expenditures unless it is accompanied by a good economic evaluation system.

Purpose of Economic Evaluation. The general purpose of the economic evaluation of capital expenditures is to provide information that indicates the economic consequences of investment decisions. This information pertains to alternatives, consistency of the proposed expenditure with other plans of the company and its goals, an evaluation of the reliability of the estimates provided, the degree to which the proposal meets some established financial criterion, and the possible consequences of failure of the proposal to realize its estimated benefits.[2]

Project Evaluation as One of Four Key Steps. Project evaluation may be regarded as one of the four key steps of the economic evaluation of capital expenditures. The other steps are: project generation, project selection, and project execution.[3] Project generation is the first important step. (See Appendix A.) Without it, project evaluation, selection, and execution could not exist. Ways should be found to assure the continuous flow of an adequate number of proposals. Generally speaking, project generation is not a problem in large corporations. One financial officer indicated that in his company it is considered a status symbol by some department heads to be able to generate more proposals than could possibly be accepted. This led to the informal name "wish list" for the initial list of proposals—undoubtedly a healthy sign. However, companies, usually smaller concerns, that do not have a long list of projects to select from should devote more time and effort to increasing project generation by encouraging employees to submit ideas.

The next step is the evaluation of these proposals to provide information about their profitability. This step includes a primary screening of all proposals to eliminate those that are obviously poor and to identify those that are attractive. Those proposals that survive the primary screening are then analyzed and subjected to various tests. To assist in the evaluation process, one or more of several methods may be used—payback, accountant rate of return, discounted cash flow rate of return, net present value, and MAPI (to be discussed in Chapters 3, 4, 5, 6, and 7, respectively).

The following five questions may be considered common to all project evaluation problems:

1. What is the amount and timing of the cash outflow(s) or investment?
2. What are the amounts and timings of the cash inflows (benefits)?
3. What is the discounted cash flow rate of return on the proposed investment?
4. Does the rate of return exceed the cost of capital?
5. What are the qualitative aspects of the proposed capital expenditure?

The first question pertains to the cash outlays or costs of the proposal. The second question is related to estimating the benefits from the proposed investment. The third and fourth questions pertain to measuring the profitability of an investment using the discounted cash flow rate of return method and comparing the resulting rate with the cost of capital. A firm that does not use the discounted cash flow rate of return method should modify questions three and four. The last question is important in emphasizing the nonmonetary aspects of a capital expenditure proposal.

Third is the selection step, which is based on, but not necessarily restricted by, the quantitative results of the evaluation process. The quantitative measures provide some clues to the advisability of undertaking a capital expenditure proposal, but the decision maker should not be enslaved by the results of these quantitative measures. In making his decision, he will have to consider also the qualitative measures and use his judgment, with the quantitative measures playing the role of aids to his judgment and not of a replacement for it.

Finally, after a proposal is selected, it is executed, and the actual results are compared with the estimates. The execution stage is concerned with the carrying out of the project, the methods of dealing with any deviations from plans, and the follow-up reports. Progress reports and other postaudits provide the feedback link necessary to assure continual improvement of the capital expenditure analysis system through identifying past mistakes (so they will not be repeated) and areas that need corrective action.

Rule 3: Classify Capital Expenditures Whenever Possible

Classification of capital expenditures is the process of grouping similar capital expenditures into separate categories or classes. (See Appendix B.) Such classification can be of great assistance to management. Classification of capital expenditures allows grouping similar items together, which helps in summarizing the expenditures for budgeting purposes. It also helps in identifying the types of projects and the types of decisions that are needed, especially when those reviewing the projects are not the originators.

Also, different types of projects may require different types of analyses. Major projects require more in-depth analysis than minor projects. Projects with a measurable rate of return may need different treatment from projects with qualitative benefits.

A single ideal classification system for capital expenditures does not exist. The best classification is that which is tailored to the firm's needs and stage of development.

Unless there is a good reason to the contrary, the firm should specify certain classifications of capital expenditures. More discussion of this subject will be found in Chapter 11.

Rule 4: Consider Future Costs–Not "Sunk Costs"

The term costs here refers to all types of expenditures directly related to the proposed investment. Initial costs are also called cash outlay or investment. The preferred way of defining costs is in terms of cash flows.

Any "sunk costs" of past decisions should not be included; only future costs are relevant. An increase in costs of any kind resulting from the proposed project should be considered a cost of the project. When assets are converted for use by the project, the estimated benefits that would have occurred from the best alternative use of these assets will determine their cost to the project.

Estimation of costs is usually easier than estimation of benefits. The firm can normally use its past records and draw upon its own experience for estimating costs. Moreover, costs are ordinarily controlled by factors that are easier to estimate, within narrower error limits, than those controlling benefits.

The concept of a sunk cost needs more emphasis because it is often hard to accept in practice. For example, a firm has just purchased a specially made machine for $20,000. The machine has a six-year life expectancy, at the end of which the salvage value is zero.

The moment the machine is purchased, the $20,000 cost is sunk. It is sunk in the sense that the $20,000 is a historical cost, something of the past, that should not influence future decisions to keep or replace the machine.

To illustrate the point further, let us exaggerate and assume that only one day later a new, more efficient machine is made available. Let us further assume that the one-day-old machine, because of its specialized nature, could not be used for anything else and that it could not be sold at all. The new machine costs $15,000 and is expected to result in *additional* savings (after taxes) of $6,000 per year for the next six years of its life.

In evaluating the profitability of the new machine, should it be charged with the $20,000 loss on the old machine? (The tax effect of the loss is ignored to simplify the discussion.) The answer is positively no. The investment in the new machine should be evaluated on the basis of the incremental (additional) benefits derived from using it and the incremental (additional) investment required. If the return on the additional investment is satisfactory, the investment should be accepted, regardless of the loss on the old machine. To charge a new investment with the loss on an old investment is, in effect, punishing a new investment for past mistakes.

Rule 5: Consider Only Future Benefits–Not Past Benefits

Benefits are inflows of income or advantage resulting from an investment. Benefits may take several forms. For example, they may take the form of cost-saving, additional revenue, or profit. Estimating benefits is not usually an easy process because of the many variables involved. Economic conditions, competitors' strategies, consumers' tastes, and the state of technology are only a few of the many factors that should be considered when estimating benefits. The estimating process is complicated further because benefits are sometimes hard to express in monetary terms.

Regardless of the form of benefits for capital expenditure analysis purposes, the only relevant benefits are future benefits, not past benefits. For example. if a firm is planning to build a new factory that is expected to be in operation 4,000 hours a year, whereas the old factory operates 2,000 hours a year, the 4,000 hours is the relevant figure, not 2,000 hours.

Rule 6: Make Computations on an After-Tax Basis

Computations of the economic worth of capital expenditure proposals should be made on an after-tax basis. Income tax is a reality and must be included in any analysis of capital expenditure proposals that purports to be meaningful.

When the method of evaluating capital expenditures ignores taxes, this should be regarded as a weakness of the method. It is not correct to assume that if all capital expenditure proposals are compared on a before-tax basis the selection will be the same. Because tax treatments are not always identical from one proposal to another, ignoring taxes could lead to wrong conclusions about the profitability or the true worth of an investment.

Also, no meaningful comparison can be made with the after-tax cost of capital unless the computations consider taxes.

Rule 7: Consider the Time Value of Money

The concept of the time value of money, which means simply that a dollar received today is more valuable than a dollar to be received tomorrow or any time later, will be explained in more detail in Chapter 5. A method of evaluating capital expenditures that considers the time value of money is superior to a method that ignores the time value of money.

Rule 8: Quantify Whenever Possible, But Do Not Overdo It

A differentiation should be made between proposals that may be subjected to quantitative analysis and proposals that do not lend themselves to such an analysis. Although, whenever possible, an attempt should be made to estimate costs and benefits quantitatively, the quantitative analysis should not be forced upon every proposal without regard to whether or not the resulting estimates are meaningful. In the decision-making process a way has to be developed to deal with those proposals that do not qualify for quantitative analysis.

To supplement the quantitative measures, some firms require that each capital expenditure proposal be accompanied by information in narrative form. The following is a part of the capital appropriations section of the corporate financial procedure of a large industrial corporation, which exemplifies the type of narrative information that may be sought:

> Information in narrative form should accompany each request to explain fully the background and reasoning that have resulted in the proposed

investment. Complete and well-documented information will expedite prompt consideration of the proposal. The narrative might include the following as appropriate:

Present Situation. If new sales are involved, summarize the present market or contract situation. Indicate share of market and details of product price structure if appropriate. For competitive contracts, new business ventures, or expansion of existing business, include an analysis of the competition, their share of the market, unique capabilities compared with [the firm]. If increased capability or cost reduction is involved, describe the present operation. Explain where, how and why it is being carried out. Then explain what is wrong with the present situation, how and why it is inefficient or otherwise unsatisfactory. Whenever possible, show future implications of continuing the present situation. Describe capital equipment presently in use to be disposed of.

Proposed Project. Describe the purpose, scope and background of the proposed project and its relationship to the long range plans of the Division and Corporation. In the case of research, development and engineering projects, indicate the amount and timing of potential sales and profits. Identify specific programs and contracts if known. Replacement equipment projects should indicate the age, past and current maintenance costs, capacity and performance of existing equipment. List individual items of new equipment and their cost. Provide sufficient information for technical evaluation. Indicate the estimated starting and completion dates of the proposed project.

Alternatives. Discuss alternative courses of action which could be followed to accomplish the objectives of the project. Mention why they were rejected in favor of the chosen plan. Indicate consideration, if any, given to use of *surplus equipment at other divisions* and/or *government provided facilities.* Indicate whether the proposed facilities can be leased. Even if the facilities are to be leased, calculate the economic results on an ownership basis with a separate lease versus purchase calculation.

Timing. Give reasons for the amount and timing of the investment of corporate funds listed on [the Schedule of Investment form]. Indicate the consequences of delaying the project for six months to a year in terms of cash flow, return on investment, etc.

Economic Justification. The majority of investment proposals can and should be evaluated on the principles of discounted cash flow. The omission of such evaluation should be the exception rather than the rule. Where an economic justification is not included, the reasons should be given. . . .

Rule 9: Avoid Excessive Necessity-type Expenditures

At times, capital expenditure is a necessity if the firm intends to stay in business. An example of necessity for a railroad company is a washed-out bridge. But trying to compute a rate of return on such a necessity-type expenditure is a futile effort. By its very nature, however, a necessity-type project should be the exception rather than the rule. Care should be taken to avoid excessive use of the necessity classification as a way of "beating the system." Projects so classified should be reviewed carefully to assure that they are in reality necessary, urgent, and indispensable, and to guard against using the necessity classification as a free pass for unprofitable "pet" proposals.

Rule 10: Do Not Subscribe to the Profit Illusion

It is sometimes argued that since a firm is making satisfactory profits, the capital expenditure evaluation system must be perfect. This is not necessarily true.

It is possible for a firm to have an obsolete and ineffective capital expenditure analysis system and yet be profitable. The profit may be realized because of excellence in other areas, such as product design and quality, advertising, channels of distribution, or engineering staff. Capital expenditures may represent a very small part of the operation of the firm and thus have little influence on profitability. Also, it is possible that more profits could have been reported if a better capital expenditure evaluation system had been employed. Profitability and the adequacy of a capital expenditure analysis system are not synonymous; one can exist without the other.

Rule 11: Benefits from the Analysis Should Exceed Costs

Methods of capital expenditure analysis, like other yardsticks or measuring devices, aspire to measure something; in this case, the profitability of a certain proposal. Thus, they disclose information but they do not add to profits. Since the use of any method of capital expenditure analysis involves costs (time and money), care should be taken that costs of the analysis do not exceed the value of the additional information provided by that analysis. This means that the costs of the analysis should be less than the expected benefits to be derived through selecting better proposals because of the additional information.

Thus, while extensive study and more detailed analyses are usually needed for major projects, routine and minor projects should not be given the same extensive treatment. This does not mean that inefficient ways of analyzing proposals for minor projects are advocated, but rather that the analysis should not be carried beyond its marginal return.

Rule 12: Do Not Shy Away from Profit Maximization

One fundamental yet very controversial question is that of the objectives of capital expenditures. Some common objectives are maximizing short-term or long-term profits, maximizing opportunities, increasing the market share of the company, achieving the highest possible return on common stockholders' investments, maximizing the present value of stockholders' wealth, assuming the social responsibilities of a good community citizenship, building a good company image, boosting employee morale, and so on.

Objectives of capital expenditures may vary from one firm to another, from one time to another, and sometimes from one investment project to another. It is consistent, accordingly, for a firm to reject a project promising a 20 percent return on investment because it is below an established minimum, yet accept another project to improve morale of its employees with little or no tangible return.

One correspondent advised that, in his firm, the following general criteria would be considered in the evaluation of a capital expenditure proposal: (1) long-range objectives, (2) government regulations, (3) capacity, (4) cost and financial returns, and (5) personnel considerations.

Generally speaking, a firm has to earn profits if it is to stay in business. A conclusion to be derived is that, overall, the objective of capital expenditures is usually profit. The word "usually" is inserted here to allow for undertaking investments that contribute in intangible ways (such as those concerned with employee morale) and investments required by an authority (such as projects to reduce or eliminate pollution).

Rule 13: Consider Alternatives Whenever Possible

Whenever it is possible, a study of alternative courses of action should be made. In every investment situation there are at least two alternatives: do something, or do nothing.

The importance of studying alternative courses of action in capital investment analysis cannot be overemphasized. The study of alternatives may reveal opportunities or guard against fatal mistakes. An investment promising a 20 percent return may be quite acceptable, but a study of alternatives may reveal a substitute with a much higher return.

What types of alternatives? The analysis should concentrate on the most promising alternatives to enable the decision maker to select the best, yet eliminate unnecessary effort of considering the obviously poor or far less promising alternatives.

Rule 14: Use the Project Concept Whenever Possible

The project concept means that all investments that are to be undertaken together or that are part of a larger project should be studied as one unit. For example, if four machines have to be kept in total or replaced in total, the project concept requires that the investment in the four machines be treated as one project and not as four separate projects. This helps to provide a better analysis of the investment and guards against getting around authorization levels. (See Appendix A.)

The capital expenditure request section of the accounting manual of one responding firm defines a project in this way: "A project is a complete, self-contained program involving the acquisition of capital assets. Its completion or effectiveness is not dependent on approval of additional expenditures. It is unrelated to other projects in the sense that it cannot be construed as a phase of a larger program."

Rule 15: Use a Multitalent Approach Whenever Possible

Capital expenditures, by their very nature, may require many talents to evaluate their worth. The bigger and more involved the project, the more the need for different talents to evaluate it. It is almost impossible for one individual to be an expert in all areas. This means that, if needed, the opinions of several individuals or a committee should be sought before approving a proposal.

Whereas a top manager may consider the overall effect of the proposal on the firm as a whole and how it fits into other plans and activities, an individual with technical expertise may pass judgment on the feasibility of the project. The production department may be asked to determine whether the project under consideration can be implemented at the estimated costs. A marketing officer may be consulted to find whether market conditions are realistic, and a financial officer may study the effect of the proposed project on the cash budget and other financial aspects. Very large projects may require the help of outside consultants.

Rule 16: Capital Expenditure Analysis Is Both an Art and a Science

Capital expenditure analysis may be regarded as both an art and a science. It is a science in that there is a well established body of theory and techniques that can be employed. This means that it does not usually pay to ignore theory and to resort to inappropriate rule-of-thumb approaches or careless ways of evaluating capital expenditures.

Capital expenditure analysis is an art in that it is not a purely scientific exercise in a controlled experiment. The excellence of an analysis depends in large part on the subjective judgment of the decision maker, on his experience, on his ability to raise the right questions, and on his way of integrating all the piecemeal data before reaching a decision.

Rule 17: There Is No Substitute for Good Judgment

It is important to emphasize at this point that no method, technique, or system can replace the good judgment of the decision maker. All methods and techniques covered here are intended to enhance the judgment of operating managers and decision makers; they are in no way a substitute for it, but rather they complement it. A corollary is that there is no substitute for experience. An individual knowledgeable in the theory of investment analysis could not automatically assume a leading role in the analysis without some experience in actual practice. Of course, a person with adequate knowledge of the theory could acquire the necessary experience in a short time.

Rule 18: Do Not Overlook the Human Side of the Enterprise

It is the same old story: no system, no matter how perfect, can work without the cooperation and support of the people involved. To help gain the support for the capital expenditure analysis system, the logic behind such a system must be well understood by the people involved. This applies to top management personnel too. Unless they understand the methods and techniques employed, they can never fully use them. A training program from the top down may be required.

Resistance to change may be reduced by participative management and an explanation of why a change is needed. Also, it is important to remember that people need time to digest new ideas before they can accept them fully.

Fortunately, a good capital expenditure analysis system usually makes life much easier for all involved individuals. Although at times a more detailed and well-thought-through analysis may be required, a good system makes it easier for project originators to justify good proposals, for reviewers to make better decisions, and for good performers to be recognized and rewarded. All those involved should feel that their system is not only effective but fair.

Human relations cannot be overlooked in any job that involves dealing with people.

NOTES

1. Donald F. Istvan, *Capital Expenditure Decisions,* Indiana Business Report 33 (Bloomington: Indiana University, 1961), p. 2.
2. *Financial Analysis to Guide Capital Expenditure Decisions,* N.A.A. Research Report 43 (New York: National Association of Accountants, 1967), p. 114.
3. G. David Quirin, *The Capital Expenditure Decision* (Homewood, Ill.: Richard D. Irwin, 1967), p. 15.

3 / The Payback Method

THE payback method deserves a standing ovation, not because of its perfection but because of its persistence. Despite all the criticisms and condemnations of the payback method by almost every writer of capital investment analysis, this method has defied all attacks and is the most commonly used method of investment analysis, not only among the small and less proficiently managed firms, but also among the largest and most successful corporations in the United States.

This popularity of the payback method makes it both interesting and informative to describe. In addition to describing it, this chapter will highlight some of its key potentials and limitations and give some comments businessmen have made about the method.

It is important to emphasize that no method is either altogether good or altogether bad. Full understanding of each method and of its potentials and limitations is prerequisite to any progressive capital expenditure analysis program.

Definition and Characteristics of Payback

What Is Payback? The payback method (also known as the years to payback, the payoff, the payout, the cash recovery period, and the return period) is one of several methods of measuring the attractiveness of a capital expenditure proposal. Here, this attractiveness is measured in terms of a payback period. The time needed to receive benefits equivalent to the initial investment is the payback period. In other words, given a certain amount of investment, the payback period is simply the time required to recover this investment through the expected stream of benefits.

In practice, several variations are found with regard to what is considered an investment and how the benefits are measured. However, the payback concept should be applied to cash flows, the investment being the initial cash outflow and the benefits being the annual cash inflows (before deducting depreciation but after taxes).

For example, given a proposed capital expenditure of $50,000 with expected uniform benefits of $10,000 per year for 10 years, the payback period ($50,000 divided by $10,000) is 5 years. The value 5 means that if undertaken, this investment is expected to be paid back in 5 years.

The payback period may be used as a way of ranking various capital expenditure proposals. Under one approach the decision maker establishes a maximum payback period for accepting proposals, and any proposal with a payback period not exceeding this maximum is generally accepted. Another practice is to group investments into specific classifications and establish a maximum for each classification; for example, a maximum of five-year payback for major projects and three-year payback for minor projects.

In still other instances, the payback period is used merely to supplement other measures of evaluating the investment. Or, as stated in the corporate financial procedure of a large industrial corporation: "All other things being equal, preference will be given to those projects demonstrating the best rate of return on investment or, if the return is approximately the same for several requests, to projects with the shortest payout period."

When the payback method is used exclusively, a proposed capital expenditure is not usually approved unless the benefits are expected to continue beyond the payback period to assure covering the investment and an additional amount as a return on the investment. This extra period is usually determined according to some arbitrary rule of thumb based on experience or the judgment of the decision maker.

Some key characteristics of the payback method are cited below.

A Time Concept–Not a Profitability Measure

The payback period is a time concept. It does not measure profitability, but rather how fast the investment will be recovered. The fact that one investment has a shorter payback period than another investment does not guarantee that the former investment is more profitable than the latter. If any generalization is to be made, it is more sensible to assume that long-lived investments could and should earn more than short-lived investments.

Since the primary purpose of economic evaluation is usually to measure the profitability of a proposed investment, and payback does not measure profitability, the payback method should *not* be used exclusively for capital investment analysis. By its very nature, the payback method has a built-in bias against longer-lived investments with initially small but constantly increasing benefits. If carried to an extreme, use of the payback method could lead to investing capital in short-lived investments at the expense of more profitable long- and intermediate-lived investments.

EXAMPLE

Two investments, A and B, cost $10,000 each, with investment A earning $2,500 per year in the following six years and investment B earning nothing for three years followed by $2,000, $2,000, $3,000, $3,000, $3,000, $4,000, and $5,000 each year during the tenth to twentieth years. Investment A has a 4-year payback period, and investment B has a 7-year payback period (0 + 0 + 0 + $2,000 + $2,000 + $3,000 + $3,000). According to payback, the shorter-lived investment with a 4-year payback period will be selected as being superior to the other, longer-lived investment with 7-year payback. However, a careful examination of the figures (a method of computing rate of return will be discussed in Chapter 5) will indicate that the longer-lived investment B is much more profitable than investment A.

Computation by Division or Subtraction

The payback period could be arrived at by a process of division or subtraction. The division method of computing payback is acceptable when the annual cash inflows are uniform or practically so. When cash inflows vary from year to year, it is better to subtract the cash flows from the investment starting with the first year and proceeding until the declining investment figure reaches zero. The number of years required to get the investment back to zero is equal to the payback period. The following examples will illustrate this point.

EXAMPLE

A piece of equipment costs $10,000 to acquire and results in the following net cash flows (after taxes) over the next 10-year period: $1,500, $1,500, $1,000, $1,000, $2,500, $2,500, $2,000, $3,000, $3,000, $2,000.

What is the payback period using, first, the division process and then the subtraction process?

SOLUTION BY DIVISION

Total cash inflows = $1,500 + $1,500 + $1,000 + $1,000 + $2,500 + $2,500 + $2,000 + $3,000 + $3,000 + $2,000 = $20,000

$$\text{Average cash inflows} = \frac{\$20{,}000}{10} = \$2{,}000$$

$$\text{Payback} = \frac{\text{initial investment}}{\text{average cash inflows}} = \frac{\$10{,}000}{\$2{,}000} = 5 \text{ years}$$

SOLUTION BY SUBTRACTION

Number of years required to recover the investment ($10,000) may be determined by subtracting the annual benefits from the outstanding investment until the initial investment is fully recovered.

Year	*Benefits per Year*	*Outstanding Investment*
0	$ 0	$10,000
1	1,500	8,500
2	1,500	7,000
3	1,000	6,000
4	1,000	5,000
5	2,500	2,500
6	2,500	0

Payback period, the number of years required to bring the investment back to zero, is 6 years.

EXAMPLE

A piece of equipment costs $20,000 to acquire and is expected to generate the following net cash inflows: $2,000, $2,000, $2,000, $3,000, $4,000, $5,000, $4,000, $4,000, $4,000, $4,000.

What is the payback period, using a subtraction process?

SOLUTION BY SUBTRACTION

Year	*Benefits per Year*	*Outstanding Investment*
0	$ 0	$20,000
1	2,000	18,000
2	2,000	16,000
3	2,000	14,000
4	3,000	11,000
5	4,000	7,000
6	5,000	2,000
7 (½ of $4,000)*	2,000	0

*Since the remaining investment after the sixth year is $2,000, an amount equal to one-half of the expected benefits in the seventh year, the payback period is 6½ years. Obviously, the payback period could include a fraction of the year.

Cash Flows Computed from Net Income

Some firms arrive at annual cash inflows by adjusting accounting income. This is a useful shortcut, particularly when accounting income is easy to determine. In this case net income after taxes is determined in the same manner used by accountants to determine profit or loss. Then, depreciation and other similar deductions from income that did not result in cash outlays are added back to the figure of net income to arrive at cash flows. Finally, the payback period is determined by dividing this adjusted net income into total cash outlays (or found by subtraction if the cash flows differ from year to year).

It is not correct, however, to use accounting income without adjustment in computing payback period since that would involve recovering the investment twice: once in the form of depreciation and again in the form of benefits.

EXAMPLE

A $10,000 investment with $2,500 expected cash inflows (after taxes and before depreciation) and $2,000 annual depreciation (straight-line over a 5-year period with no salvage value) has a payback period of 4 years and not 20 years ($10,000 divided by $500 of cash inflows after depreciation). The latter method is wrong because the deduction of $2,000 from cash inflows results in recovering the investment twice: once in the form of $2,000 depreciation and another time in the form of $500 cash inflows.

Cash Flows After the Payback Period

The payback period does not consider cash flows after the investment is recovered. Thus, proceeds and any salvage value that occur after the payback period are usually ignored in the computations, although the profitability of an investment is dependent upon them. The following example illustrates what may be regarded as a shortsightedness inherent in the payback concept when used to evaluate capital expenditure proposals.

EXAMPLE

Compute the payback period for two investments, A and B, of $10,000 each. Cash inflows are:

Year	*Investment A*	*Investment B*
1	$2,500	$2,500
2	2,500	2,500
3	2,500	2,500
4	2,500	2,500

Year	*Investment A*	*Investment B*
5	$2,500	$2,500
6	2,500	0
7	2,500	0
8	2,500	0
9	2,500	0

SOLUTION

The cash inflows are uniform for both proposals. Therefore, the averaging method is used:

$$\text{Payback period for investment A} = \frac{\text{initial investment}}{\text{average cash inflows}} = \frac{\$10{,}000}{\$2{,}500} = 4 \text{ years}$$

$$\text{Payback period for investment B} = \frac{\$10{,}000}{\$2{,}500} = 4 \text{ years}$$

Investment A has the same payback period as investment B, which could lead to the conclusion that they are equally desirable. However, it is clear that investment A is superior to investment B since it continues to generate income after the fifth year for an additional 4-year period.

Time Value of Money

The payback method does not consider the time value of money. (A method of computing payback that considers the time value of money—discounted payback—will be discussed in Chapter 8.) However, in our world where interest exists, a dollar received today should be treated as worth more than a dollar to be received tomorrow or any time later. The fact that the payback method ignores the time value of money is illustrated by the following example.

EXAMPLE

Two proposals (again using investments A and B, of $10,000 each) are under consideration, with the following estimates of benefits:

Year	*Investment A*	*Investment B*
1	$5,000	$1,000
2	3,000	1,000
3	1,000	3,000
4	1,000	5,000
5	2,000	2,000

Year	*Investment A*	*Investment B*
6	$2,000	$2,000
7	2,000	2,000

Compute the payback period and comment on the answers.

SOLUTION

The payback period in both cases is 4 years. Investment A is much better than investment B considering the time value of money, since the higher cash inflows are received earlier. Despite this obvious difference between the two proposals, the payback method ranks them equally. Thus, payback treats all benefits received during the payback period equally, as if a dollar to be received one year from now were of the same value to the firm as a dollar to be received three or five years from now.

	Investment A		*Investment B*	
Year	*Annual Benefits*	*Outstanding Investment*	*Annual Benefits*	*Outstanding Investment*
0	$ 0	$10,000	$ 0	$10,000
1	5,000	5,000	1,000	9,000
2	3,000	2,000	1,000	8,000
3	1,000	1,000	3,000	5,000
4	1,000	0	5,000	0

Payback Reciprocal and DCFR

When the annual cash flows from the investment are uniform and are expected to continue for much longer than the payback period (approximately twice as long as the payback period), the reciprocal of the payback (1 divided by the payback period) gives a rate close to that found by using the theoretically superior DCFR (discounted cash flow rate of return) method. This method will be discussed in detail in Chapter 5.

EXAMPLE

A $10,000 investment that returns $2,000 per year for 30 years has a payback period of 5 years and a reciprocal payback period of one-fifth, or 20 percent. The discounted cash flow rate of return for this project is about 19.92193 percent, which is very close to 20 percent.

Since these assumptions of uniform cash flows and extensive life are not very common, it is not justifiable to generalize by saying that the reciprocal of payback always gives a close approximation to the discounted cash flow rate of return.

Risk

The payback period may provide some indication of risk. (The term "risk" is used here instead of "uncertainty" since it is common practice to use the word "risk" in this regard.) The assumption here is that the longer the payback period, the more chance that things could go wrong. Insofar as providing one clue to indicate an element of risk, the payback is useful; however, to say that the payback offers a full measurement of risk is incorrect.

EXAMPLE

A 2-year investment in any venture is commonly regarded as more risky than a 20-year purchase of U. S. government bonds, which are, for all practical purposes, risk-free. In other words, it should be emphasized that payback does not necessarily measure risk but rather how long capital would be invested with risk.

When Payback Is Useful

The payback period becomes an ideal measure of the desirability of an investment in situations in which the speed of recovering the investment is critical. These situations occur when a company has cash problems, when the product a company is selling usually lasts for a short period of time, when the proposed investment is known to have a high degree of obsolescence, when a company is working under a government contract that may be canceled on short notice, or, in foreign investments, when the possibility of adverse governmental action exists.

Payback is useful when used as a supplementary method. For example, it can be used as a quick screening device to identify very poor or very good investments. Also, it can be used to indicate the cash return pattern of an investment and the effect of a proposal on the cash budget. It can help in evaluating the sensitivity of the returns of an investment to different estimates of its life (sensitivity analysis is discussed in Chapter 9). The payback method can be used for evaluating minor capital expenditure proposals when the investments are small and the cost of using more sophisticated methods of analysis exceeds the possible benefits from the refinement in such analysis. Finally, payback may be used if estimates of cash flows are unreliable and the life of the proposed investment is undeterminable.

Payback in Practice

Despite all the shortcomings of payback from the theoretical viewpoint, it is very popular in practice. The responses to the author's questionnaire indicate that the payback method is used extensively by large industrial corporations in the United States. Of the responding firms 80 percent use payback for evaluating major projects such as new facilities, major replacements, and overhauling. An accurate perspective of the popularity of payback may be obtained by comparing it with the other basic methods that are used. The basic methods for evaluating major projects, in order of usage, are shown in Table 1.

Table 1. Basic methods used for evaluating major projects.

Method	*No. of Companies**
Payback	158
DCFR (yield, or internal rate of return)	136
Accountant rate of return	113
Net present value	49
MAPI	18

*The total number of responding firms is 197 for major projects. The total of this column exceeds the total number of responding firms because a majority of the respondents use more than one method.

Thus, payback is the most commonly used method of evaluating major capital expenditure proposals by large industrial corporations, followed by DCFR, accountant rate of return, net present value, and MAPI formula.

For undertakings other than major projects, referred to here as "all other projects" (such as projects of a routine nature, regular replacements, cost savings, and other minor capital expenditures), the payback method is used by 80 percent of the responding firms. The methods for "all other projects," ranked in order of usage, are shown in Table 2.

Table 2. Basic methods used for evaluating "all other projects."

Method	*No. of Companies**
Payback	151
Accountant rate of return	105
DCFR	102
Net present value	37
MAPI	16

*The total number of responding firms is 189. The total of this column exceeds the total number of responding firms because a majority of the respondents use more than one method.

Again, payback is the most commonly used method of evaluating the "all other projects" category of capital expenditure proposals. Payback is followed by accountant rate of return, DCFR, net present value, and MAPI formula.

These results strengthen and support the common belief, and the data provided by preceding studies, that payback is the most popular method of evaluating capital expenditures.

Over the past 20 years several studies have been made of practices of business firms with regard to evaluating capital expenditure proposals generally. All these studies indicate that the payback method is the most commonly used method of evaluation. A 1956 study of equipment replacement and depreciation policies and practices, by the Machinery and Allied Products Institute, found that 60 percent of the surveyed firms used payback.[1] Two years later, Frank Schwab, Jr., after surveying 75 of the 500 largest corporations, concluded that the payback method was the most common evaluation method used by these corporations.[2]

Donald F. Istvan found that 34 of 48 large firms (71 percent) were using payback. Of these, 13 firms used payback as the primary method, whereas the remaining 21 firms used it to supplement other methods.[3]

In a study of 127 "well-managed" companies, James H. Miller found that 66 of 127 firms (52 percent) used payback, and of these, 18 firms used it exclusively.[4]

The National Association of Accountants' Research Report 43 issued in 1967 indicated that, of 28 companies studied, practically all used payback to evaluate capital expenditure proposals. Only one of these firms used payback exclusively.[5]

Very few studies have been made of capital expenditure analysis practices in small businesses; however, it seems that payback is extensively used in small businesses also.[6]

Despite the continuing popularity of payback, two basic changes have occurred over the years. First, the payback method is not as commonly used by large industrial corporations as the only method of evaluating capital expenditure proposals as was the case about 20 years ago. Of the 158 responding firms that indicated they use payback for major projects, only 7 use it exclusively. For "all other projects," only 20 of 151 firms use payback alone.

The second change is that the payback method has lost its ranking as the most important method of capital expenditure evaluation. Respondents were asked to rank the methods used in the order of their importance. The results are given in Tables 3 and 4.

Table 3. Importance of methods used for major projects.

Method	*No. of Firms That Consider the Method Most Important*	*Percentage**
DCFR	93	68
Accountant rate of return	58	51
Net present value	14	29
Payback	45	28
MAPI	1	6

*Those respondents who consider the method most important, as a percentage of the number of firms using the method.

Table 4. Importance of methods used for "all other projects."

Method	*No. of Firms That Consider the Method Most Important*	*Percentage**
Accountant rate of return	56	53
DCFR	53	52
Payback	57	38
Net present value	8	22
MAPI	3	19

*Those respondents who consider the method most important, as a percentage of the number of firms using the method.

Thus, the respondents place payback fourth in importance for evaluating major projects, preceded by DCFR, accountant rate of return, and net present value. Payback is placed third in importance for evaluating "all other projects."

Advantages

Each respondent was given a list of thirteen suggested advantages* and was asked to appraise each advantage, with respect to the methods, as "great advantage," "slight advantage," or "no advantage."

The list of suggested advantages was checked with respect to the payback method by 133 respondents. It is felt that an advantage should not be con-

*These advantages are enumerated on page 3.

sidered a real advantage unless at least half of the respondents regard it as either a great or a slight advantage. Furthermore, it is felt that if the respondent thinks that a suggested advantage is an advantage to him, it is in effect a real advantage, regardless of what others may feel or believe. Accordingly, there are nine practical advantages to the payback method.

These advantages may be ranked in the order of being an advantage (either great or slight) as shown in Table 5.

Table 5. Chief advantages of the payback method.

Advantage	*Percentage of Respondents*
Easy to understand	94
Simple in use	93
Well known	88
Easy to sell to operating personnel	83
Easy to sell to top management	81
Low in cost	70
Easy to postaudit	64
Requires few assumptions	50
Can be used for evaluating different types of investment proposals	50

It is not surprising that the top three advantages of using payback are that it is easy to understand, simple in use, and well known. All that is required to use payback is an estimate of the investment and the expected benefits, and in many cases these benefits are estimated on an average basis. Unlike the discounted cash flow method, to be discussed in Chapter 5, the payback method does not require detailed estimates of cash flows and their timings after the payback period.

Two advantages of payback are believed worthy of further analysis: easy to sell to operating personnel, and easy to sell to top management. During the course of personal interviews and other contacts with financial officers, these two advantages were cited as primary reasons for using simple methods like payback, even though some of these individuals stated that they were personally convinced that other, more refined methods could be more beneficial to the company.

Because it is easy to understand, the payback method is popular with operating personnel who have an interest in a capital expenditure proposal. But should popularity be the criterion for selecting a method for capital expenditure evaluation?

Because of the importance of capital expenditure decisions, top management usually maintains the final authority to approve or disapprove those decisions. It is possible, furthermore, that the head of financial planning or the top analyst of capital expenditure proposals might find it difficult to convince top management personnel because of their varied backgrounds to accept the results of more complex, but more refined, methods of evaluating capital expenditure proposals.

Weaknesses

As was the case with advantages, each respondent was given a list of 12 suggested weaknesses* and was asked to appraise each weakness as minor, major, or no weakness. The list of weaknesses with respect to payback was checked by 116 respondents. None of the 12 suggested weaknesses are considered *real* weaknesses by the respondents.

Familiarity with Payback

The respondents were asked to indicate whether the analysts, reviewers, and decision makers in their company were familiar with selected methods of evaluation. Of 188 respondents, 99 percent feel that such persons are familiar with payback. This degree of familiarity is very high when compared to that of other methods, such as accountant rate of return (91 percent), DCFR (77 percent), net present value (59 percent), and MAPI formula (22 percent). The fact that payback is so familiar to analysts, reviewers, and decision makers offers a good explanation for its popularity.

Evaluation of Payback Performance

Each respondent was asked to check the phrase (very satisfactory, fairly satisfactory, unsatisfactory, or no opinion) that best describes the results achieved by the method or methods used by his firm. The 159 responses related to payback are distributed as follows: 38, very satisfactory (24 percent); 103, fairly satisfactory (65 percent); 15, unsatisfactory (9 percent); and 3, no opinion (2 percent). When the total of very satisfactory is expressed as a percentage of total responses, these five methods are ranked as follows: DCFR, payback, net present value, accountant rate of return, and MAPI formula. However, when the totals of very satisfactory and fairly

*These weaknesses are enumerated on page 5.

satisfactory are combined and expressed as a percentage of total responses, a minor change in the order occurs: DCFR, payback, accountant rate of return, net present value, and MAPI.

These results suggest that payback, as it is used in practice, is placed second as a very satisfactory or satisfactory method of evaluating capital expenditure proposals.

Discontinued as Unsatisfactory

Each respondent was asked to check whether his company has used any of the listed methods within the last five years and subsequently discontinued its use because of unsatisfactory results. The replies regarding payback are: 17 yes, 112 no, and 6 not sure. The 17 yes replies, expressed as a percentage of yes, no, and not sure, represent 13 percent for payback. This compares to 20 percent for accountant rate of return, 9 percent for MAPI, 8 percent for net present value, and 6 percent for DCFR. Thus, payback is placed second among methods discontinued as unsatisfactory. The number of companies that discontinued this method is not large enough to indicate general dissatisfaction with payback.

Typical Comments

The assistant financial vice-president of a large metal manufacturing company pointed out that there are at least three instances in which payback is the best method. In these instances, investments with short payback periods are desirable. First, for very risky projects (such as projects undertaken in foreign countries where it is hard to forecast the attitude of the foreign government toward American investments), generally the shorter the payback period, the more desirable the investment. Second, in some types of mining activities, where the extracted product could discontinue flowing at any time, the importance of a short payback period is increased. Finally, for investments in certain products, such as plastics, if the firm does not recover its investment in a short period a loss is certain to occur since it is known that competitors will quickly produce similar products and thus dilute the market.

According to the treasurer of a subsidiary of a large electronics manufacturer, it is important to get back invested capital as soon as possible because of the nature of the company's business. The company depends on government contracts, which are likely to be canceled at any time Congress wishes. The company requires, generally, a maximum of four years' payback period from proposed investments. Furthermore, whenever it is possible, facilities are leased rather than purchased because they would be of little use to the company if its contract were canceled or not renewed because of a cut in the government's budget.

The controller of a large tobacco manufacturing company who uses payback and DCFR methods was asked to explain why he uses payback even though he indicated that it is not a perfect method. He explained that individuals who have final authority to approve capital expenditure proposals know the method and ask for it. This or a very similar statement was made by financial officers time and again.

"Payback is great," said the executive vice-president of a large electronics manufacturing company. "It is easy to understand and it makes sense." In the same company the director of capital expenditure investment planning, who assumes a large role in capital investment analysis and decision making, stated that payback backfires.

When asked, "Why do you use payback?" the vice-president and chairman of the capital expenditures committee of a large beverage and food manufacturing company, who uses a combination of methods (DCFR, accountant rate of return, and payback), explained that payback is an easy early indicator, a primary screening device.

All the above remarks by financial officers of different corporations lead to the basic conclusion that payback is lasting because top management, at the highest level, nourishes it and fosters it.

Conclusion

It is incorrect to say that payback is altogether good or altogether bad. The payback method should not be viewed as a measure of profitability. Used to supplement other methods, it can provide useful information. Any firm that uses payback exclusively for capital investment analysis should examine its position periodically to see whether its exclusive use of payback is still warranted or is due to resistance to change.

NOTES

1. *Equipment Replacement and Depreciation Policies and Practices: A Survey* (Washington, D.C.: Machinery and Allied Products Institute, 1956), p. 7.
2. Frank Schwab, Jr., "Capital Expenditure Evaluation," *The Controller,* Vol. 26, No. 8 (August 1958), p. 359.

3. Donald F. Istvan, "The Capital-Expenditure Decision-Making Process in Forty-eight Large Corporations" (D.B.A. dissertation, Indiana University School of Business, 1959), p. 177.
4. James H. Miller, "A Glimpse at Practice in Calculating and Using Return on Investment," *N.A.A. Bulletin,* Vol. 41, No. 10 (June 1960), p. 72.
5. *Financial Analysis to Guide Capital Expenditure Decisions,* N.A.A. Research Report 43 (New York: National Association of Accountants, 1967), p. 66.
6. The reader will find more information about capital expenditure decisions in small businesses in *Investment Decisions in Small Business,* by Martin B. Solomon, Jr. (Small Business Management Research Reports prepared by the University of Kentucky for the Small Business Administration, Washington, D.C., published under the University of Kentucky Studies Program [Lexington: 1963]).

4 / Accountant Rate of Return

NEXT to payback popularity comes the accountant rate of return (ARR) method of evaluating capital expenditure proposals. It is so called because the benefits are usually measured in terms of accounting concepts. However, the term does not reflect a general acceptance of the method by accountants. Basically, this method compares the annual expected benefits from an investment with the amount to be invested in a project and expresses this relationship as a percentage return on investment.

The accountant rate of return method is also known as the accounting method, the simple rate of return method, the initial year rate of return method, the average rate of return method, the average annual return on investment method, the unadjusted rate of return method, the financial statement method, the simple return on investment method, the net return on investment method, and the return on investment by the financial statement method.

It is quite legitimate to say, then, that there are, in essence, many accounting rate of return methods. These variations are due to the wide differences in practices of computing the accountant rate of return. However, two features common to all these variations justify studying them as a unit and referring to the accountant rate of return as one method. The two features commonly shared by all versions of accountant rate of return are: using accounting concepts in determining benefits, and making no adjustment for the time value of money (the idea that a dollar received today is more valuable than a dollar to be received any time later).

The popularity of this method of evaluating capital expenditures may be attributed to the familiarity of businessmen with both rate-of-return language and accounting concepts.

A question frequently raised is, If accounting concepts and methods are good enough for reporting the results of operations and the financial condition of the firm, is the accountant rate of return good enough for evaluating capital expenditures? Not necessarily.

45 / Accountant Rate of Return

What Is Accountant Rate of Return?

Like payback, the accountant rate of return method is designed to measure the attractiveness of a proposed capital expenditure. Whereas the payback method is a time concept, the ARR is a measure of profitability.

For example, if an investment of $100 will result in an annual return of $6, the rate of return on this investment is 6 percent ($6 return divided by $100 investment). The objective of using this method is to obtain a figure that represents the rate of return expected to be earned on a proposed investment. This rate is determined by dividing an income figure by an investment figure.

The accountant rate of return calculated by this method is considered superior to the payback method, not only because it measures profitability, but also because it usually includes the proceeds after payback and it allows ranking investments according to their respective returns. Furthermore, the computed return could be compared with an established minimum to determine the degree of attractiveness of a proposed investment.

Characteristics of Accountant Rate of Return

Several characteristics of the accountant rate of return are discussed here to provide a better understanding of this method.

Ways of Computing Accountant Rate of Return

There are at least 864 possible ways of computing the accountant rate of return. Differences exist because of the wide variance in ways of determining the benefits and the investment.

Benefits. Benefits can be determined in a number of ways. They may be defined as first year's income, each year's income, or an average income (the total benefits during the life of the investment divided by the number of years). Income may be figured before or after depreciation, and more possibilities result from considering also the types of depreciation that could be used, such as straight-line, declining-balance, or sum-of-the-years-digits. The income may also be figured before or after deducting a financing cost for use of capital, and before or after corporate taxes.

1. Advocates of *first year's income* argue that most likely the first year will be representative of other years, the estimate will be a conservative one, and it is easier to forecast benefits for one year than for a longer period of time. Advocates of *each year's income* argue that without estimating income for each year of the life of the investment the analysis is incomplete, and that quite often income from an investment fluctuates from one year to another.

Some firms select certain typical years rather than a single year or every year. For example, in one company, the financial officer in charge of capital expenditures indicated that he figures the benefits (and the rate of return) for three years of the life of the project: the first, third, and fifth. These three years are usually found by that company to be the most important and representative years of the life of an investment. Fluctuations in the benefits and the extent and direction of such fluctuations are usually uncovered from the first-, third-, and fifth-year estimates of benefits.

2. Those who believe in *averaging benefits* argue that an investment should be viewed as one unit and that the best estimate is one based on an average of all years. Furthermore, errors in forecasting each year's benefits are minimized by averaging.

3. Whether to deduct *depreciation* or not is another issue. To some people, depreciation represents an allocation of the cost of the asset and should be deducted before arriving at net income. To others, depreciation is irrelevant for capital expenditure analysis since it does not represent an actual cash outlay but rather a journal entry. The usual practice when using accountant rate of return is to deduct depreciation in accordance with financial accounting practice before arriving at net income reported on the profit-and-loss statement.

4. The handling of *finance charges* is also a controversial issue. Proponents of charging the cost of financing to the investment maintain that capital is not free—it costs money. Therefore, the cost of money in the form of a finance charge on the amount of capital tied up in the investment should be considered. The opposing viewpoint, of ignoring finance charges, is more acceptable on the grounds that any finance charge would be an unrealistic, arbitrary value; if the same finance charge is applied to all projects, it would not affect their relative standing and would be unnecessary. Furthermore, the practice of using different finance rates with different types of investments is usually unacceptable since funds available should be treated as one unit, with one cost. Allowing different finance charges for different investments is discriminatory but warranted under very special conditions (for example, in some foreign investment projects financed specifically from an identifiable source). Finally, if the finance charge is considered, the result is then a double counting: first when computing the accountant rate of return, and again when computing the cost of capital or cutoff point.

5. Figuring income from an investment *before or after deducting taxes* is another debatable issue. Advocates of using income before taxes argue that taxes complicate but do not change the relative standing of proposals and that the typical manager, since he has no control over taxes, should be con-

cerned only with benefits before taxes. Advocates of deducting taxes have the stronger argument that tax is a reality; that different proposals may require different treatment, and this should be reflected in the evaluation of the project; and that only profits after taxes are relevant when comparing the rate of return with the after-tax cost of acquiring long-term capital.

Figure 2. Ways of computing benefits using accountant rate of return.

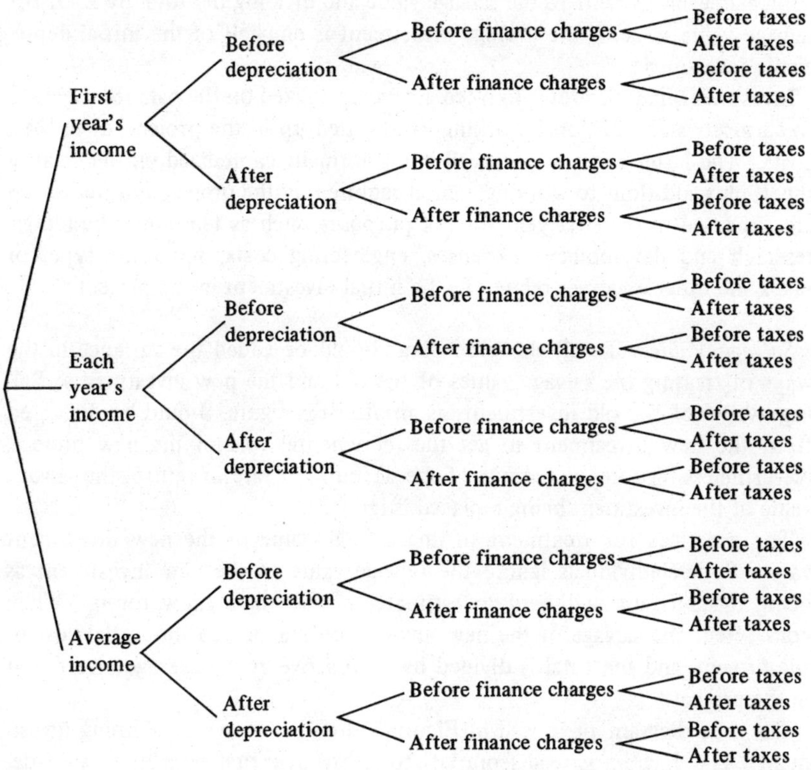

Figure 2 is a tree diagram that shows 24 ways of computing benefits. The diagram is read from left to right. The first possible way of defining income may be read, for example, as the first year's income before depreciation, before finance charges, and before taxes. The last possibility, then, is read as average income after depreciation, after finance charges, and after taxes.

Investment. Another source of variation lies in the way of computing the investment figure. Investment may be defined as the original investment, the average investment for a given year, or the average investment for the life of the project. The use of the average rather than initial investment in the calculations is more acceptable because it is assumed that part of the investment is recovered through depreciation and because the use of the initial investment underestimates the rate of return on the investment. The average investment for the life of the project may be computed by adding the initial depreciable investment to the salvage value and dividing the total by 2. If the salvage value is zero, the average investment is one-half of the initial depreciable investment.

Investment may also refer to fixed assets capitalized on the balance sheet, to fixed assets and additional working capital tied up in the project, or to total costs. The latter reference is to all items normally capitalized on the balance sheet, plus additions to working capital required by the project and items that are expensed in the first year for tax purposes, such as temporary buildings, research and development expenses, engineering costs, and some types of taxes and other expenses related to the initial investment in the project.

Salvage Value. To all the preceding should be added the variance in the ways of treating the salvage values of the old and the new investments. Salvage value of the old investment, as an after-tax figure, should be deducted from the new investment to get the incremental cost of the new project. Nevertheless, in some variations of the accountant rate of return, the salvage value of the investment being replaced is ignored.

The practices for treatment of the salvage value of the new investment vary. Some individuals ignore the salvage value of the new investment as being insignificant and hard to estimate, while others allow for it. When considered, the salvage of the new investment is added to the initial cost of the project, and the total is divided by 2 to arrive at the average investment in the project.

The tree diagram presented in Figure 3 shows 36 ways of defining investment. The diagram is read from left to right. The first possible way of defining investment may be read, for example, as the original investment in fixed assets, adjusted for the salvage values of both the old and the new investments. The last possibility, then, is read as the average investment in fixed assets, working capital, and expenses, not adjusted for the salvage value of either the old investment or the new investment.

It has been shown that there are 24 possible ways of determining benefits and 36 possible ways of computing investment. The combined number of

Figure 3. Ways of defining investment using accountant rate of return.

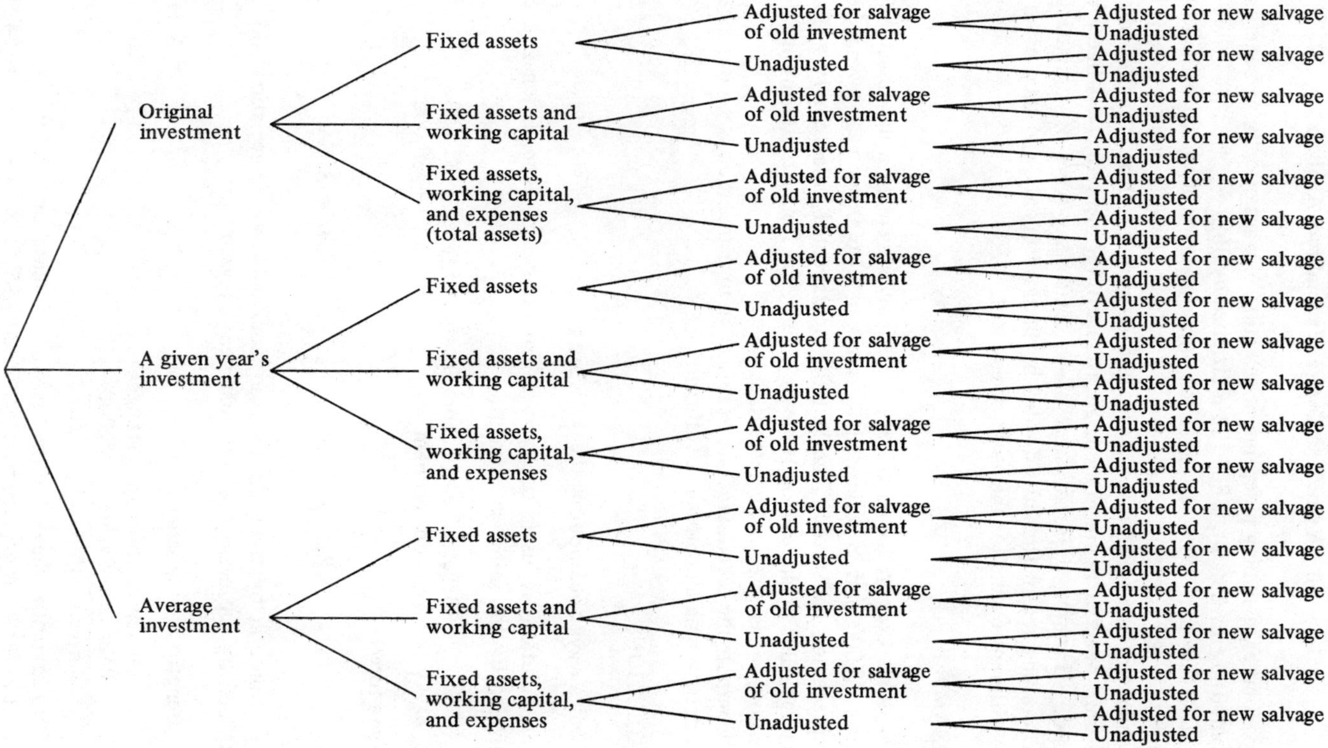

possibilities, assuming independent selection of ways of defining benefits and computing investment, is 864 (24 multiplied by 36).

It is true that some variations are more common in practice than others and that the selection of the way of defining benefits is not totally independent of the way of computing the investment. For example, when an average benefits figure is used, an average investment figure is likely to be used. However, even so, there are a great many ways of computing the accounting return (benefits divided by the investment), and they often lead to different results for the same investment.

EXAMPLE

The XYZ Corporation is considering an investment in a new machine that costs $5,000 and is estimated to result in $1,600 per year savings before depreciation and taxes. The benefits are expected to last for 10 years; the salvage value at the end of 10 years is zero; the firm uses straight-line depreciation, and is taxed at 50 percent.

Compute the accountant rate of return on investment using various methods of determining income and investment.

SOLUTIONS

Twelve ways of computing the ARR are presented.

(1) Solution by using the average benefits before depreciation and taxes, divided by the initial investment:

Benefits before depreciation and taxes	= $1,600
Initial investment	= $5,000

Therefore:

$$\text{Rate of return} = \frac{\$1{,}600}{\$5{,}000} \times 100 = 32\%$$

(2) Solution by using the average benefits before depreciation and taxes, divided by the average of the first year's investment:

Benefits are the same as in (1) = $1,600

Annual depreciation using straight-line

$$= \frac{\text{depreciable value}}{\text{investment life}} = \frac{\$5{,}000}{10} = \$\ 500$$

Investment at the end of the first year = initial investment less first-year depreciation = $5,000 − $500 = $4,500

Average of the first year's investment = ½ (initial investment + investment at year end) = ½ ($5,000 + $4,500) = $4,750

Therefore:

$$\text{Rate of return} = \frac{\$1,600}{\$4,750} \times 100 = 34\%$$

(3) Solution by using the average benefits before depreciation and taxes, divided by the average investment (over the entire life of the machine):

Benefits are the same as in (1) = $1,600

Average investment = ½ (initial investment + salvage) = ½ ($5,000 + 0) = $2,500

Therefore:

$$\text{Rate of return} = \frac{\$1,600}{\$2,500} \times 100 = 64\%$$

(4) Solution by using the average benefits after depreciation and before taxes, divided by the initial investment:

Benefits = benefits before depreciation and taxes – depreciation = $1,600 – $500 = $1,100
Investment = $5,000

Therefore:

$$\text{Rate of return} = \frac{\$1,100}{\$5,000} \times 100 = 22\%$$

(5) Solution by using the average benefits after depreciation and before taxes, divided by the average of the first year's investment:

Benefits = $1,100
Investment = $4,750

Therefore:

$$\text{Rate of return} = \frac{\$1,100}{\$4,750} \times 100 = 23\%$$

(6) Solution by using the average benefits after depreciation and before taxes, divided by the average investment:

Benefits = $1,100
Investment = $2,500

Therefore:

$$\text{Rate of return} = \frac{\$1,100}{\$2,500} \times 100 = 44\%$$

Table 6. Calculations for solution 7.

Benefits before depreciation and taxes	= $1,600
Less depreciation (deduct)	500
Benefits after depreciation and before taxes	= $1,100
Less taxes (50%)	550
Benefits after depreciation and taxes	= $ 550
Plus depreciation (add)	500
Benefits before depreciation and after taxes	= $1,050

(7) Solution by using the average benefits before depreciation and after taxes, divided by the initial investment. Calculation of benefits before depreciation and after taxes is shown in Table 6. Thus:

$$\text{Rate of return} = \frac{\$1{,}050}{\$5{,}000} \times 100 = 21\%$$

(8) Solution by using the average benefits before depreciation and after taxes, divided by the average of the first year's investment:

Benefits = $1,050
Investment = $4,750

Therefore:

$$\text{Rate of return} = \frac{\$1{,}050}{\$4{,}750} \times 100 = 22\%$$

(9) Solution by using the average benefits before depreciation and after taxes, divided by the average investment:

Benefits = $1,050
Investment = $2,500

Therefore:

$$\text{Rate of return} = \frac{\$1{,}050}{\$2{,}500} \times 100 = 42\%$$

(10) Solution by using the average benefits after depreciation and after taxes, divided by the initial investment:

Benefits after depreciation and taxes, as shown in Table 6 = \$550
Investment = \$5,000

Therefore:

$$\text{Rate of return} = \frac{\$550}{\$5{,}000} \times 100 = 11\%$$

(11) Solution by using the average benefits after depreciation and taxes, divided by the average of the first year's investment:

Benefits = \$550
Investment = \$4,750

Therefore:

$$\text{Rate of return} = \frac{\$550}{\$4{,}750} \times 100 = 12\%$$

(12) Solution by using the average benefits after depreciation and taxes, divided by the average investment:

Benefits = \$550
Investment = \$2,500

Therefore:

$$\text{Rate of return} = \frac{\$550}{\$2{,}500} \times 100 = 22\%$$

The most accepted practices require deducting depreciation and taxes. Depreciation should be deducted because it is part of the cost in any determination of accounting income.

The above 12 approaches used to calculate the ARR resulted in the following rates of return: 11, 12, 21, 22, 22, 22, 23, 32, 34, 42, 44, and 64 percent. The question to be asked now is, Which rate is correct, particularly since the range is so large (from 11 to 64 percent)? The answer will depend upon the philosophy of top management and the person doing the computation. But the impartial answer to this question is that all of them are right!

A common practice in computing the ARR is to use average income over average investment. The average income is a simple average of expected benefits from the investment, computed after depreciation and taxes but before financing charges. The investment is an average of fixed assets plus working capital. The following example, which illustrates this common technique, is more elaborate than the previous one, since uniformity of benefits is not assumed and the investment is defined to include working capital.

EXAMPLE

A machine costs $10,500 and requires an additional investment in working capital of $600 that will be recovered fully at the end of the project. This machine is expected to have a 5-year useful life, at the end of which the salvage value is expected to be $500. The expected benefits before depreciation, finance costs, and taxes in the five years are as follows: $3,000, $4,000, $3,000, $4,000, and $6,000. The company uses straight-line depreciation and is taxed at 50 percent.

Compute the accountant rate of return using the average rate of return after depreciation and taxes on average investment.

SOLUTION

Table 7 shows the calculation of benefits after depreciation and taxes.

Table 7. Calculation of benefits after depreciation and taxes.

Total benefits before depreciation and taxes = $3,000 + $4,000 + $3,000 + $4,000 + $6,000	= $20,000
Average benefits = $\frac{\text{total benefits}}{\text{number of years}} = \frac{\$20,000}{5}$	= $ 4,000
Depreciable value = capitalized cost of the asset − salvage = $10,500 − $500	= $10,000
Annual depreciation = depreciable value ÷ life of the investment = $\frac{\$10,000}{5}$	= $ 2,000
Benefits before depreciation and taxes	= $ 4,000
Less depreciation	= $ 2,000
Benefits after depreciation and before taxes	= $ 2,000
Less taxes (50 percent)	= $ 1,000
Benefits after depreciation and taxes	= $ 1,000

Next, the average investment in fixed assets and working capital is found by concentrating on each of these two components.

Average investment in the machine = ½ (initial cost + salvage)
= ½ ($10,500 + $500) = $5,500

Additional working capital required by the purchase of the machine is assumed to be used from the beginning of the project and released at the end of the project. The average investment in working capital is

$$\tfrac{1}{2}\text{(beginning + ending amount)} = \tfrac{1}{2}(\$600 + \$600) = \$600$$

If working capital is fixed throughout the period, the investment in working capital is that amount. If working capital declines regularly from beginning to end, then it is one-half of the total of the working capital for the first year plus the working capital for the last year. If working capital varies from year to year, it is the average of working capital obtained by adding the working capital required for each year and dividing by the number of years.

$$\text{Average investment} = \$5{,}500 + \$600 = \$6{,}100$$

Therefore:

$$\text{Rate of return} = \frac{\text{average benefits}}{\text{average investment}} \times 100$$

$$= \frac{\$1{,}000}{\$6{,}100} \times 100 = 16\%$$

To summarize, there are numerous ways of computing the accountant rate of return. No single approach is considered absolutely right or absolutely wrong. For this reason, it is important to study the approach taken to assure that it is the best for the firm. Once the decision is made to follow a certain approach, it should be continued. Changes in the way of computing the return would make it difficult, if not impossible, to study proposals on an equal basis. When it is found to be extremely important and beneficial to the firm to change its way of computing the ARR, care should be taken to explain the change to all concerned individuals and to consider it when comparing present and past proposals.

Capital Consumption Allowances Versus Tax Depreciation

When computing the accountant rate of return for the first year of the life of the investment, or for a specific year, care should be taken to differentiate between depreciation as a measure of capital consumption and tax depreciation. A difference may result if one method of depreciation is used for tax purposes and another method is used for reporting actual performance.

EXAMPLE

The purchase of a $10,000 machine with a 5-year life is proposed; the salvage value at the end of 5 years is zero. The firm uses double-declining-balance for tax purposes, the actual capital consumption follows a straight-line pattern, and the firm is taxed at 50 percent. First-year benefits before depreciation and taxes are $4,500.

Compute first-year benefits after depreciation and taxes using double-declining-balance for both capital consumption allowance and tax purposes, and then compute these benefits using double-declining-balance for tax purposes and straight-line for capital consumption.

SOLUTIONS

The two methods of solution are shown in Tables 8 and 9.

Table 8. Solution by using double-declining-balance only.

First-year depreciation using double-declining-balance	= $4,000
(Straight-line rate = $\frac{100\%}{5}$ = 20%; double-declining-balance = 2 X 20% = 40%; 40% of $10,000 = $4,000.)	
Benefits before depreciation and taxes	= $4,500
Less depreciation (double-declining) for tax purposes	4,000
Benefits after depreciation	= $ 500
Less taxes (50 percent)	250
First-year benefits after depreciation and taxes	= $ 250

Table 9. Solution by using double-declining-balance and straight-line.

Benefits before depreciation and taxes	= $4,500
Less depreciation (double-declining) for tax purposes (deduct)	4,000
	$ 500
Less taxes (50 percent)	250
	250
Plus tax depreciation (add)	4,000
First-year benefits before depreciation and after taxes	= $4,250
Less actual depreciation using straight-line ($10,000 ÷ 5 yrs.)	2,000
First-year benefits after taxes and depreciation	= $2,250

If the accelerated double-declining depreciation method is used for both tax and book purposes, the benefits are $250 in the first year. However, if straight-line is used for book purposes and double-declining for tax purposes only, benefits are $2,250.

Payback Reciprocal

The payback reciprocal (average cash inflows divided by investment) is used by some firms to measure return on investments. This measure is very similar to the accountant rate of return since it is the ratio of some form of benefits to an investment. Strictly speaking, however, payback reciprocal is not an accountant rate of return; the benefits usually refer to cash flows and not to accounting income.

Accounting Income, Not Cash Flows

The income figure (the benefits) used in computing the accountant rate of return is determined by accounting methods. Unfortunately, accounting income is not best suited for capital expenditure analysis. At the very least, a conceptual problem is bound to exist because of basic differences between financial accounting and capital expenditure analysis. On the one hand, financial accounting is designed primarily for reporting past events for an accounting unit, for a given accounting period of time (usually a year), and it is based on accounting conventions and tax considerations.

On the other hand, capital expenditure analysis is mainly concerned with future events for a given investment project, for the life of the project covering several accounting periods, regardless of accounting conventions and tax considerations that do not affect that investment.

Financial accounting methods concern themselves with actual data, whereas capital expenditure analysis recognizes alternatives and opportunity costs. Financial accounting methods would treat the rent of an empty space to be occupied by a machine either by charging the machine with an allocated amount of actual rent or by treating the rent as a period cost to be closed in the income statement at the end of the year. For capital expenditure analysis purposes, however, rent would be considered only if that space could be used for another purpose, in which case the income that could be drawn from the best possible alternative use of that space would be considered and regarded as an opportunity cost because this income must be sacrificed when assigning the space to the machine.

The concept of accounting income is considered inferior to the concept of cash flows for capital expenditure analysis. Basically, the purpose of making an investment is to spend cash now with the expectation of receiving cash in the future in amounts large enough to recover the original investment and provide a sufficient return on that investment. The reason for placing emphasis on receiving cash is that, until amounts are received in the form of cash, free of any restrictions, they cannot be reinvested at face value and, accordingly, should not be considered benefits received from the project.

Annual accounting income can be manipulated, for instance, by changing the depreciation method. Accelerated depreciation methods lead to lower net income figures in the early years of the project and higher net income figures in the latter years of the project. Decelerated depreciation methods have the opposite effect. Errors in estimating the salvage value or the life of the investment could affect the rate of the return computed by the accounting method.

For example, a $1,000 machine with an estimated useful life of 5 years and no salvage value would have the following depreciation figures for the first year of the life of the investment:

$200 using straight-line ($1,000 ÷ 5)
$333 using sum-of-the-years-digits
$$(\$1{,}000 \times \frac{5}{5+4+3+2+1} = \$1{,}000 \times \frac{1}{3})$$
$400 using double-declining-balance

The same machine with an estimated useful life of 4 years would have a first-year depreciation of:

$250 using straight-line ($1,000 ÷ 4)
$400 using sum-of-the-years-digits ($\$1{,}000 \times \frac{4}{10}$)
$500 using double-declining-balance ($1,000 × 0.50)

Again the same machine, with salvage value of $100 and an estimated useful life of 5 years, would result in a first-year depreciation of:

$180 using straight-line ($1,000 − $100 = $900 ÷ 5 years)
$300 using sum-of-the-years-digits ($900 depreciable value × $\frac{1}{3}$)
$400 using double-declining-balance (the 40% rate is applied to the original amount before deducting salvage)

To say the least, accounting income is not a unique figure. It can be determined in a number of ways, which can lead to a number of figures. When one speaks of accounting income (based on the same books of accounts), he is not speaking of a single value, but of a range of possible values.

There are several generally accepted ways of treating depreciation, evaluating inventory, allocating costs, and so on, which makes it possible for ten accountants, working with the same books of accounts, to produce ten different net income figures. Even worse, each of these ten accountants can *honestly* claim that he is right![1]

It is frequently argued that the ARR method should be used for evaluating capital expenditure proposals, the reason being that it is an extension of the usual use of the method—that is, evaluating the performance of a firm or a segment thereof. The accountant rate of return (also known as the return on investment or Du Pont formula) may be computed directly by dividing operating income by operating assets or indirectly by multiplying operating margin (operating income divided by sales) by asset turnover (sales divided by operating assets). However, because of differences between capital expenditure analysis (future-oriented) and actual performance analysis (historically oriented), the accountant rate of return is not considered a generally acceptable method of evaluating capital expenditure proposals.

Time Value of Money

The time value of money, the idea that a dollar received today is better than a dollar to be received tomorrow, is ignored by the accountant rate of return method. This represents a serious shortcoming of the method since all benefits, regardless of timing, are treated equally. Under unusual conditions of having uniform benefits and a short investment life, mistakes in computing rate of return are not critical. However, highly unreliable results can occur when the life of the proposed investment is relatively long and the benefits from the proposal are not uniform.

EXAMPLE

A 10-year-life investment costs $27,500. It has no salvage value and has the following annual benefits after depreciation and taxes: $1,000, $2,000, $3,000, $4,000, $5,000, $6,000, $7,000, $8,000, $9,000, $10,000. This investment has an average rate of return of 40 percent ($5,500 average benefits divided by $13,750 average investment). Another similar investment of $27,500 with a reversed (decreasing) benefit in 10 years ($10,000, $9,000, $8,000, $7,000, $6,000, $5,000, $4,000, $3,000, $2,000, $1,000) would have the same 40 percent accountant rate of return.

According to the 40 percent accountant rate of return, these two investments are equally desirable. However, a closer look at the figures shows that the latter investment is the more favorable since its higher benefits are drawn, and thereby available, for reinvestment in early years. This example shows that the accountant rate of return is insensitive to the time value of money.

Ignoring the time value of money is a serious shortcoming with long-lived investments when the benefits vary from year to year. The longer the life of the asset and the less uniform the annual benefits, the more important is the use of a discounted cash flow method.

Comparability with Cost of Capital

The accountant rate of return may be compared with a cutoff point to determine the desirability of an investment proposal. However, the ARR is not readily comparable with the cost of capital since it ignores the time value of money. (See Chapter 6 on net present value for a more detailed coverage of the cost of capital.)

Ease in Postauditing

It is often argued that the ARR method, being based on accounting concepts of income, makes the task of postauditing capital expenditures from the normally kept books of accounts an easy one. This argument, though widely used, is far from the truth. The books of accounts are usually designed for reporting events with reference to accounting periods and for profit centers. As such, they are not usually designed for reporting on single investments. Thus, ease of postauditing projects evaluated by the accountant rate of return method is more a myth than a reality.

Simplicity and Popularity

Use of the ARR method for capital expenditure analysis is often justified on the grounds of simplicity and popularity. It is often stated that the method is well known and well understood by analysts, evaluators, and decision makers; that it uses readily available figures from projected income statements; and that the rate-of-return language is very familiar to businessmen.

A careful examination of these claims reveals their fallacies. Because of the many ways of calculating the rate of return by the accountant method, it is hard to believe that all the concerned people in a company would be able to comprehend it unless extensive and intensive efforts are made to explain to them and to justify the version or versions used by the firm. Moreover, because of the dependence of the method on accounting concepts, an individual has to be very familiar with accounting to be able to understand and interpret a rate of return so computed.

Simplicity and popularity should not be considered key factors in the choice of a method of evaluating capital expenditures since the large dollar amounts and the risks involved outweigh any possible advantage to be drawn from simplicity and popularity of the evaluation method. The criterion should not be how simple a method is but how accurately it measures the profitability of an investment proposal. Because it ignores the time value of money and because of its heavy reliance on accounting concepts, the accountant rate of return method falls short of being a theoretically acceptable method of evaluating capital expenditures.

Accountant Rate of Return in Practice

Responses to the author's evaluation questionnaire confirm that the accountant rate of return is a popular method of evaluating capital expenditures. Of 197 large industrial corporations, 57 percent use this method for evaluating major projects, and 56 percent of 189 firms use it for evaluating "all other projects." Accordingly, at least one of every two large corporations uses the ARR method for evaluating capital expenditures. This also seems to be true of small and medium-size corporations.

In order of usage for evaluating major projects, the ARR method is placed third. It is preceded by payback and DCFR methods, and followed by net present value and MAPI.

The ARR method plays a major role in evaluating the "all other projects" category. It is placed as the second method (considering the total number of firms using each method), preceded by payback and followed by the other three methods (DCFR, net present value, and MAPI). It is not unusual for the accountant method to assume a key role in the evaluation of minor projects. It is often argued that minor projects do not justify a more sophisticated analysis and that the accountant rate of return method is best suited for such evaluation.

This method is more commonly used in some industries than in others. For major projects, when the replies were classified by industry and ranked according to the extent of use of the method, usage was found to range from as low as 33 percent in the food and beverages industry to as high as 100 percent in the rubber industry. The accountant rate of return method is used the most for evaluating major projects by five industries: rubber; chemicals; metal manufacturing; motor vehicles and trucks; and stone, clay, glass, and concrete products.

Data for the "all other projects" category show that usage of the method ranges from 22 percent in the crude petroleum and natural gas industry to 86 percent in the rubber industry. It is used the most for evaluating "all other projects" in the following five industries: rubber; mining; metal manufacturing; chemicals; and stone, clay, glass, and concrete products.

The role played by a method of evaluation is dependent upon two factors: first, how often it is used, and, second, percentage of users that consider it the preponderant method of evaluation. When the respondents were asked to rank the methods according to their relative importance for capital expenditure evaluation, accountant rate of return was placed as the second most important method for major projects (preceded by the discounted cash flow rate of return), and as the most important method for evaluating "all other projects."

As is the trend in current practice, very few respondent companies use the ARR method exclusively for evaluating capital expenditure proposals.

Advantages

Of the nine practical advantages of the accountant rate of return method (that is, more than half of the respondents consider them advantages), the top three are that it is easy to understand, simple in use, and well known. These three advantages undoubtedly explain why at least one of every two large corporations surveyed uses the ARR method.

The next three advantages of the method are that it is easy to sell to operating personnel, easy to sell to top management, and easy to postaudit. Ease of postauditing is often cited as an advantage; however, careful examination shows its illusionary character. Nevertheless, until this mythical advantage is recognized as such, it will be regarded as a real advantage of the accountant method by some of those using it.

Ease of selling to operating personnel, as an advantage, may reflect the importance of selling capital expenditure evaluation methods, not only to top management, but also to operating personnel down the line. Many businessmen confirmed in personal interviews that, to assure the success of capital investment analysis, as many people as possible should be involved and know something about the logic and reasoning behind such evaluation.

The last three advantages are that the accountant rate of return is low in cost, can be used for evaluating different types of investment proposals, and analyzes future data—not historical. The latter advantage is due to the use of future estimates, rather than past-performance figures as is the case with some rules of thumb that are sometimes used for capital expenditure analysis (for example, replacing a car after so many miles or so many years).

Weaknesses

The main weaknesses of the accountant rate of return method are ignoring the time value of money and depending excessively on accounting concepts. From the respondents' viewpoint, none of the other 12 suggested weaknesses are considered real weaknesses of the method.

Familiarity with Accountant Rate of Return

Analysts, evaluators, and decision makers in business firms usually feel that they are familiar with the accountant rate of return method. This conclusion was supported by the evaluation survey results.

Of 189 respondents, 91 percent feel that analysts, reviewers, and decision makers are familiar with the ARR method. The high degree of familiarity with this method (exceeded only by that with payback) is undoubtedly one of the key reasons for its popularity.

Evaluation of Accountant Rate of Return Performance

Although the accountant method of evaluating capital expenditures is usually considered a theoretically inefficient method, it is regarded as a satisfactory method by the majority of top managers.

Of 143 responding firms that appraised the overall performance of the ARR method, 20 percent consider it very satisfactory; 58 percent, fairly satisfactory; 15 percent, unsatisfactory; and 7 percent had no opinion. When the totals of very satisfactory and fairly satisfactory are combined and expressed as a percentage of total responses, the accountant rate of return is placed third, with DCFR and payback in the first two positions, and followed by net present value and MAPI.

Discontinued as Unsatisfactory

The accountant rate of return method is at the top of the list of methods discontinued because of unsatisfactory results. It is followed by payback, MAPI formula, net present value, and DCFR. Although this may indicate more dissatisfaction with the accountant rate of return than with the other methods studied, no definite conclusions can be reached in this regard because of the small number of companies (28 of 141 firms) that indicated such dissatisfaction with the method.

Typical Comments

The treasurer of an American subsidiary of a large foods corporation indicated that it does not make sense to use refined discounted cash flow measures on estimates that are of doubtful accuracy beyond five years. He added that his company had to concentrate on making a profit first and justifying expenditures second, and that the combination of the payback and accountant rate of return was satisfactory for those purposes. When asked about ease of postauditing expenditures, he indicated that postauditing is a problem regardless of the method of evaluation used.

In a subsidiary of a large chemical corporation, where the accountant rate of return is used as the key method of evaluating capital expenditures supplemented by cash flow analysis when needed, the industrial engineer in charge of evaluating a major portion of these expenditures indicated that the accountant rate of return is computed by dividing the earnings after depreciation and taxes (on an annual basis) by the total investment (including fixed assets plus working capital). This is done for the first, third, and fifth years. He felt that by computing the return for three years, a better picture of the return and its trend could be seen. He cited the following reasons for using the accountant rate of return: it is considered simple and easy to understand by managers, and it includes revenue, cost, and investment considerations.

The assistant financial vice-president of a large metal manufacturing company that uses both payback and accountant rate of return indicated that the ARR method carries more weight in his company's investment analysis system because computations are easier to postaudit. He went on to say that it is not practical to use discounted cash flow methods, because the projects evaluated by these methods would be hard to postaudit since reliable estimates are difficult, or even impossible, to make and because the figures used with the accounting rate of return are comparable to those used in profit and loss statements. The rate of return is computed by dividing profit before taxes (for example, sales estimate less standard costs and selling and general expenses) by the gross additional investment (capital assets plus additional working capital required by the investment).

One executive was asked why he uses the figure before taxes and not after taxes. He answered by explaining that taxes go up and down and make it difficult to relate one project to another, and that tax treatments are full of tricks and could be subjected to manipulation.

Another financial executive indicated why his firm is using accountant rate of return rather than the discounted cash flow method. He stated that if the estimates are not very reliable, it is hard for him to accept the idea that by discounting them a more useful figure would be produced.

The vice-president and treasurer of a large mining corporation that uses payback, accountant rate of return, and discounted rate of return methods was asked why his firm is using a combination of methods rather than one single method. He stated that it is a matter of individual preference; he related it to an individual in a marketplace buying a combination of apples, oranges, and bananas.

One respondent to the evaluation questionnaire indicated that his company had traditionally used the accountant rate of return and cash payback methods for evaluating capital expenditure proposals. He added that his company had recently started using the DCFR method and has experienced some difficulties with this change because of the unfamiliarity of both analytical and management personnel with the theory and concepts involved.

Another respondent had this to say about using the accountant rate of return rather than discounted cash flow: "Generally, errors in estimates in a system that is not understood and supported in principle by operating personnel will outweigh all the nice mathematical advantages of the more esoteric approaches."

Still another respondent, in justifying methods that do not consider the time value of money, said: "For major projects, the use of sophisticated expenditure analysis is overshadowed by the unknowns such as market share, attainable manufacturing costs, selling price, and so on, and for minor projects actual costs and projected costs are many times more difficult to obtain for comparative purposes in equipment replacement, and so forth."

Conclusion

The accountant rate of return method is superior to the payback method since it measures profitability and the analysis is usually extended over the entire life of the proposal. It allows ranking proposals by rate of return and produces a rate that can be compared with a predetermined cutoff point. The ARR method is considered, in theory, inferior to discounted cash flow methods.

The accountant rate of return should generally be used only to supplement other methods. However, when used by itself, the ARR may give acceptable results for evaluating some minor capital expenditure proposals. It may also be acceptable when the lives of the investments to be compared are similar, when the investments are short-lived, or when the benefits of each proposal under consideration are uniform or very similar.

This method can provide useful information if used to supplement other methods or as an initial screening device. Consistency in computing the rates of return is important since different ways of computation can give different answers. The ARR method is not the ideal method to use for evaluating major capital expenditures since it does not recognize the time value of money and it uses accounting income instead of cash flows in the analysis. The method is considered unsatisfactory as a general method of evaluating capital expenditures.

In terms of usage, the accountant rate of return is a common method of evaluating capital expenditures because of its simplicity and because analysts, reviewers, and top management personnel are familiar with it.

One cannot help but wonder why a firm, particularly a large firm, would use the accountant rate of return method exclusively, with its known deficiencies, when better, discounted cash flow methods are available.

NOTE

1. For an excellent discussion of basic accounting concepts and their drawbacks, the reader is referred to John W. Coughlan, *Guide to Contemporary Theory of Accounts* (Englewood Cliffs, N.J.: Prentice-Hall, 1965).

5 / Discounted Cash Flow Rate of Return

THE discounted cash flow rate of return (DCFR) is becoming more and more a status symbol in capital investment analysis. Increasing numbers of firms are adopting the DCFR method. Many companies are redrafting their capital expenditure policies and procedures to reflect the adoption of DCFR. While some companies are converting to the method as a result of extensive study of the available methods, others are converting merely because they want to "move with the crowd." The DCFR method has become so "in" that financial officers of companies not using it often feel intimidated to the point of being apologetic. While the use of DCFR is far from the 100 percent level, especially in small and medium-size companies (in many of these companies the DCFR method is practically unknown), there is definitely a welcome trend toward extensive use of the DCFR method by large industrial corporations in the United States.

In 1956, the Machinery and Allied Products Institute conducted a survey with reference to equipment replacement practices and reported that only 2 percent of the respondents made use of the discounted cash flow method for evaluating equipment replacement proposals.[1] Istvan's frequently quoted 1959 study of the decision-making process in 48 large industrial corporations in the United States concluded that only 29 percent (14 of 48 firms studied) used the time adjusted rate of return method (the DCFR). Of these, 5 firms used it as the primary measure, and the remaining 9 as a supplementary measure.[2]

"Discounted cash flow" refers to methods that take into consideration the time value of money. There are, basically, two such methods: discounted cash flow rate of return (DCFR) and net present value (NPV). The primary concern in this chapter is with the first of these methods. The net present value method will be discussed in Chapter 6.

The discounted rate of return method is also known as the discounted return method, the discounted cash flow rate method, the yield method, the investor's method, the after-tax investor's rate of return, the scientific method, the actuarial rate of return method, the time adjusted rate of return method, the internal rate of return method, and the industrial rate of return method.

The time adjusted rate of return concept is not new. It has been used for many years in investment circles for mortgages and loans, but its extensive use for capital investment analysis is a recent practice.

From a theoretical viewpoint, the DCFR method is generally regarded as one of the two most advanced and efficient methods of evaluating capital expenditures, the other method being the net present value method. Although there are many arguments regarding the advisability of using one method versus the other, both are generally regarded as theoretically advanced methods of evaluating capital expenditures.

What Is DCFR?

The DCFR is a rate of return method. The resulting analysis figure may be regarded in general the same as the accountant rate of return figure, except that, whereas the accountant rate of return ignores the time value of money, the DCFR takes it into consideration. Roughly speaking, a 10 percent DCFR means that a project is expected to earn 10 percent on the *outstanding investment.* This 10 percent means that during the life of the project enough cash payments will be received to amount to 10 percent interest on the remaining investment plus return of the capital invested. Each amount of cash flows received in this case would, in effect, consist of two payments: one for the interest on the amount of the outstanding investment, and another for the reduction or amortization of the initial investment.

Formally speaking, the DCFR is that rate of interest that discounts the expected stream of benefits (cash flows) to be received from a proposal (may be called the present value of the cash inflows) to an amount equal to the initial investment. It is that interest rate that will equate the present value of cash inflows (benefits) with the present value of cash outflows (investment), thus making the net present value of all cash flows (present value of cash inflows less present value of cash outflows) equal to zero.

For example, an initial investment of $610,510, which would result in net cash flows of $161,051 each year for 5 years, has a 10 percent DCFR (assuming that the benefits are net after taxes and are received at the end of each year). (See calculations in Table 10 for this example. The 10 percent DCFR is found by a trial-and-error process, which will be explained later in this chapter.)

Table 10. Calculations for the example.

Year (1)	*Investment at Beginning of Year (Outstanding Investment less Amortization)* (2)	*Interest (10% of Investment)* (3)	*Cash Flows Received at End of Year* (4)	*Reduction in Investment (Cash Flows less Interest)* (5)
1	$610,510	$61,051	$161,051	$161,051 – $61,051 = $100,000
2	$610,510 – $100,000 = $510,510	51,051	161,051	161,051 – 51,051 = 110,000
3	510,510 – 110,000 = 400,510	40,051	161,051	161,051 – 40,051 = 121,000
4	400,510 – 121,000 = 279,510	27,951	161,051	161,051 – 27,951 = 133,100
5	279,510 – 133,100 = 146,410	14,641	161,051	161,051 – 14,641 = 146,410
6	146,410 – 146,410 = 0			

In the calculations for this example, the first row may be read as follows: In the first year (column 1), the investment at the beginning of the year is \$610,510 (column 2); the 10 percent interest on this investment is \$61,051 (column 3); the amount of cash flows received from the investment at the end of the first year is \$161,051 (column 4); and, after the \$61,051 interest (10 percent) is deducted from the \$161,051 cash inflow, this leaves \$100,000 for the amortization of the initial investment (column 5). The outstanding investment at the beginning of the second year is shown in the second row as \$510,510 (\$610,510 less \$100,000 amortization).

The fifth row may be read as follows: At the beginning of the fifth year (column 1) the initial investment is \$146,410 (column 2); the 10 percent interest on this amount is \$14,641 (column 3); a \$161,051 cash flow is received (column 4); and, after the interest is deducted from this last amount, \$146,410 is left for amortization of the investment (column 5).

The last row shows that when the \$146,410 is used to amortize the investment, a zero balance is left. This means that the amounts to be received are sufficient to pay 10 percent interest and amortize the investment. The 10 percent interest is applied to the outstanding investment, not to the initial investment.

Thus, the 10 percent return is *a return on the outstanding* (remaining) *investment* and not the initial investment. This point will be explored further when the reinvestment assumption is discussed.

Characteristics of DCFR

Some of the main characteristics of the DCFR method are discussed here to provide a better understanding of the method.

The Time Value of Money

The most important characteristic of the DCFR method is that it takes into consideration the time value of money. This means that a differentiation is made between cash flows received at different points in time. Before adding cash flows to be received at different times, they are adjusted. This adjusting process is called discounting.

The concept of time value of money is often explained by stating that a dollar received today is better than a dollar to be received tomorrow or any time later. We cannot treat dollars received at different points in time as if they were equal since the earlier we receive a dollar, the earlier we can put it to use to earn money. Thus, a dollar received today is worth more than a dollar to be received tomorrow, and a dollar received tomorrow is worth more than a dollar to be received a year from now.

The underlying assumption here is that, in an economy in which interest and opportunities for investment exist, a dollar received today could be invested to earn money immediately. A dollar to be received one year hence could not be invested until it is received; therefore, it is less valuable than a dollar received today. In other words, there is a price for waiting to receive benefits; the longer we have to wait, the more return we should expect on our money.

Suppose we receive a dollar today and invest it at 3 percent. One year from now we will get the dollar back plus \$0.03 interest, or a total of \$1.03. This means that, at a 3 percent rate, a dollar today is worth \$1.03 one year from now, or, we would feel the same about receiving a dollar now or \$1.03 one year hence (if the prevailing interest rate is 3 percent). Using compound interest, if we were to keep the new amount, \$1.03, for another year at the same 3 percent rate, it would earn \$0.0309 interest, and the new sum would then be \$1.0609. A simple way of figuring the total is by using the formula:

$$S = P(1 + i)^n$$

where S = the sum of the principal and interest at the end of a given period
P = initial amount or principal
n = the number of periods in which the principal amount would be compounded
i = interest rate

For example, \$100 invested at 6 percent for one year would be \$100(1 + 0.06) = \$106; the same amount invested for 2 years at 6 percent would be $\$100(1 + 0.06)^2 = \$112.36$, and for 3 years it would be $\$100(1 + 0.06)^3 = \$119.1016$. This process is called compounding, and tables are available to facilitate the process for different interest rates and compounding periods.

The opposite of compounding is called discounting, which can be figured by manipulating the same formula to get:

$$P = \frac{S}{(1 + i)^n}$$

where P = the present value of a single amount S
S = single amount received at the end of period n
i = interest rate
n = number of periods during which interest is calculated

Using this formula, the present value of $1.00 received a year hence at a 6 percent annual interest rate is

$$\frac{1}{(1 + 0.06)} = 0.9434$$

This is the present value of $1.00 to be received a year hence at 6 percent. This means that if we invest $0.9434 at 6 percent for a year, the combined total of interest ($0.0566) and principal ($0.9434) would be a dollar ($0.9434 + 0.0566 = $1.000). It also means that you can accept $0.9434 today in place of $1.00 a year from now and be just as well off. In other words, the present value (value today) of $1.00 to be received a year hence is $0.9434 (assuming you can earn 6 percent). Where interest exists, the present value of future cash flows is always lower than the face value.

Fortunately, tables that reduce the necessary arithmetical computations for present value are available for various commonly used interest rates and compounding assumptions. There are tables that assume receiving the cash flows at the end of the period once a year, twice a year, or continuously.[3] *For simplicity, all computations here will be based on present-value tables that assume receiving the amount at the end of the year.* Usually, the answer given when it is assumed that the benefits are to be received at the end of the year is not much different from that found by monthly or continuous compounding approaches.

Using the end-of-period assumption for receiving benefits, two basic tables are available: one for the present value of a single dollar received at the end of a given period at a given interest rate, and another for the present value of a series showing one dollar received annually at the end of each period at selected interest rates for a given number of periods. (See Tables 11 and 12.) Excerpts from both tables are shown below to illustrate how to use them.

Selected entries from Table 11 for a single dollar:

No. of Years	*10%*	*20%*	*30%*
1	$0.909	$0.833	$0.769
2	0.826	0.694	0.592
3	0.751	0.579	0.455
4	0.683	0.482	0.350
5	0.621	0.402	0.269

From this information it can be seen that the present value (value today) of $1 to be received 5 years hence (see the fifth row) at 10 percent is $0.621, whereas at a 20 percent rate it is $0.402, and at 30 percent it is $0.269. Also, the $0.579 value in the 20 percent column may be read as the present value of $1 to be received 3 years hence if it is discounted at 20 percent.

Two conclusions may be drawn from the above tabulation. First, at a given interest rate, the more distant the time in the future that the amount is to be received, the lower its present value. At 10 percent, $1 to be received a year hence has a present value of $0.909; the present value of $1 to be received 2 years hence is $0.826, and 5 years hence is $0.621.

Second, the higher the interest rate for the same waiting period, the lower the present value. The present value of $1 to be received 4 years hence is $0.683 at 10 percent, $0.482 at 20 percent, and $0.350 at 30 percent.

To use the table for an amount other than a dollar, multiply that amount by the appropriate value from the table. The present value of $10,000 to be received 5 years hence at 10 percent is $6,210 ($0.621 multiplied by $10,000).

If we add the present value as found in Table 11 for a dollar to be received a year later at 10 percent to the present value of a dollar to be received 2 years later at 10 percent, we will have the present value of an annuity of $1 to be received at the end of each year for 2 years at 10 percent ($0.909 + $0.826 = $1.735).

This value is shown in the following excerpt from Table 12 for annuity (the difference between $1.735 and the value shown in the table of $1.736 is due to rounding). The table for annuity is the result of repeatedly adding present-value figures (Table 11) for different rates of interest and different time periods.

Excerpt from Table 12 for the present value of an annuity of $1 received at the end of each period:

No. of Years	*10%*	*20%*	*30%*
1	0.909	0.833	0.769
2	1.736	1.528	1.361
3	2.487	2.106	1.816
4	3.170	2.589	2.166
5	3.791	2.991	2.436

The values in the excerpt may be interpreted as follows: The present value of $1 to be received at the end of each year for 3 years at 10 percent (a face value of $3) is $2.487 (third row, second column), at 20 percent the present value is $2.106, and at 30 percent it is $1.816. The $1.528 value in the 20 percent column is the present value of an annuity of $1 for 2 years at 20 percent interest rate.

Table 11. Present value of $1.00.

Years Hence	1%	2%	4%	6%	8%	10%	12%	14%	15%	16%	18%	20%	22%	24%	25%	26%	28%	30%	35%	40%	45%	50%
1	0.990	0.980	0.962	0.943	0.926	0.909	0.893	0.877	0.870	0.862	0.847	0.833	0.820	0.806	0.800	0.794	0.781	0.769	0.741	0.714	0.690	0.667
2	0.980	0.961	0.925	0.890	0.857	0.826	0.797	0.769	0.756	0.743	0.718	0.694	0.672	0.650	0.640	0.630	0.610	0.592	0.549	0.510	0.476	0.444
3	0.971	0.942	0.889	0.840	0.794	0.751	0.712	0.675	0.658	0.641	0.609	0.579	0.551	0.524	0.512	0.500	0.477	0.455	0.406	0.364	0.328	0.296
4	0.961	0.924	0.855	0.792	0.735	0.683	0.636	0.592	0.572	0.552	0.516	0.482	0.451	0.423	0.410	0.397	0.373	0.350	0.301	0.260	0.226	0.198
5	0.951	0.906	0.822	0.747	0.681	0.621	0.567	0.519	0.497	0.476	0.437	0.402	0.370	0.341	0.328	0.315	0.291	0.269	0.223	0.186	0.156	0.132
6	0.942	0.888	0.790	0.705	0.630	0.564	0.507	0.456	0.432	0.410	0.370	0.335	0.303	0.275	0.262	0.250	0.227	0.207	0.165	0.133	0.108	0.088
7	0.933	0.871	0.760	0.665	0.583	0.513	0.452	0.400	0.376	0.354	0.314	0.279	0.249	0.222	0.210	0.198	0.178	0.159	0.122	0.095	0.074	0.059
8	0.923	0.853	0.731	0.627	0.540	0.467	0.404	0.351	0.327	0.305	0.266	0.233	0.204	0.179	0.168	0.157	0.139	0.123	0.091	0.068	0.051	0.039
9	0.914	0.837	0.703	0.592	0.500	0.424	0.361	0.308	0.284	0.263	0.225	0.194	0.167	0.144	0.134	0.125	0.108	0.094	0.067	0.048	0.035	0.026
10	0.905	0.820	0.676	0.558	0.463	0.386	0.322	0.270	0.247	0.227	0.191	0.162	0.137	0.116	0.107	0.099	0.085	0.073	0.050	0.035	0.024	0.017
11	0.896	0.804	0.650	0.527	0.429	0.350	0.287	0.237	0.215	0.195	0.162	0.135	0.112	0.094	0.086	0.079	0.066	0.056	0.037	0.025	0.017	0.012
12	0.887	0.788	0.625	0.497	0.397	0.319	0.257	0.208	0.187	0.168	0.137	0.112	0.092	0.076	0.069	0.062	0.052	0.043	0.027	0.018	0.012	0.008
13	0.879	0.773	0.601	0.469	0.368	0.290	0.229	0.182	0.163	0.145	0.116	0.093	0.075	0.061	0.055	0.050	0.040	0.033	0.020	0.013	0.008	0.005
14	0.870	0.758	0.577	0.442	0.340	0.263	0.205	0.160	0.141	0.125	0.099	0.078	0.062	0.049	0.044	0.039	0.032	0.025	0.015	0.009	0.006	0.003
15	0.861	0.743	0.555	0.417	0.315	0.239	0.183	0.140	0.123	0.108	0.084	0.065	0.051	0.040	0.035	0.031	0.025	0.020	0.011	0.006	0.004	0.002
16	0.853	0.728	0.534	0.394	0.292	0.218	0.163	0.123	0.107	0.093	0.071	0.054	0.042	0.032	0.028	0.025	0.019	0.015	0.008	0.005	0.003	0.002
17	0.844	0.714	0.513	0.371	0.270	0.198	0.146	0.108	0.093	0.080	0.060	0.045	0.034	0.026	0.023	0.020	0.015	0.012	0.006	0.003	0.002	0.001
18	0.836	0.700	0.494	0.350	0.250	0.180	0.130	0.095	0.081	0.069	0.051	0.038	0.028	0.021	0.018	0.016	0.012	0.009	0.005	0.002	0.001	0.001
19	0.828	0.686	0.475	0.331	0.232	0.164	0.116	0.083	0.070	0.060	0.043	0.031	0.023	0.017	0.014	0.012	0.009	0.007	0.003	0.002	0.001	
20	0.820	0.673	0.456	0.312	0.215	0.149	0.104	0.073	0.061	0.051	0.037	0.026	0.019	0.014	0.012	0.010	0.007	0.005	0.002	0.001	0.001	
21	0.811	0.660	0.439	0.294	0.199	0.135	0.093	0.064	0.053	0.044	0.031	0.022	0.015	0.011	0.009	0.008	0.006	0.004	0.002	0.001		
22	0.803	0.647	0.422	0.278	0.184	0.123	0.083	0.056	0.046	0.038	0.026	0.018	0.013	0.009	0.007	0.006	0.004	0.003	0.001	0.001		
23	0.795	0.634	0.406	0.262	0.170	0.112	0.074	0.049	0.040	0.033	0.022	0.015	0.010	0.007	0.006	0.005	0.003	0.002	0.001			
24	0.788	0.622	0.390	0.247	0.158	0.102	0.066	0.043	0.035	0.028	0.019	0.013	0.008	0.006	0.005	0.004	0.003	0.002	0.001			
25	0.780	0.610	0.375	0.233	0.146	0.092	0.059	0.038	0.030	0.024	0.016	0.010	0.007	0.005	0.004	0.003	0.002	0.001	0.001			
26	0.772	0.598	0.361	0.220	0.135	0.084	0.053	0.033	0.026	0.021	0.014	0.009	0.006	0.004	0.003	0.002	0.002	0.001				
27	0.764	0.586	0.347	0.207	0.125	0.076	0.047	0.029	0.023	0.018	0.011	0.007	0.005	0.003	0.002	0.002	0.001	0.001				
28	0.757	0.574	0.333	0.196	0.116	0.069	0.042	0.026	0.020	0.016	0.010	0.006	0.004	0.002	0.002	0.002	0.001	0.001				
29	0.749	0.563	0.321	0.185	0.107	0.063	0.037	0.022	0.017	0.014	0.008	0.005	0.003	0.002	0.002	0.001	0.001	0.001				
30	0.742	0.552	0.308	0.174	0.099	0.057	0.033	0.020	0.015	0.012	0.007	0.004	0.003	0.002	0.001	0.001	0.001					
40	0.672	0.453	0.208	0.097	0.046	0.022	0.011	0.005	0.004	0.003	0.001	0.001										
50	0.608	0.372	0.141	0.054	0.021	0.009	0.003	0.001	0.001	0.001												

Reproduced with permission from Robert N. Anthony, *Management Accounting,* 4th ed. (Homewood, Ill.: Richard D. Irwin, © 1970).

Table 12. Present value of $1.00 received annually for N years.

Years (N)	1%	2%	4%	6%	8%	10%	12%	14%	15%	16%	18%	20%	22%	24%	25%	26%	28%	30%	35%	40%	45%	50%
1.......	0.990	0.980	0.962	0.943	0.926	0.909	0.893	0.877	0.870	0.862	0.847	0.833	0.820	0.806	0.800	0.794	0.781	0.769	0.741	0.714	0.690	0.667
2.......	1.970	1.942	1.886	1.833	1.783	1.736	1.690	1.647	1.626	1.605	1.566	1.528	1.492	1.457	1.440	1.424	1.392	1.361	1.289	1.224	1.165	1.111
3.......	2.941	2.884	2.775	2.673	2.577	2.487	2.402	2.322	2.283	2.246	2.174	2.106	2.042	1.981	1.952	1.923	1.868	1.816	1.696	1.589	1.493	1.407
4.......	3.902	3.808	3.630	3.465	3.312	3.170	3.037	2.914	2.855	2.798	2.690	2.589	2.494	2.404	2.362	2.320	2.241	2.166	1.997	1.849	1.720	1.605
5.......	4.853	4.713	4.452	4.212	3.993	3.791	3.605	3.433	3.352	3.274	3.127	2.991	2.864	2.745	2.689	2.635	2.532	2.436	2.220	2.035	1.876	1.737
6.......	5.795	5.601	5.242	4.917	4.623	4.355	4.111	3.889	3.784	3.685	3.498	3.326	3.167	3.020	2.951	2.885	2.759	2.643	2.385	2.168	1.983	1.824
7.......	6.728	6.472	6.002	5.582	5.206	4.868	4.564	4.288	4.160	4.039	3.812	3.605	3.416	3.242	3.161	3.083	2.937	2.802	2.508	2.263	2.057	1.883
8.......	7.652	7.325	6.733	6.210	5.747	5.335	4.968	4.639	4.487	4.344	4.078	3.837	3.619	3.421	3.329	3.241	3.076	2.925	2.598	2.331	2.108	1.922
9.......	8.566	8.162	7.435	6.802	6.247	5.759	5.328	4.946	4.772	4.607	4.303	4.031	3.786	3.566	3.463	3.366	3.184	3.019	2.665	2.379	2.144	1.948
10......	9.471	8.983	8.111	7.360	6.710	6.145	5.650	5.216	5.019	4.833	4.494	4.192	3.923	3.682	3.571	3.465	3.269	3.092	2.715	2.414	2.168	1.965
11......	10.368	9.787	8.760	7.887	7.139	6.495	5.937	5.453	5.234	5.029	4.656	4.327	4.035	3.776	3.656	3.544	3.335	3.147	2.752	2.438	2.185	1.977
12......	11.255	10.575	9.385	8.384	7.536	6.814	6.194	5.660	5.421	5.197	4.793	4.439	4.127	3.851	3.725	3.606	3.387	3.190	2.779	2.456	2.196	1.985
13......	12.134	11.343	9.986	8.853	7.904	7.103	6.424	5.842	5.583	5.342	4.910	4.533	4.203	3.912	3.780	3.656	3.427	3.223	2.799	2.468	2.204	1.990
14......	13.004	12.106	10.563	9.295	8.244	7.367	6.628	6.002	5.724	5.468	5.008	4.611	4.265	3.962	3.824	3.695	3.459	3.249	2.814	2.477	2.210	1.993
15......	13.865	12.849	11.118	9.712	8.559	7.606	6.811	6.142	5.847	5.575	5.092	4.675	4.315	4.001	3.859	3.726	3.483	3.268	2.825	2.484	2.214	1.995
16......	14.718	13.578	11.652	10.106	8.851	7.824	6.974	6.265	5.954	5.669	5.162	4.730	4.357	4.033	3.887	3.751	3.503	3.283	2.834	2.489	2.216	1.997
17......	15.562	14.292	12.166	10.477	9.122	8.022	7.120	6.373	6.047	5.749	5.222	4.775	4.391	4.059	3.910	3.771	3.518	3.295	2.840	2.492	2.218	1.998
18......	16.398	14.992	12.659	10.828	9.372	8.201	7.250	6.467	6.128	5.818	5.273	4.812	4.419	4.080	3.928	3.786	3.529	3.304	2.844	2.494	2.219	1.999
19......	17.226	15.678	13.134	11.158	9.604	8.365	7.366	6.550	6.198	5.877	5.316	4.844	4.442	4.097	3.942	3.799	3.539	3.311	2.848	2.496	2.220	1.999
20......	18.046	16.351	13.590	11.470	9.818	8.514	7.469	6.623	6.259	5.929	5.353	4.870	4.460	4.110	3.954	3.808	3.546	3.316	2.850	2.497	2.221	1.999
21......	18.857	17.011	14.029	11.764	10.017	8.649	7.562	6.687	6.312	5.973	5.384	4.891	4.476	4.121	3.963	3.816	3.551	3.320	2.852	2.498	2.221	2.000
22......	19.660	17.658	14.451	12.042	10.201	8.772	7.645	6.743	6.359	6.011	5.410	4.909	4.488	4.130	3.970	3.822	3.556	3.323	2.853	2.498	2.222	2.000
23......	20.456	18.292	14.857	12.303	10.371	8.883	7.718	6.792	6.399	6.044	5.432	4.925	4.499	4.137	3.976	3.827	3.559	3.325	2.854	2.499	2.222	2.000
24......	21.243	18.914	15.247	12.550	10.529	8.985	7.784	6.835	6.434	6.073	5.451	4.937	4.507	4.143	3.981	3.831	3.562	3.327	2.855	2.499	2.222	2.000
25......	22.023	19.523	15.622	12.783	10.675	9.077	7.843	6.873	6.464	6.097	5.467	4.948	4.514	4.147	3.985	3.834	3.564	3.329	2.856	2.499	2.222	2.000
26......	22.795	20.121	15.983	13.003	10.810	9.161	7.896	6.906	6.491	6.118	5.480	4.956	4.520	4.151	3.988	3.837	3.566	3.330	2.856	2.500	2.222	2.000
27......	23 560	20.707	16.330	13.211	10.935	9.237	7.943	6.935	6.514	6.136	5.492	4.964	4.524	4.154	3.990	3.839	3.567	3.331	2.856	2.500	2.222	2.000
28......	24.316	21.281	16.663	13.406	11.051	9.307	7.984	6.961	6.534	6.152	5.502	4.970	4.528	4.157	3.992	3.840	3.568	3.331	2.857	2.500	2.222	2.000
29......	25.066	21.844	16.984	13.591	11.158	9.370	8.022	6.983	6.551	6.166	5.510	4.975	4.531	4.159	3.994	3.841	3.569	3.332	2.857	2.500	2.222	2.000
30......	25.808	22.396	17.292	13.765	11.258	9.427	8.055	7.003	6.566	6.177	5.517	4.979	4.534	4.160	3.995	3.842	3.569	3.332	2.857	2.500	2.222	2.000
40......	32.835	27 355	19.793	15.046	11.925	9.779	8.244	7.105	6.642	6.234	5.548	4.997	4.544	4.166	3.999	3.846	3.571	3.333	2.857	2.500	2.222	2.000
50......	39.196	31.424	21.482	15.762	12.234	9.915	8.304	7.133	6.661	6.246	5.554	4.999	4.545	4.167	4.000	3.846	3.571	3.333	2.857	2.500	2.222	2.000

Reproduced with permission from Robert N. Anthony, *Management Accounting,* 4th ed. (Homewood, Ill.: Richard D. Irwin, © 1970).

Two observations may be drawn from Table 12. First, for the same number of periods, the value of the annuity decreases as the rate increases (because of using large discounting factors). The present value of a 5-year annuity of $1 is $3.791 at 10 percent, $2.991 at 20 percent, and $2.436 at 30 percent. Second, at the same interest rate, the increase in value because of additional periods occurs at a decreasing rate. At 10 percent the present value of $1 to be received at the end of each year for 2 years is $1.736; for 3 years it is $2.487 (an increment of $0.751); for 4 years, $3.170 (a smaller increment of $0.683); for 5 years, $3.791 (a still smaller increment of $0.621). An understanding of these two observations will be of help in learning the mechanics of computing the DCFR.

A Process of Trial and Error

A question to be raised at this time is, How do we determine the rate of return by the DCFR method? The answer—by trial and error. Consider the simple example of an investment of $3,791 at the beginning of the first year (or at the end of year zero) that will result in net cash flows of $1,000 at the end of each year for 5 years.

This may be represented graphically as follows:

End of year:	0	1	2	3	4	5
Cash outflows:	$3,791	0	0	0	0	0
Cash inflows:	0	$1,000	$1,000	$1,000	$1,000	$1,000

Since the cash inflows are uniform, the annuity table may be used. The question to be asked is, At what rate is the present value of a $1 annuity for 5 years multiplied by $1,000 to equal $3,791? In other words, if we let x be the value in the table (the rate that will equate cash inflows with cash outflows), then

$$1{,}000x = 3{,}791$$
$$x = 3.791$$

The rate that will result for a value of $3.791 in 5 years is the rate of return on the project.

An inspection of the values in the annuity table for the 5-year period shows that the entry in the 10 percent column is exactly $3.791. Accordingly, the DCFR is 10 percent.

How can we get the answer when no entry in the table exactly equals the amount we are looking for? It can be found by a trial-and-error process.

EXAMPLE

The ABC Corporation is considering the purchase of a new machine. The purchase price is $10,000 and it is expected to generate net cash inflows of $2,500 a year over the next 5 years. What is the DCFR on the proposed investment?

SOLUTION

End of year:	0	1	2	3	4	5
Cash outflows:	$10,000	0	0	0	0	0
Cash inflows:	0	$2,500	$2,500	$2,500	$2,500	$2,500

The DCFR is the rate that will make the present value of the five annual $2,500 cash inflows equal to the initial investment of $10,000. This means that the $2,500 multiplied by the present value from the annuity table (the present value of $1 received each year for 5 years) should equal $10,000. Since 4 multiplied by $2,500 is equal to $10,000, the rate of interest that will equate the cash inflows with the cash outflows is that rate that will make the present value of an annuity of $1 for 5 years equal to $4.

An examination of the values in the annuity table for a 5-year period indicates that the rate lies between 6 and 8 percent.

Rate	*Present Value of an Annuity of $1 for 5 Years*	*Present Value of Cash Inflows*
6%	4.212	$2,500 X 4.212 = $10,530.00
8%	3.993	$2,500 X 3.993 = $ 9,982.50

Thus, at 6 percent, the present value of cash inflows is $10,530. Since this amount is higher than the $10,000 investment, the investment must be earning more than 6 percent. At 8 percent, the present value of the cash flows is $9,982.50. Since the latter amount is less than the $10,000 investment, the rate of return must be lower than 8 percent. This trial-and-error process indicates that the rate of return lies between 6 and 8 percent.

To find the percentage or rate of return that lies between two rates is known as an interpolation process. This interpolation assumes linear progression.

Consequently, the computed return, strictly speaking, is an approximation because the actual function is nonlinear. This is quite acceptable, however, since the difference between the exact rate and the interpolated rate is always small.

At 6% the present value is $10,530.
At ? the present value is $10,000.
At 8% the present value is $9,982.5.

A 2 percent difference between 6 and 8 percent corresponds to $547.5 ($10,530 - $9,982.5). The difference between the present value of $10,530 at 6 percent and the $10,000 present value of the project's unknown rate is $530. If $547.5 is due to a 2 percent rate, then $530 is due to 0.019.

$$0.02 \times \frac{530}{547.5} = 0.019$$

Therefore, the DCFR on the proposed investment is 7.9 percent (0.06 + 0.019).

EXAMPLE

The ABC Corporation is considering the purchase of a piece of automated equipment that will result in annual after-tax cash flows of:

Year	*Cash Flows*
1	$1,000
2	2,000
3	3,000
4	3,000
5	4,000
6	3,000
7	1,000

The purchase price is $8,052. Compute the DCFR on this investment.

SOLUTION

To find the DCFR, a trial-and-error process is needed. First, a rate is selected, by guess, and tested to find if it will equate the cash inflows and outflows. If not, another rate is selected, and so on.

Suppose 18 percent is the first guess at the rate of return. The present-value table for single values is used because the cash inflows differ from year to year. The present value of the cash inflows at 18 percent is $8,830, found as follows:

$$\begin{aligned}\text{Present value} &= \$1{,}000(0.847) + \$2{,}000(0.718) + \$3{,}000(0.609)\\ &\quad + \$3{,}000(0.516) + \$4{,}000(0.437) + \$3{,}000(0.370)\\ &\quad + \$1{,}000(0.314)\\ &= \$847 + \$1{,}436 + \$1{,}827 + \$1{,}548 + \$1{,}748\\ &\quad + \$1{,}110 + \$314\\ &= \$8{,}830\end{aligned}$$

Since the purchase price is only $8,052, the investment must be earning more than 18 percent; therefore, another rate (the next rate in the table) is tried, the 20 percent rate.

The present value of the cash inflows at 20 percent is $8,296, found as follows:

$$\begin{aligned}\text{Present value} &= \$1{,}000(0.833) + \$2{,}000(0.694) + \$3{,}000(0.579)\\ &\quad + \$3{,}000(0.482) + \$4{,}000(0.402) + \$3{,}000(0.335)\\ &\quad + \$1{,}000(0.279)\\ &= \$833 + \$1{,}388 + \$1{,}737 + \$1{,}446 + \$1{,}608\\ &\quad + \$1{,}005 + \$279\\ &= \$8{,}296\end{aligned}$$

Again, the $8,296 is more than the initial outlay of $8,052, and, accordingly, the investment must have a higher rate of return. Let us try 22 percent.

The present value of the cash inflows at 22 percent is $7,808, found as follows:

$$\begin{aligned}\text{Present value} &= \$1{,}000(0.820) + \$2{,}000(0.672) + \$3{,}000(0.551)\\ &\quad + \$3{,}000(0.451) + \$4{,}000(0.370) + \$3{,}000(0.303)\\ &\quad + \$1{,}000(0.249)\\ &= \$820 + \$1{,}344 + \$1{,}653 + \$1{,}353 + \$1{,}480\\ &\quad + \$909 + \$249\\ &= \$7{,}808\end{aligned}$$

The $7,808 present value is less than the initial outlay, which means that the actual rate of return is less than 22 percent.

So far, it is obvious that the rate of return is somewhere between 20 and 22 percent. This answer may be acceptable. However, to find a single rate, an interpolation process is needed.

At 20% the present value is $8,296.
At ? the present value is $8,052.
At 22% the present value is $7,808.

A 2 percent difference between 20 and 22 percent corresponds to $488 ($8,296 - $7,808). The difference between the $8,296 (at 20 percent) and the present value of $8,052 is $244. Thus, the dollar difference corresponds to 244/488 of the 2 percent difference between 20 and 22 percent:

$$0.02 \times \frac{244}{488} = 0.02 \times \frac{1}{2} = 0.01$$

Therefore, the DCFR on this investment is 21 percent (0.20 + 0.01).

As can be seen, the trial-and-error process may prove to be time-consuming and tedious. However, there are shortcuts for determining the rate to start with, such as using the reciprocal of some form of the payback period (the cash inflows are averaged and divided by the cash outflows). Also, computer programs are available to facilitate the process.

A simple procedure (a form of payback period) may be used to help select the first rate to be tried and thereby reduce the number of necessary trials. To use this procedure, add all the cash inflows to be received in the future, including salvage value and recovery of working capital if applicable ($1,000 + $2,000 + $3,000 + $3,000 + $4,000 + $3,000 + $1,000 = $17,000). Divide this total of cash inflows by the years of life of the project ($17,000 ÷ 7 = $2,429). Divide the initial cash outlay by the last figure calculated ($8,052 ÷ $2,429 = $3.315). Finally, consult the annuity table, in the row indicating the years of life of the project, for the rate that will make the present value of a dollar received annually closest to the figure found in the previous step. (The entries of the 7-year row show that $3.315 lies between 22 and 24 percent.) Thus, according to this simple procedure, the first rate to apply should be 22 percent or 24 percent; usually, we start with the smaller rate. If the 22 percent rate is selected as the starting point, it will take one more trial to find that the actual rate lies between 20 and 22 percent.

Cash Flows, Not Accounting Income

The DCFR method uses the superior concept of cash flows in the analysis. An investment is basically an exchange of immediate cash (expenditure) for a future stream of cash (benefits) that extends over a number of years to come. Until benefits are received in the form of cash, they should not be considered realized because, until they are received in cash, they cannot be reinvested at face value.

The cash flow concept is different from the accrual accounting concept, which tries to charge expenses to benefiting periods regardless of when they are paid. For example, according to accounting concepts, whether the rent is paid for one year or for five years in advance, at the end of the first year an accounting adjustment is made to charge the income statement with only one year's rent.

For DCFR purposes, cash payments are all that matter, and, using the latter example, the full amount is considered cash outflows when it is paid, regardless of the accounting treatment of the expenditure. The reason for such treatment is that paying the rent in advance results in tying up an extra amount of cash. The same analogy holds with respect to benefits. Credit sales, from a cash-flow viewpoint, should not be considered realized until they are collected in cash. In other words, for DCFR purposes, we are mainly concerned with cash, not accounts receivable or other transitory forms before cash is received.

Cash flows may be divided into cash inflows and cash outflows. Cash inflows are receipts or benefits from the investment. Cash outflows are payments related to the investment that are made by the company. "Net cash flows" means the excess of one over the other. Net cash flows can be positive (when cash inflows exceed cash outflows), or negative (when cash outflows exceed cash inflows).

To appreciate the concept of cash flows one has only to point to the problems avoided by using cash flows instead of accrual accounting. Accrual accounting involves a never-ending process of allocating costs among different accounting periods and different financial statements. It is much easier for a group of individuals to agree on cash flows than on accounting income.

Although our main concern is with cash, this does not mean we are to follow this concept blindly. It is usually acceptable to use an approximation or shortcut to estimate cash flows when the difference between the long method (calculating everything on a cash basis) and the approximation method is insignificant. A common shortcut is to start with accounting income as determined in the normal way (especially when it is readily available) and to add to it the depreciation charges and other similar non-cash charges to obtain the figure for cash flows.

Do Not Deduct Depreciation. A word of caution is needed here to point out a source of possible errors. Some individuals feel that a depreciation allowance should be deducted from the cash flows to compensate for capital consumption of the assets used. This practice is absolutely wrong since it involves a double counting of the investment. As a part of the DCFR mechanism, each cash flow includes a capital recovery and a return on the capital used. To deduct depreciation from cash flows would mean allowing for the recovery of the asset twice—once as part of the DCFR computation and again through deductions for depreciation.

Do Not Deduct Charges for Financing. Generally, the proper way to deal with finance charges (or the cost of funds) is to consider them when figuring the cost of capital (to be discussed in detail in Chapter 6). It is incorrect to deduct a finance charge from the cash inflows because that will result in double consideration of these charges—once when comparing the rate of return with the minimum cutoff or desirable rate, and again when figuring net cash flows. The proper way is to keep the evaluation of capital expenditures separate from financing since it is difficult, and theoretically unacceptable, to identify a given source of funds with each investment project.

Even when funds can be borrowed at a given rate for a specific project, this is not considered cost of capital. The cost of capital is usually much higher. Incurring additional debt affects the cost of *future* capital (makes it harder to borrow more funds) and the rate charged for borrowed funds is a result of the credit standing of a company. The credit standing of a company may change as a result of the increased debt, and the cost of common equity may increase as a result of a change in its capital structure.

Always Deduct Taxes. Cash flows should be determined net, after all taxes. Taxes have to be paid in cash, thereby qualifying as cash outflows. Considering government practice of accelerating deadlines for paying taxes, it is quite legitimate to treat taxes as immediate cash outflows as soon as taxable gains are realized. Reduction in tax payments due to investment tax credit (when applicable) and accelerated depreciation methods should be considered when determining cash flows. If taxes were ignored, a meaningful comparison of proposals would not be possible; nor would an intelligent comparison with cost of capital be feasible.

The Reinvestment Assumption

One of the most controversial issues surrounding the DCFR method is the so-called reinvestment assumption. Some writers and practitioners believe that this assumption is implied whenever the DCFR method is used, while others deny that it even exists. Reinvestment assumption centers around what the DCFR method assumes is done with the cash flows received from an investment.

Believers in the reinvestment assumption maintain that, through the DCFR mechanism, cash flows received during the life of an investment are assumed to be reinvested at the rate of return of that investment. For example, a 20 percent DCFR on a given investment assumes that cash flows received during the life of the investment are reinvested at 20 percent and that, similarly, a 15 percent DCFR assumes reinvestment of proceeds at 15 percent.

The question now is whether reinvestment assumption exists or not, and what to do about it. The answer to the first part of the question is both yes and no. If you interpret the DCFR as the rate of return on the initial investment, the answer is yes. If you interpret the rate of return in another way, the answer is no. For example, consider two investments, A and B. Investment A has initial outlays of $1,589 and is expected to bring an annual cash flow of $1,000 for 3 years.

By trial and error, it will be found that the rate of return on project A is 40 percent. This is the case because, when the $1.589 present-value factor of an annuity of $1 at 40 percent for 3 years is multiplied by $1,000, the product, $1,589, equals the initial investment.

Investment B has the same initial outlays of $1,589 and is expected to have a single cash inflow (benefits of $4,366 to be received at the end of the third year). The present value of $1 to be received 3 years later at 40 percent is $0.364 and, accordingly, the present value is $1,589 ($4,366 × $0.364). This means that the rate of return on project B is also 40 percent.

Advocates of the reinvestment assumption argue that although the two projects seem equal (each is expected to earn 40 percent), the two investments are not of equal profitability.[4] Unless the $1,000 received each year from project A is reinvested at the 40 percent rate, the actual return on the $1,589 initial investment is less than 40 percent. To see the difference, consider the possibility that the firm would be able to reinvest the proceeds at only 10 percent.

At 10 percent, the $1,000 received at the end of the first year will be equal to $1,210 ($1,000 $[1 + 0.1]^2$) at the end of the third year. The $1,000 received at the end of the second year will be equal to $1,100 ($1,000 [1 + 0.1]) at the end of the third year. The value of all cash flows at the end of the third year is $3,310 ($1,210 from first-year benefits, plus $1,100 from second-year benefits, plus $1,000 from third-year benefits).

Thus, project A will accumulate the equivalent to total benefits of $3,310 at the end of the third year, whereas project B will bring the larger amount of $4,366. Obviously, under these conditions, the true rate of return on the *initial* investment for project A is below 40 percent (between 26 and 28 percent).

The reinvestment assumption does not exist if the rate of return is viewed as a return on the outstanding amount of the investment. From this viewpoint, the DCFR is the actual rate on the amount of investment outstanding. Once the cash flows are received, what is done with them is not relevant.[5]

Since each argument is right in a way, it is hard to say that one is more right than the other. However, the latter viewpoint seems more consistent with a typical evaluation situation. An investment is supposed to earn a return on the capital employed. Once an amount is returned, it seems unfair to punish a project because of future inability to find equally desirable investments.

If we take the reinvestment viewpoint, then we must select a rate of reinvestment to apply to the cash flows received before the end of the life of the investment. This rate is hard to justify since it should depend in part upon the opportunities for investment that will be open several years hence, an almost impossible determination. Also, if the present cost of capital is used as the reinvestment rate, this practice will lead to unfair treatment of projects since future cash flows should be considered reinvested at the best possible rate and not at the cost (usually lower) of obtaining funds.

In summary, it is preferable to overlook the reinvestment assumption unless it is certain that opportunities for reinvestment will be scarce in the future and thus at a materially reduced rate. Furthermore, when such a situation exists, it is better to use instead the net present value method, to be discussed in Chapter 6.

The Unconventional Investment with Multiple DCFR

When an investment results in a series of negative and positive net cash flows, it is called unconventional investment. Some unconventional investments may have more than one rate of return.

EXAMPLE

An investment requires cash outlays of $100 at the beginning of the project and results in the following net cash flows:

End of Year	*Net Cash Flows*[6]
1	$360
2	–428
3	168

Calculate the DCFR for this investment.

SOLUTION

Three DCFR solutions will make the present value of cash flows equal to the $100 investment: 0 percent, 20 percent, and 50 percent. First, since a $100 investment results in total cash inflows of $100 ($360 – $428 + $168 = $100), the DCFR is zero.

Second, at 20 percent DCFR, the cash flows are as shown in Table 13. Present value of cash flows is equal to the $100 initial investment.

Table 13. Cash flows at 20 percent DCFR.

Year (1)	Cash Flows (2)	Present Value of $1 at 20% (3)	Present Value of Cash Flows (2 X 3) (4)
1	$360	0.833	$299.880
2	-428	0.694	-297.032
3	168	0.579	97.272
			$100.12
		rounded to	$100.00

Finally, at a 50 percent rate, the cash flows are as shown in Table 14. Present value of cash flows is equal to the $100 initial investment.

Table 14. Cash flows at 50 percent DCFR.

Year (1)	Cash Flows (2)	Present Value of $1 at 50% (3)	Present Value of Cash Flows (2 X 3) (4)
1	$360	0.667	$240.120
2	-428	0.444	-190.032
3	168	0.296	49.728
			$ 99.816
		rounded to	$100.00

The possibility of multiple DCFR solutions is one of the shortcomings of the DCFR method. However, unconventional investments do not occur frequently enough (they occur very rarely) to warrant advising against the use of DCFR. It means simply that when an investment with unconventional cash flows is analyzed, the DCFR method should not be used (unconventional cash flows may result in incremental analysis of projects of different sizes).

Arguments For and Against the DCFR Method

The DCFR method has its own advocates and opponents; each uses some commonly known arguments, some of which are cited here. These arguments should not be taken as absolute truths since for each one of them there is a counter-argument. Also, in some particular situations an argument will be more valid than in others.

Arguments For the DCFR Method

Some of the arguments used by those favoring the DCFR method were mentioned earlier, among the characteristics of the method. Therefore, they are discussed only briefly here.

Time Value of Money. Undoubtedly, the key argument is that the DCFR method allows for the time value of money. This enables the rate of return so computed to accommodate the different patterns of cash flows associated with different investment proposals.

Cash Flows. The DCFR computations are based on cash flows, not accounting income. For capital expenditure analysis purposes, the concept of cash flows is more applicable than that of accounting income. This enables the DCFR method to be less dependent on accounting conventions than is the case with methods that use accounting income.

Ranking Proposals. The rate of return computed by the DCFR method may be used as a basis for ranking proposals. This makes it easier to select from these proposals. It is further argued that the use of DCFR results in a consistent system of ranking and selecting investment proposals.

Mistakes in Later Years. Due to the discounting process, the further in the future the amount is expected to be realized, the less its present value and the less its influence on the rate of return. It is argued, accordingly, that the discounting process reduces the impact of errors in estimating very distant future values, such as cash flows in later years or salvage value.

Proper Treatment of Taxes. The DCFR method provides for correct treatment of taxes. Taxes affect cash flows, and cash flows are used in the computations; consequently they are considered.

Comparability with Cost of Capital. The rate of return computed by the DCFR method may easily be compared with the cost of capital. This is found to be true because the DCFR method computes a rate of return, and that rate is computed on the outstanding or used part of capital. Comparison with the cost of capital does not necessarily require specifying an exact value but rather a range.

DCFR Versus Net Present Value. As will be seen when the net present value (NPV) is discussed, the NPV method requires prior knowledge of the cost of capital (or some substitute rate) for use in the computations. The DCFR is computed independently from the cost of capital. Since the cost of capital is, to say the least, a highly controversial issue, and an agreement on a cost-of-capital figure is often impossible to achieve, it can be a big relief to use a method that does not require specifying it.

Familiarity with Rate of Return Concepts. One of the main reasons for favoring the DCFR method over its competitor, the net present value method, is that top management and operating personnel are familiar with the rate of return language used in financial circles. It is similar to the amortization of debt. Also, it seems easier to interpret and understand a rate of return than a dollar present value. This idea will be explained in more detail in Chapter 6.

Easy to Continue Updating. Although the introduction and installment of a sound, discounted rate of return system may involve additional costs to a company, little effort and few costs are required to keep the system going once it is installed.

More Complete Analysis. Another argument is that the use of the DCFR method forces all individuals concerned to estimate cash flows and to consider many factors that would otherwise be ignored. Through bringing these factors out in the open, they can be recognized, studied, and dealt with. In other words, the method encourages more in-depth analysis of capital expenditures.

Arguments Against the DCFR Method

Recently, some writers and practitioners have voiced their concern about the increasing use of the DCFR method. They say that the method has many drawbacks that may outweigh its advantages.

The Need for Education and Training. It is argued that the main problem with DCFR seems to be that many people are uncomfortable with compound interest and discounting. This is especially true for some operating managers. Even when the idea of discounting is quite acceptable, introduction and implementation of such an idea in actual situations take a long time and require extensive and intensive efforts to educate and train the people involved to understand the method, to use it properly, and to develop the necessary administrative changes to accommodate it.

Because of common resistance to change and the need not only to learn the new method but to unlearn the old, much time and effort are consumed.

Heavy Demands on Analysis Staff Personnel. Another common argument is that the use of DCFR results in excessive demands on analysis staff personnel. This is not always the case since, first, if more savings are to be expected from proper analysis, it may be worthwhile to hire more analysts. Second, computer programs are available to do most of the tedious and time-consuming routine DCFR computations. Third, if all concerned individuals are well trained and properly educated in the use of DCFR, they can do most of the analysis themselves without having to depend heavily on analysis staff personnel. Finally, it could be argued that the additional time spent by analysis staff personnel would be more than compensated for by the time saved by top management personnel.

However, regardless of the counter-arguments, the DCFR method requires more in-depth analysis and computations than other rough or informal methods of evaluation.

Difficult to Compare with Accounting Data. Since the accounting books are not usually kept on a cash flow basis or on a project basis, it is not easy to compare the actual with the estimated cash flows for an investment project. It could be countered that this difficulty is true with all other methods. Nevertheless, comparability with accounting data is a problem when the DCFR method is used.

Revising Policies and Procedures. It is often necessary to change forms, procedures, and manuals to accommodate the introduction of the DCFR method.

Multiple Yields. The DCFR method may result, under extreme conditions of having unconventional cash flows, in finding more than one rate of return on the same investment. Opponents of the method argue that even though this will be the exception rather than the rule, it is still a defect of the DCFR method.

The Reinvestment Assumption. The reinvestment assumption, discussed earlier, is considered a major drawback of the method. The DCFR is not a return on the initial investment but on the outstanding amount of the investment. Opponents of the DCFR method assert that what is to be done with cash flows is very important and that the DCFR method, by ignoring this subject, is misleading.

Overemphasis on Allocation of Capital. It could be argued that the DCFR method overemphasizes the scarcity of capital, whereas capital is not that difficult to obtain. It is harder to find good investments than it is to find the funds to finance them.

DCFR Cannot Be Used Under All Conditions. Selection of the higher rate of return alternative of the DCFR method does not always result in selection of the best investment when the alternative proposals have different lives. Furthermore, the DCFR method does not always result in the correct selection of projects from among mutually exclusive investments (if one is selected, the others have to be rejected). This is by far the most serious argument against the DCFR method.

Inflation. It is also argued that the DCFR method does not deal with the problem of inflation. However, no existing method does deal properly with inflation.

Evaluation of the Arguments

A study of the arguments will show that, overall, the arguments in favor of the DCFR method are stronger than those against it.

Misuses of DCFR

Like any other tool, the DCFR is useful when used properly and less useful or even harmful when abused or used beyond its capabilities. An example of misuse of DCFR, as told by one of the financial officers of a large mining company, is that decision makers often treat the rate of return as an absolute truth, overlooking the simple fact that all the figures are based on assumptions and that at best the rate of return is no better than the assumptions on which it is based. The DCFR is not designed to replace judgment; nor is it designed to be used blindly.

A misunderstanding of the DCFR method and its limitations occurs when decisions to ration funds among projects are based on very small differences in the rates of return. Because of dealing with estimates, the exact DCFR cannot be determined; therefore, decisions should not be based on small differences in rates of return among projects. When the computed rates are insignificantly different, other methods should be used to supplement the DCFR method.

Some individuals assume that the DCFR measures risk. This assumption is far from the truth, since the discounting process takes into consideration the time value of money–not risk. Risk refers to the distribution and certainty of achieving the estimates. The possible distribution of various estimates is an important topic in its own right and must be dealt with in other ways. The DCFR should not be construed as a substitute for ways of treating risk. (See Chapter 9.)

A common misunderstanding assumes that DCFR is a cure-all for problems of capital expenditure analysis. A closely related issue is that some managers think that the use of DCFR will relieve them of the tedious process of estimating cash flows and that they can use sloppy forecasting and administrative methods as long as the DCFR is used. The DCFR method is not a panacea for capital investment analysis problems, and it is not a substitute for good estimates or good judgment. Proper use of DCFR requires more–not less–refined and more detailed estimates of cash flows.

Another common misuse of DCFR is to "compute DCFR and actually use payback or other methods in the evaluation." Some managers require the use of the DCFR method on paper, but when it comes to the final analysis and evaluation, the decision is based on other methods. This practice is dangerous. Unless top management is planning to use the figures computed by the DCFR method, there is no need for wasting the money or the time and effort of employees to compute them. A human relations problem is bound to exist when it is found that top management consistently asks for figures that are seldom used. If it becomes known that top management pays lip service to DCFR and that decisions are made regardless of DCFR results, employees down the line will also pay lip service to the use of DCFR in the evaluation process. If top management does not believe in DCFR, it is better not to use it.

It is commonly assumed that just because the DCFR method makes sense to analysts and evaluators, every concerned individual in the organization will be able to understand it and support it. The experience of corporations does not support this assumption. In fact, their experience shows that it is important to educate and train all levels in proper investment analysis. This education process is not by any means a one-exposure affair; it is a continuous process. Further, education and training should start from the highest managerial level and proceed down, for the obvious reason that unless top management understands and supports DCFR, it will never be successful.

Another misuse of DCFR is requiring that all projects, regardless of their nature, be evaluated by using DCFR. This is bad practice since there are projects that cannot be subjected to such analysis and should be dealt with in a different manner. Examples of such projects include those that are intended to improve the morale of employees, where meaningful quantitative cash flows cannot be realistically estimated.

It is sometimes assumed that efficient investment analysis requires evaluating all proposals in the same manner. This is not necessarily true since a more elaborate analysis should be made for major projects and a less detailed analysis for minor ones. Analysis, like most operations, has a cost, and this cost should be more than compensated by the expected benefits from such refinement. Major projects are more likely to benefit from elaborate analysis than are minor projects. In other words, the analysis should not be carried beyond its beneficial point.

When DCFR Should Be Used Cautiously

The DCFR method may not give the correct measure of ranking capital expenditure proposals when selecting from among mutually exclusive projects with unequal lives or unequal sizes. Under conditions of capital rationing (when limited funds are allocated among competing projects that demand more funds) it is not always desirable to judge projects only on the basis of their DCFR figures when the projects are not equal in size, economic life, or risk class (distribution and certainty of cash flows). In Chapter 6, the net present value method will be introduced, and a suggestion will be made regarding what to do about these types of projects and where to find further discussion of ways of dealing with them.

DCFR in Practice

The DCFR is gaining constantly wider acceptance. Although not as popular as payback, it is placed second to payback for major projects, and it ranks as the third most commonly used method of evaluating "all other projects." The present survey shows that the DCFR method is used by 136 of 197 responding firms (69 percent) for major projects and by 102 of 189 responding firms (54 percent) for "all other projects."

Of those using DCFR for evaluating major projects, 68 percent consider it the most important method, 21 percent place it second in importance, and 10 percent place it third or lower (the percentages do not add to 100 because of rounding). The corresponding percentages of "all other projects" are: first, 52 percent; second, 27 percent; and third, 21 percent.

The DCFR method is used the most for evaluating major projects by the following five industries: crude petroleum and natural gas; petroleum refining; paper and allied products; appliances, electronics; and mining.

The data for the "all other projects" category show that usage of the method ranges from 20 percent in the mining industry to 80 percent in the textiles industry. It is used the most for evaluating "all other projects" in the following five industries: textiles; appliances, electronics; crude petroleum and natural gas; petroleum refining; and metal products.

One observation, based on a study of the percentage of users to total replies in each industry, is that in every case the degree of use of DCFR for major projects is at least equal to or more than that for "all other projects." This means that, generally speaking, and as would be expected, the DCFR is used more often for major projects than for "all other projects."

A second observation is that the range for major projects is higher than that for "all other projects." For major projects, usage ranges from as low as 25 percent in the motor vehicle and truck industry to as high as 100 percent in the crude petroleum industry. For "all other projects" (as mentioned above), the corresponding percentages are 20 percent for the mining industry and 80 percent for the textiles industry.

A third observation is that the rankings of industries according to the extent they use DCFR for major projects is not the same as those for "all other projects."

Advantages

Four practical advantages of the DCFR method (that is, more than half of the respondents consider them advantages) are: it considers the time value of money (95 percent of 116 respondents who evaluated DCFR), can be used for evaluating different types of investment proposals (85 percent), analyzes future data—not historical (74 percent), and is accurate (72 percent).

It is not surprising that the preponderant advantage of DCFR is that it considers the time value of money. Being accurate is considered a practical advantage of three methods only: DCFR, net present value, and MAPI. It is not generally considered a practical advantage to the accountant rate of return and payback methods.

Weaknesses

According to the survey responses, the DCFR method has five practical weaknesses (at least half of the respondents consider them a major or a minor weakness). They are: imposes heavy demands on analysis staff personnel (68 percent of 129 respondents), difficult to sell to operating personnel (67 percent), difficult to compare with accounting data (62 percent), unnecessarily complicated (62 percent), and difficult to sell to top management (52 percent).

A preponderant weakness of the DCFR is that it is difficult to sell to operating personnel. This is a problem that can be solved only by more education and training in the theory and practice of capital expenditure analysis. It also points to a relatively new idea—the importance of understanding by operating personnel of the logic behind evaluation and the methods used in such evaluation.

Familiarity with DCFR

Overall, the analysts, evaluators, and decision makers in the responding firms are less familiar with the DCFR method than with payback or accountant rate of return. On the other hand, these individuals are more familiar with the DCFR method than with net present value or MAPI.

Of 190 respondents, 147 (77 percent) feel that analysts, reviewers, and decision makers are familiar with the DCFR method.

Evaluation of DCFR Performance

The DCFR method is regarded highly by the responding firms. Of 137 respondents, 63 (46 percent) consider the performance of the DCFR very satisfactory; 65 (47 percent), fairly satisfactory; only 3 (2 percent), unsatisfactory; and 6 respondents had no opinion. This means that 93 percent of the respondents consider the DCFR either fairly satisfactory or very satisfactory. This percentage indicates by far the highest degree of satisfaction of any of the five methods. It compares with 89 percent for payback, 78 percent for the accountant rate of return, and 75 percent for net present value.

Discontinued as Unsatisfactory

Of the methods that had been used within the last five years and subsequently discontinued because of unsatisfactory results, the DCFR is ranked as the least unsatisfactory. Those companies that had discontinued its use (9 of 147 respondents) represent only 6 percent of the possible replies of yes, no, and not sure, compared to 8 percent for net present value, 9 percent for MAPI, 13 percent for payback, and 20 percent for accountant rate of return.

Typical Comments

A respondent to the evaluation questionnaire discussed the problem of introducing and implementing a discounted cash flow approach. The more sophisticated methods have been studied by his concern and are reasonably well understood by a few. However, they are not readily accepted by the management and operating management because of their complicated nature and time element necessary to understand them.

Another respondent explained how use of a computer can help with capital expenditure analysis in general, and the DCFR method in particular. The methods of present value and discounted cash flow return are used extensively by this company in evaluating capital expenditure proposals. These methods, in addition to other economic evaluation techniques, have been programmed on a remote terminal computer system. The awkwardness usually associated with the use of these techniques is obviated by the computer assistance, which is on line in real time.

The manager of capital investment planning of a large electronics firm indicated that the literature on capital expenditure analysis is confusing, especially on the reinvestment assumption (some say it exists while others state that it does not exist). As an evaluator, he is not convinced that there is a reinvestment assumption associated with the DCFR. He explained that if a $1 million investment is expected to bring annual net cash flows of $50,000, once these cash flows are received they are earned, and what is done with the money after that is irrelevant.

When asked about the possibility of getting more than one rate of return when using DCFR, he indicated that this is not a problem because, from a practical viewpoint, it is unlikely to happen.

The financial vice-president of a successful electronics company warned against excessive emphasis being placed on the DCFR method. He stated that in the final analysis capital expenditure evaluation is a matter of judgment, and knowledge of one's business is necessary for sound decisions. This statement is quite true, since all of the capital expenditure analysis methods and techniques should be regarded as ways of supplementing, enhancing, and aiding the decision maker's judgment, but not replacing it. To be able to exercise sound judgment, familiarity with the business, through experience and other means, is a must.

The vice-president of finance of a large chemical company stated that from his experience it would be easier to manipulate figures to justify a pet proposal if DCFR was used by itself, whereas such manipulation would be revealed if a combination of payback, DCFR, and accountant rate of return were used. The reinvestment assumption, he felt, poses a problem. To overcome it, he suggested it could be assumed that the cash flows received are reinvested at cost of capital.

One executive emphasized the importance of simplifying the analysis when the DCFR method is used. He suggested that the DCFR should be well explained in a company manual that is continuously updated. The tendency in these revisions should be toward more simplified ways of handling the data on a DCFR basis, with the objective of imposing fewer demands on the time of busy operating executives.

Another questionnaire respondent said his company had traditionally used the accountant rate of return and cash payback methods in evaluating capital expenditure proposals. Recently, however, the company instituted the use of discounted cash flow techniques, particularly the DCFR method, in its evaluation procedure. Like many companies, his has experienced difficulties with this innovation due to the unfamiliarity of both analytical and management personnel with the theory and concepts involved.

To justify the use of the discounted cash flow approach, another respondent stated that management had worked with the accountant rate of return and the net present value methods. However, the discounted cash flow, which considers the time value of money, gave a stable base for making comparisons and decisions.

One executive complained about what he considered an undue emphasis on allocation of capital. He indicated that discounted cash flow methods assume that the company is resource-restricted. This is not a correct assumption, in his view, since any successful company can always get the capital if a project is good. There seems to be undue emphasis in the theory of capital expenditure decision making on the unavailability of capital.

Conclusion

The DCFR method is a theoretically sound method. It is used by more business firms now than was the case 10 to 15 years ago.

Like any other tool, the DCFR method should be used with care. Before using it, an individual has to be aware of its capabilities and its limitations. The DCFR method should never be viewed as a panacea for all problems of capital expenditure analysis, but it is certainly an excellent method when used properly.

NOTES

1. *Equipment Replacement and Depreciation Policies and Practices: A Survey* (Washington, D.C.: Machinery and Allied Products Institute, 1956), p. 12.
2. Donald F. Istvan, *Capital-Expenditure Decisions: How They Are Made in Large Corporations,* Indiana Business Report 33 (Bloomington: Indiana University, 1961), p. 69.
3. For an example of available tables, see Jerome Bracken and Charles J. Christenson, *Tables for Use in Analyzing Business Decisions* (Homewood, Ill.: Richard D. Irwin, 1965).
4. Statements supporting the reinvestment assumption are found in the following: James Van Horne, *Financial Management and Policy* (Englewood Cliffs, N.J.: Prentice-Hall, 1968), p. 37; and W. W. Haynes and M. B. Solomon, Jr., "A Misplaced Emphasis in Capital Budgeting," *Quarterly Review of Economics and Business,* No. 2 (February 1962), pp. 39–46.
5. Examples of references that deny the existence of the reinvestment assumption are: *Return on Capital as a Guide to Managerial Decisions,* N.A.A. Research Report 35 (New York: National Association of Accountants, 1959), p. 62; and J. B. Weaver and R. J. Reilly, "Interest Rate of Return for Capital Expenditure Evaluation," *Chemical Engineering Progress* (October 1956), p. 408.
6. This example is based on an illustration in A. J. Merrett and Allen Sykes, *The Finance and Analysis of Capital Projects* (London: Longman, 1961), p. 160.

6 / Net Present Value

THE net present value (NPV) is another discounted cash flow method. It is similar to the discounted cash flow rate of return (DCFR) method, but rather than finding the rate of return that equates the cash inflows with the cash outflows, it discounts the cash flows at an assumed (required or desirable) rate of return. Through the discounting process the present value of the benefits is determined. Then, the initial investment is subtracted from this present value (PV) to determine the net present value (NPV) of the investment. A positive NPV indicates that the proposed investment is profitable.

Accordingly, the total discounted value of the cash inflows is called the present value, and the amount (positive or negative) that would result after deducting the initial investment from this present value is called the net present value. However, in practice the terms NPV and PV are sometimes used interchangeably.

The net present value method is also known as the net present worth method, the present worth method, the discounted cash flow by the present value method, and the discounted cash flow method. The latter term is ambiguous since it could also mean the DCFR method.

In terms of popularity, the NPV method may be placed after the payback, the accountant rate of return (ARR), and the DCFR methods and before the MAPI method. Thus, the NPV ranks fourth among the five commonly known methods of evaluating capital expenditures.

From a theoretical viewpoint, the NPV method is considered by many writers in the field (such as Harold Bierman and Seymour Smidt) to be more desirable than and far superior to the DCFR method. From a practical viewpoint, however, NPV is less well known and less commonly used than the DCFR method. It is often argued that the NPV method is here to stay and that more and more firms are going to shift to the method in the near future.

What Is NPV?

The net present value (NPV) method expresses the attractiveness of a proposed capital expenditure in dollar terms. The starting point is the desired rate of return. A rate has to be selected. This rate may be some form of the cost of capital to the firm or an arbitrary figure that represents the minimum return below which an investment would be undesirable. Determination of this desired return is the most difficult aspect of the NPV computations. Once a rate is selected, the process of computation is simple.

All the cash inflows are discounted at the selected rate, and the net present value is found by deducting the initial investment from the present value of the cash proceeds. If the NPV is positive, the investment is considered desirable, and vice versa.

Consider, for example, a proposed capital expenditure of $12,000 that is expected to result in annual cash inflows after taxes of $4,000 for 4 years. If the desired rate is 10 percent, the present value of the benefits will be computed in this way: $4,000 multiplied by the present value of an annuity of $1 received at the end of the year for 4 years discounted at 10% = $4,000 × 3.170 = $12,680.

The net present value is $680—the present value of the benefits less the initial investment ($12,680 less $12,000).

The same investment would be undesirable if the required rate were 20 percent. In that case, the present value of the cash inflows (benefits) would be $10,356 ($4,000 × 2.589), and the net present value would be - $1,644 ($10,356 - $12,000).

A negative net present value indicates that the proposed investment would not be able to generate the minimum 20 percent rate required for capital expenditures. Unless there are other qualitative reasons to undertake such investment, it should be rejected.

The main difficulty associated with using the net present value method lies in determining the rate of discount to be used in the calculations. A logical rate to use is the cost of capital. However, the cost of capital is difficult to determine because of the wide differences of opinion as to exactly what is meant by the term, the various alternative ways of defining capital and costs (actual or opportunity), and the disagreements over whether, for a given firm, there is one cost of capital or several. The subject is discussed more fully later in this chapter.

Characteristics of NPV

The main characteristics of the NPV method are similar to those of DCFR. Some differences can be attributed to the role assumed in the computations by the desired rate and the way the profitability of the proposed investment is measured.

Ease of Computation

The NPV method, by specifying the discount rate to apply, relieves the analyst of the tedious trial-and-error process. Once the cash inflows and outflows are determined, the NPV computation is a simple matter. Even though the investment may be spread over a period of years, computing the NPV poses no problem, for the cash outflows can be treated as a deduction from the cash inflows, or they can be discounted separately.

EXAMPLE

The XYZ Corporation is considering the purchase of a large piece of equipment that will require overhauling during its lifetime. The benefits and the investments (last year's benefits include the salvage value) are given in Table 15. If it is assumed that the required minimum return is 10 percent, the NPV can be found by two methods. Table 16 gives the solution by treating cash inflows separately from cash outflows, and Table 17 gives the solution by discounting net cash inflows only.

Table 15. Data on proposed equipment purchase.

End of Year	*Cash Inflow*	*Investment*
0	$ 0	$120,000
1	20,000	–
2	20,000	–
3	20,000	20,000
4	30,000	–
5	40,000	–
6	40,000	20,000
7	30,000	–
8	20,000	–
9	20,000	–
10	30,000	–

Dependence on Cost of Capital

An essential requirement of the NPV method is the prior determination of a minimum rate of return to be used in the computations. Often, this minimum is the cost of capital. Some people prefer to use an adjusted cost of capital figure, whereas others simply use an arbitrary figure. Since a change in this

Table 16. Solution by treating cash inflows separately from cash outflows.

End of Year	*Present Value at 10%*	*Present Value of Cash Inflows*	*Present Value of Investment (Cash Outflows)*
0	1.000	\$ 0 × 1.000 = \$ 0	\$120,000 × 1.000 = \$120,000
1	0.909	20,000 × 0.909 = 18,180	
2	0.826	20,000 × 0.826 = 16,520	
3	0.751	20,000 × 0.751 = 15,020	20,000 × 0.751 = 15,020
4	0.683	30,000 × 0.683 = 20,490	
5	0.621	40,000 × 0.621 = 24,840	
6	0.564	40,000 × 0.564 = 22,560	20,000 × 0.564 = 11,280
7	0.513	30,000 × 0.513 = 15,390	
8	0.467	20,000 × 0.467 = 9,340	
9	0.424	20,000 × 0.424 = 8,480	
10	0.386	30,000 × 0.386 = 11,580	
		\$162,400	\$146,300

NPV = PV of cash inflows − PV of cash outflows = \$162,400 − \$146,300 = \$16,100

Table 17. Solution by discounting the net cash inflows only.

End of Year (1)	*Net Cash Inflows (Cash Inflows – Cash Outflows)* (2)	*PV of $1 at 10%* (3)	*PV of Net Cash Inflows (2 X 3)* (4)
0	$ 0 – $120,000 = –$120,000	1.000	–$120,000
1	20,000 – 0 = 20,000	0.909	18,180
2	20,000 – 0 = 20,000	0.826	16,520
3	20,000 – 20,000 = 0	0.751	0
4	30,000 – 0 = 30,000	0.683	20,490
5	40,000 – 0 = 40,000	0.621	24,840
6	40,000 – 20,000 = 20,000	0.564	11,280
7	30,000 – 0 = 30,000	0.513	15,390
8	20,000 – 0 = 20,000	0.467	9,340
9	20,000 – 0 = 20,000	0.424	8,480
10	30,000 – 0 = 30,000	0.386	11,580
		NPV =	$ 16,100

established minimum could result in changing the status of a proposal from desirable to undesirable, or vice versa, the minimum should be determined with care. An excessively high minimum results in an ultra-conservative capital expenditure program, and an excessively low minimum results in the acceptance of a host of unprofitable investments. Since the cost of capital usually plays a major role in establishing this minimum, it is more fully discussed later in this chapter. It is sufficient now to mention the need of establishing a minimum desirable rate of return and to point out that doing so is not an easy task.

NPV for Different Types of Investment Proposals

Unlike the DCFR, from which it is possible to obtain more than one rate of return on the same investment, there is only one NPV figure for an investment at a given discount or interest rate.

The NPV may be used for evaluating different types of investment proposals, regardless of the pattern of the cash flows. There is no problem with unconventional cash flows (an assorted combination of positive and negative net cash flows).

In addition, it is often argued that the NPV method is far superior to the DCFR method for selecting among mutually exclusive investment proposals with significantly different useful lives. Bierman and Smidt go to the extent of recommending net present value as usually being the best method of evaluating capital expenditure proposals.[1]

Other Characteristics

Time Value of Money. The NPV method considers the time value of money through the discounting of cash flows. Both the cash inflows and the cash outflows are discounted to a single point in time (usually the start-up time).

Cash Flows. The NPV method uses the superior concept of cash flows (not accounting income) in the analysis.

The Reinvestment Assumption. The reinvestment assumption poses no significant problem with the NPV method because the cash flows are discounted at the desired rate.

Difficulty of Interpreting the Profitability Measure. The NPV method measures the profitability of a proposed investment. However, the end result of the computation is a dollar net present value, not a rate of return. Unfortunately, it is hard to interpret this dollar value.

A related difficulty is the unfamiliarity of businessmen with the NPV concept. Businessmen usually feel more at ease with a rate of return that can be compared with market rates.

Insensitivity to the Required Investment. One of the main arguments against the NPV method is that a net present value by itself may not tell the whole story about the profitability of a capital expenditure proposal. A $1,000 NPV on a $2,000 investment, other things being equal, is more profitable than a $1,000 NPV on a $200,000 investment. To help overcome such an argument, a profitability index was developed.

The Profitability Index

The P.I. or profitability index, also known as benefit/cost ratio, desirability index, or discounted profitability index, is the ratio of the present value of the cash inflows (benefits) divided by the present value of the cash outflows (investment). By relating the benefits to the investment in such a manner, it is possible to compare one project with another even though the required investments are different.

A profitability index of 1 means that the present value of benefits is exactly equal to the present value of the investment. A P.I. of more than 1 indicates that the proposed investment is profitable, and a less-than-1 P.I. indicates that the project is unprofitable. The profitability index for the XYZ Corporation example introduced earlier in this chapter is:

$$\frac{\text{Present value of benefits}}{\text{Present value of investment}} = \frac{\$162{,}400}{\$146{,}300} = 1.11$$

The profitability index is often criticized as being difficult to interpret. Another criticism, which can also be made of any rate of return calculation, is that of being insensitive to the size of net benefits. Given a choice between a 1.1 index for a million-dollar investment ($100,000 net present value) and a 2.0 index for a $1,000 investment ($1,000 net present value), the former investment with the lower P.I. should be selected since it will result in much higher benefits. Therefore, the P.I. is not generally regarded as the ideal measure of the profitability of a capital expenditure proposal.

The Cost of Capital

The cost-of-capital theory may be best described by borrowing Harold Koontz's term "management theory jungle" and referring to it as the "cost-of-capital theory jungle." The cost of capital is one of the most controversial financial management topics. Differences of opinion exist regarding what it is, how to measure it, what is meant by capital, what is meant by cost, and how to determine the overall cost of capital for different firms under different conditions.

The combined or weighted-average after-tax cost of long-term sources of capital is one definition of the cost of capital. It is often computed by using a weighted average of the cost of the components of capital—various forms of long-term debt, preferred stock, common stockholders' equity. The latter includes common stock, retained earnings, and other forms of stockholders' equity such as contributions in excess of par and other proprietary reserves.

To appreciate the real complexity of this apparently straightforward definition and the diversity of opinions, a selected sample of controversial questions may be cited. Is depreciation part of capital, and if so, what is its cost? Does the cost of capital include the cost of short-term debt? Is there one cost of capital, or are there several costs of capital? Is it a single point or a range? Is it constant, or does it change over time? If so, how often does it change? Is the cost of capital independent, or is it dependent upon the debt-equity mix? Does the cost of capital vary with the change in the risk class of capital investments? Does the cost of capital have a constant, increasing, or decreasing function with respect to volume? What are the role and the effect of taxes on cost of capital? If an overall cost of capital is computed, what weights should be used to combine the costs (that is, market values or book values)? What is the role played by dividends? What is the cost of capital for a stable industry in comparison with that of a growth industry? Should the cost of capital be used in the net present value computations, or should a risk-adjusted rate be used? Are retained earnings cost-free? If they are not, how can their cost be determined?

Obviously, an adequate discussion of cost of capital in a limited space and at a simple level of mathematical sophistication is not an easy task and could be the subject of a separate book. Since the cost of capital is presented here as a means to an end, that end being its use for capital expenditure analysis, a simplified approach is used. The underlying assumption is that the interested reader, having been warned of the complexity of the subject, will go to some of the referenced sources for more refined analysis.

Uses of Cost of Capital

Why does a firm need to know its cost of capital? The answers to this question may vary; nevertheless, several basic reasons can be cited. Management needs to know its firm's cost of capital for use as a guide when appraising capital expenditures. If a firm's cost of capital is 10 percent, a capital expenditure promising a 4 percent return should not be undertaken unless qualitative benefits or other considerations warrant its acceptance. If the cost of capital is not known, managers are working in the dark.

The cost of capital (or some version of the cost of capital) may be used as a basis for selecting the discount rate to be applied in the net present value computations. Knowledge of the firm's cost of capital provides an objective basis for selecting a discount rate to use instead of an arbitrary figure.

For those who believe that the capital structure of the firm (the mix of debt and equity) affects the cost of capital, guidelines for an optimal capital structure (the mix of debt and equity that will minimize the cost of capital at a given risk level) could be determined for the firm. The cost of capital may be observed over time, to study its trend and compare it with the economic trend and, if feasible, with other firms. The cost of capital may be regarded as the minimum target rate of return that the firm must exceed if it is to survive for a long period.

The results of a written questionnaire on the cost of capital are shown to give an idea of how this concept is viewed in practice. The questionnaire data on cost of capital presented in this chapter are based on a questionnaire sent to a selected sample of the 1,000 largest industrial corporations listed by *Fortune,* as described on page 6 of this book. The questionnaire data do not provide all the answers because of the known drawbacks of the questionnaire methodology, although the questionnaire was pretested to overcome part of this problem. Nevertheless, the answers of the 229 responding companies give some idea about the practices of large business firms.

Of 141 responding companies that compute a cost of capital, 104 (74 percent) use the cost of capital as a cutoff or guide when appraising capital expenditures, 77 (55 percent) use it in net present value computations when evaluating capital expenditures, 39 (28 percent) use it to determine the optimal capital structure for the firm, and 27 (19 percent) use it for miscellaneous reasons. The miscellaneous reasons include using cost of capital as a guide for performance evaluation, in evaluating acquisitions and selecting a diversification policy, for charging operating divisions for capital usage, for studying cost of investment in receivables and the inventory's economic order quantity and reorder point, and for some lease-buy decisions. (The responses total more than 141 because some firms checked more than one use of cost of capital.)

Who Should Compute Cost of Capital?

In theory, knowing the cost of capital is essential to progressive management. Unless there is good reason to the contrary, cost of capital should be computed by every business firm.

Of the 229 responding firms, 141 (62 percent) compute a cost of capital, 86 (38 percent) do not, and 2 respondents are not sure—saying, in essence, that it is not computed regularly or in the academic sense.

The percentage of firms that compute a cost of capital (62 percent) is rather low, especially since these firms are large industrial corporations.

Industries differ in the extent to which the cost of capital is computed, ranging from as low as 20 percent of the firms in the pharmaceuticals and motor vehicle and truck industries to as high as 100 percent in the aircraft industry.

Single Value Versus Range

The cost of capital may be expressed as a single value (for example, 15 percent) or as a range (for example, 13–15 percent). A single value is easier to use for net present value computations. The use of a range rather than a single value is sometimes advocated because it is more likely that the cost of capital will fall into a range than exactly coincide with a single value. In addition, a range allows fluctuations in the cost of capital and reflects the rather commonly held view that the cost of capital is not a very precise statistical measure.

Of 136 responding firms, 75 (55 percent) use single values, 57 (42 percent) use ranges, and 4 (3 percent) use both single values and ranges. Although both the single-value and range approaches are used, the single-value approach seems more common in practice among the largest corporations in the United States.

One Cost Versus More Than One Cost

Theoretically, the cost of capital should be computed for the firm as a whole (based on the combined cost of all sources of long-term capital).

Of 140 respondents to this question, 124 (89 percent) compute one cost-of-capital figure for the firm as a whole; 16 (11 percent) compute several cost-of-capital figures, one for every major division; 15 (11 percent) compute several cost-of-capital figures, one for each investment project. (The total is more than 140 because some firms checked more than one answer.) Thus, the majority of reported practices coincides with the theory of computing one cost of capital for the firm as a whole.

How Often Should Cost Be Updated?

In theory, the cost of capital involves a rather long-term approach that does not usually change from one day to another. This being the case, the cost of capital may be updated annually or semiannually.

The question was asked of the respondents, "How often do you update computing your cost of capital?" The responses indicate a range from monthly to infrequently or seldom, as the prime rate changes. The period most often cited is annually (62 of 135 responses, or 46 percent). To show the diversity of practices, the responses are listed in Table 18.

Table 18. Frequency with which respondents update cost of capital.

Frequency of Computations	*No. of Firms*
Twice a year	10
Annually	62
Each 2 years	2
Each 3 years	3
Each 3–5 years	2
Each 5 years	1
Each 5–10 years	1
Infrequently	8
Miscellaneous	46
	135

The miscellaneous category of frequency of computations includes some interesting responses: "as the economy dictates," "as needed," "with significant capital structure changes and/or changes in interest rates," or "when substantial variations in capital markets occur." Others recompute "as required to reflect current cost factors and objectives," "as prime interest rate changes," or "whenever a major change occurs in philosophy of capital structure or significant change in stockholders." One firm said its cost of capital was "fixed at 10%," in contrast to some who recomputed "constantly," "periodically," "monthly or quarterly," or "on irregular schedule."

What Is Meant by Capital?

The cost of capital cannot be determined before there is agreement on what is meant by capital. Knowing that differences of opinion exist, the term capital may be used to refer to long-term capital. One reason for including only long-term capital is that we are interested in sources relevant to long-term uses of capital, which are by necessity long-term sources. Long-term capital includes long-term debt (bonds or long-term loans), preferred stock and common equity (includes common stock and all types of retained earnings, often disguised under separate names to curb stockholders' appetite for dividends and governmental frowning upon excessive accumulation of undistributed profits).

Although long-term capital is the more common definition of capital here, an exception may be made with respect to short-term debt when it is used as a permanent source of financing through continuous renewal.

Each respondent was asked to check his definition of "capital" from a list of six items—short-term debt, long-term borrowed capital, preferred stock, common stock, retained earnings, and other. The responses varied. Some firms do not have preferred stock, and others do not have a significant amount of long-term debt. Those who define capital as strictly debt (short-term and/or long-term) are among the minority, 17 of 141 firms (12 percent). A majority of the responding firms define capital as a combination of debt and equity.

Should Cost of Capital Be Computed Before or After Taxes?

If a selection has to be made between computing cost of capital before or after taxes, it should be computed after taxes.

Of 141 respondents, 71 (50 percent) compute cost of capital after taxes, 28 (20 percent) compute it before taxes, and 42 (30 percent) compute it both before and after taxes. Thus, the majority of the responding firms compute cost of capital in accordance with the theory—after taxes.

Of the 42 respondents who compute the cost of capital using both the before-tax and the after-tax approach, 40 indicate which figure they use in capital expenditure analysis. Of these 40 respondents, 16 (40 percent) use the after-tax basis; 9 (23 percent), the before-tax basis; and the remaining 15 (38 percent), the before- and after-tax cost of capital.

Thus, the after-tax cost of capital is used most often in practice with respect to capital expenditure analysis.

Cost of Long-Term Borrowed Capital

The cost of long-term borrowed capital (debt) may be computed in a number of ways. The more accurate method ascertains the interest rate that will equate annual cash outflows with the net proceeds. An approximate method may be used instead that is basically the amount of annual cost divided by average proceeds. For a bond issue, the cost before taxes will be:

$$\text{Cost of bonds before taxes} = \frac{\text{annual interest} + \dfrac{\text{maturity} - \text{net proceeds}}{\text{years to maturity}}}{\dfrac{\text{net proceeds} + \text{maturity}}{2}}$$

The annual interest is the dollar amount resulting from multiplying the face value of the bond by the interest rate of the bond. Maturity is the amount to be paid to the bondholders at the date of retirement of the debt. The net proceeds figure is basically the amount actually received by the firm, adjusted for discounts and premiums. (For outstanding bonds, market price may be used in place of net proceeds.) Years to maturity is the duration of the debt. (Other complications such as sinking fund requirements, serial bonds, and convertible bonds require more refinements in the methods.)

Since the interest is tax-deductible, an adjustment is needed to compute the after-tax cost of debt (each dollar of interest costs less than a dollar because of its tax shield):

$$\text{After-tax cost of debt} = \text{before-tax cost} \times (1 - \text{tax rate})$$

EXAMPLE

The ABC Corporation sold $100,000 of bonds at 6 percent interest. The bond issue will mature after 20 years. The face (and maturity) value of each bond is $1,000, and the net proceeds were $960 per bond. The corporation is taxed at 40 percent. What is the after-tax cost of the bond issue?

SOLUTION

$$\text{Approximate yield before taxes} = \frac{60 + \dfrac{1{,}000 - 960}{20}}{\dfrac{1{,}000 + 960}{2}}$$

$$= \frac{60 + 2}{980} = \frac{62}{980}$$

$$= 0.0633$$

$$\text{After-tax rate} = 0.0633 \times (1 - 0.40)$$

$$= 0.0633 \times 0.6 = 0.038$$

EXAMPLE

Given the same information from the example above, what is the after-tax cost if the net proceeds are $1,020 per bond?

SOLUTION

$$\text{Approximate yield before taxes} = \frac{60 + \dfrac{1{,}000 - 1{,}020}{20}}{\dfrac{1{,}000 + 1{,}020}{2}}$$

$$= \frac{59}{1{,}010} = 0.0584$$

$$\text{After-tax rate} = 0.0584 \times (1 - 0.40)$$
$$= 0.0584 \times 0.60 = 0.035$$

Each respondent was asked to indicate how the cost of long-term, borrowed capital is determined by his firm. The responses to the question indicate a wide variety of practices. An approach frequently cited is that of using actual after-tax interest cost on current debt. Other approaches include the use of an estimate of what has to be paid now (present market rate) on newly borrowed funds, an estimate of average interest cost over the next five to ten years, the prime rate plus an added percentage, and the yield to maturity.

Other practices include several that are similar to those stated above and many that are different:

- Estimates based on historical rates and trends.
- Average cost of existing borrowing plus or minus an adjustment for anticipated changes.
- Estimates from investment bankers and rates furnished by lenders.
- Estimated interest rates over the next year.
- Cost of the recent debentures.
- Actual interest paid divided by net proceeds.
- The same cost as common stock (considering the increased risk).
- $$\frac{\text{Interest} + \dfrac{\text{maturity} - \text{proceeds}}{\text{years to maturity}}}{\dfrac{\text{maturity} + \text{proceeds}}{2}}$$

Cost of Preferred Stock

The cost of preferred stock is relatively easy to determine. It is the ratio of expected preferred dividends to market price or to estimated net proceeds. Since the preferred dividends are paid from earnings after taxes, no tax adjustment is needed.

Preferred stocks are not very commonly used by the responding firms. The tax disadvantage of preferred stock dividends may be responsible in part for this phenomenon. Responses to the question "How do you determine the cost of preferred stock?" show that two methods are most frequently used: coupon rate (dividend rate), and the ratio of dividend rate to market price (yield rate). An interesting answer cited by some respondents is that they treat the cost of preferred stock the same as the cost of common stock. Reasons indicated for such treatment include the fact that preferred stocks are convertible to common, and the fact that they represent a small percentage of the capital structure.

Other miscellaneous methods of determining the cost of preferred stock include the use of:

- Dividends divided by net proceeds.
- Dividends per share divided by 92½ percent of average market price.
- Average cost of preferred stock sold by the firm in the last five to ten years.
- Estimated rate in the next five years.
- Prevailing money market rates on preferred issues of corporations of comparable financial standing.
- Dividends plus sinking fund divided by net proceeds.
- Estimates made by the firm's banker.
- Double the dividend rate since there is no deduction for taxes (this approach is not theoretically correct).

Cost of Common Stock

The method of computing the cost of common stock depends on the philosophy of the individual concerned and the assumptions used. Differences are found with regard to stable versus growth companies, cost of present common stock versus cost of newly issued stock, and the use of an average approach versus the use of a discounting approach.

Two formulas are advocated. The first is based on expected earnings and estimated net proceeds after costs of security flotation. The expected earnings represent what the common stockholder expects to get as earnings if he invests in the company.

$$\text{Cost of common stock} = \frac{\text{expected earnings}}{\text{net proceeds}}$$

This formula is advocated for its simplicity. Nevertheless, it is subject to many criticisms. For example, a question may be raised regarding what is meant by "expected earnings." Who expects them, for how long are they expected, and how could such expected value be measured for a large corporation with many stockholders? The formula may also be criticized for its failure to differentiate between a company in a stable industry and a company in a growth industry. It could be argued that the formula is more applicable to a new issue of stock than to an outstanding issue.

Another formula advocated by many writers is this:

$$\text{Cost of common stock} = \frac{\text{expected dividend at end of first year}}{\text{current market price of stock}} + \text{expected annual growth of dividends per share}$$

The rationale behind adding growth in dividends is that it is assumed that the stockholders' wealth, as reflected in the market price of the stock, is dependent upon next year's dividends as related to market price and the expected growth in dividends. The expected growth in dividends explains how the stockholders would be satisfied by a small dividend as long as it is expected that more dividends will be forthcoming.

EXAMPLE

Given the following information, compute the cost of common stock.

Expected annual dividend per share at end of first year	= $4
Current market price of stock	= $100
Expected annual growth in dividends per share	= 0.06

SOLUTION

$$\text{Cost of common stock} = \frac{4}{100} + 0.06$$

$$= 0.04 + 0.06 = 10\%$$

For new issues of common stock, a modification is needed because the net proceeds (because of costs of flotation and underpricing) would be less than the market price. The suggested formula is:

$$\text{Cost of new issues of common stock} = \frac{\text{cost of common stock as indicated in previous formula}}{\text{net proceeds as a percentage of market price}}$$

EXAMPLE

Given the following information, what is the cost of the new issue of common stock?

Cost of outstanding common stock	= 0.09
Flotation costs and underpricing	= 10% of market price

SOLUTION

$$\text{Cost of outstanding common stock} = \frac{0.09}{0.9} = 10\%$$

Since common stock dividends are paid from net earnings after taxes, no tax adjustment is needed.

Each respondent was asked to indicate how the cost of common stock is determined in his firm. The responses indicate a host of different approaches.

Practically every company uses its own concept. Given such a variety of answers, four broad methods are indicated:

1. Some form of the formula:

$$\frac{\text{Dividends (or earnings per share)}}{\text{Price per share}} + \text{growth rate}$$

2. Some figure of earnings per share divided by some figure of price per share.
3 Some form of earnings per share divided by some form of market value per share.
4. A desired (estimated or assumed) target rate selected on the basis of judgment of senior managers.

The diversity of methods used may be better appreciated by a listing of some of the practices. They include the following:

1. Return on equity (earnings available to common stockholders divided by the book value of owners' equity).
2. Estimated earnings per share (for a given number of years) divided by market price per share.
3. Earnings per share divided by market price per share net of issuing costs.
4. Actual earnings divided by price.
5. Estimated earnings divided by price.
6. Estimated earnings divided by net proceeds.
7. Dividend rate plus growth rate.
8. Earnings divided by price adjusted for growth.
9. Dividends divided by net proceeds.
10. Pretax earnings divided by price.
11. Growth rate.
12. Earnings divided by price adjusted for risk.
13. Combination of current and past return on equity.
14. Current prime interest rate (the same as debt).

The term growth in items 7 and 8 refers to growth in expected dividends, whereas in item 11 it refers to the growth in the market price of the stock.

Cost of Retained Earnings

From a theoretical viewpoint, retained earnings are not cost-free. The cost of retained earnings may be handled in a variety of ways. It may be treated in the same manner as the cost of common stock, adjusted for the lack of costs of flotation and underpricing.

Of 130 respondents, 21 (16 percent) treat retained earnings as cost-free, and 109 (84 percent) do not. This means that the practices of the majority of large corporations coincide with the theory that retained earnings are not cost-free. Some of the respondents who treat retained earnings as cost-free indicate that they do not feel justified in their practice. A majority of the respondents (88 of 109, or 81 percent) who do not treat retained earnings as cost-free consider the cost of retained earnings the same as the cost of common stock.

Weighted Average

After determination of after-tax cost of each source of capital, the overall cost of capital may be calculated by using a weighted average. The weighted average is found by multiplying the cost of each source of capital by its percentage of the capital structure.

EXAMPLE

The XYZ Corporation's capital structure consists of 60 percent common owners' equity, 10 percent preferred stock, and 30 percent bonds. The after-tax cost of capital for these items in the order given is 12, 8, and 5 percent. What is the overall weighted average cost of capital for this firm?

SOLUTION

	Cost	*Weight*	*Cost X Weight*
Common equity	0.12	0.60	0.072
Preferred equity	0.08	0.10	0.008
Bonds	0.05	0.30	0.015
	Weighted average cost of capital =		0.095

One of the questions to be raised is, What values should be used as weights? Differences of opinion exist regarding what weights to assign to each item of capital. Some individuals advocate using an ideal percentage that represents what the capital structure should be; other individuals prefer to use market values of the different capital items, and still others prefer to use book values.

A majority of the responding firms determine their overall cost of capital by a weighted average. In response to the question, "Do you determine your overall cost of capital by a weighted average?" the following replies were given: 89, yes; 39, no; and 3, not sure. Ten did not answer the question.

Thus, of 128 respondents (the yes and no answers), 89 (70 percent) use a weighted average method in computing their cost of capital.

In practice, there are wide variations in the figuring of the weights by the various firms that use a weighted average method. Some firms use book values, some use current market values, some use capital-mix projections, some use fixed weights (for example, 60 percent equity and 40 percent debt), and some use an ideal debt-to-equity target for the firm.

The 39 firms that do not use a weighted average in determining the overall cost of capital include those that define capital as debt, that associate a given investment with specific sources of capital, that treat the cost of capital as a multiple of the prime interest rate, that subscribe to a proposition by Modigliani and Miller[2] that the cost of capital is independent of the capital structure (the debt-equity mix), and that use a simple average cost of capital (the sum of the rates divided by the number of rates).

Overall Cost of Capital

The cost of capital for different industries may be used as a guide for operating managers to compare with their own estimate. It should be used not as a precise measure, but to give some idea about what others think their costs of capital are.

Each respondent was asked to indicate the range within which his firm's latest computed overall weighted average after-tax cost of capital falls. A summary of the responses by industry is given in Table 19.

The figures in Table 19 show that a majority of the 122 respondents fall into three categories: 6 percent and less than 8 percent, 8 percent and less than 10 percent, and 10 percent and less than 12 percent. For the "other" category, four firms have a cost of capital between 6 and 12 percent. Thus, of 122 respondents (141 less 19 not answering), 80 (76 plus 4 in the "other" category), or 66 percent, have a cost of capital between 6 and 12 percent.

Typical Comments About Cost of Capital

Many misconceptions surround the cost of capital in practice. One correspondent said: "We finance our needs from retained earnings, so we do not have any need for cost of capital." This statement is not always applicable, particularly if it is agreed that the capital provided from retained earnings is not cost-free.

Another correspondent said: "We equate cost of capital with the effective interest rate on incremental borrowing necessary to finance capital expenditures. The specific type of borrowing determines the cost of capital." This statement does not coincide with the theory.

Table 19. Ranges of overall weighted average after-tax costs of capital, for selected industries.

		Cost of Capital (%)										Other	
Industry	*No. of Firms*	*2–4**	*4–6*	*6–8*	*8–10*	*10–12*	*12–14*	*14–16*	*16–18*	*18–20*	*20–22*	*No.*	*Cost of Capital (%)*
Food and beverages	18	2	–	2	4	6	2	1	1	–	–	–	
Textiles	5	1	–	–	1	1	–	–	1	–	–	1	9–11
Paper and allied products	6	–	–	2	2	–	2	–	–	–	–	–	
Chemicals	6	–	1	2	–	–	–	1	1	–	–	1	8–12
Stone, clay, glass, and concrete products	6	1	–	1	1	1	1	1	–	–	–	–	
Metal manufacturing	8	1	1	4	–	2	–	–	–	–	–	–	
Metal products	4	–	–	–	2	1	–	–	–	–	–	1	10–15
Farm and industrial machinery	13	–	–	1	4	3	3	2	–	–	–	–	
Appliances, electronics	3	–	1	–	–	–	–	1	–	–	–	1	12–16
Aircraft	6	–	–	2	1	–	–	2	–	–	–	1	8–12
Measuring, scientific and photographic	3	–	1	1	–	–	–	–	–	1	–	–	
Miscellaneous	44	1	4	10	11	11	2	1	1	–	2	1	8–12
	122	6	8	25	26	25	10	9	4	1	2	6	

*2–4% means equal to or greater than 2% and less than 4%, and so on.

Other comments that may help explain the cost of capital as viewed in practice follow.

The treasurer of an apparel manufacturing company explained why his firm does not need to compute a cost of capital:

> Due to the fact that apparel manufacturing is not a capital intensive industry, we do not have formal manuals and policies as you have in mind. In addition, for the same reason, we do not utilize, as such, cost of capital computations for capital expenditure analysis . . .
>
> Of course, we do consider profitability, return on equity, etc., on acquisition, but not on an individual capital expenditure basis.

In the words of one correspondent, the vice-president of a large manufacturer of distilled, rectified, and blended liquors:

> We do not consciously compute cost of capital. Rather we compare return on investment for a given project to a "return" objective. Our objective changes from time to time as the environment in which we operate changes.

One executive had this to say about the cost of capital:

> One of the important considerations in our evaluation of capital investments is the company's overall cost of capital. The cost reflects the composite of the estimated long-range costs of borrowed funds and shareholders' funds. For practical purposes we develop a single figure which is updated from time to time. The composite is relatively insensitive to changes in the components of the cost of capital and our estimates of future interest rates and the shareholders' opportunity costs are necessarily imprecise. The cost of capital is calculated on an after-tax basis so as to be comparable with the after-tax discounted cash flow returns on investment. . . .

Problem Investments

A relevant question remains to be asked: Which method—DCFR or NPV—would be the better to use? Unfortunately, a single, unconditional answer is hard to give. However, there are some guidelines. When a firm is in a position to approve all capital expenditure proposals that meet a minimum profitability rate, both the DCFR and the NPV usually give the same answer. Accordingly, if the decision is simply to accept or reject a capital expenditure proposal, the NPV and the DCFR are equally acceptable. Here, the selection of either method will depend on management preference.

A Case for NPV

It is hard to find the ideal method of evaluation when only one of two projects may be selected (for example, for what are called mutually exclusive proposals, where the selection of one excludes the other completely, such as building a two-lane or four-lane bridge), or when only limited funds are to be allocated among competing projects from which some proposals have to be selected and others postponed or rejected. (The latter situation may be called capital rationing, and is due to top management's desire to limit the capital appropriations to a fixed amount, or to the inability to raise more funds at a reasonable cost.) The problem of ranking proposals according to their degree of profitability can be further complicated because of unequal lives of the proposals, different investment requirements, and different risk classes. (Risk analysis is described in Chapter 9.)

There is no ideal method to be used indiscriminately under capital rationing conditions or when selecting among mutually exclusive proposals with unequal lives. However, it seems that the majority of writers find the NPV method with modifications to be superior to the DCFR method. The NPV seems to serve better than the DCFR in maximizing the stockholders' wealth as expressed in the highest total dollar return.

For a refined treatment of evaluating capital expenditure proposals under capital rationing conditions and to accommodate risk and uncertainty, the reader should consult other sources.[3] Selected examples of how to handle some mutually exclusive proposals and a problem of allocating funds are given below.

EXAMPLE

Two mutually exclusive capital expenditure proposals are available to the PQR Corporation. The corporation has a 10 percent cost of capital. The following information is available:

	Project A	*Project B*
Initial investment	–$26,350	–$42,960
Benefits	$10,000	$15,000
Economic life	5 years	5 years
Salvage	0	0
DCFR	26%	22%
NPV (at 10%)	$11,560	$13,905

Which project should be selected?

SOLUTION

First, according to the DCFR method, project A should be selected because its 26 percent return is higher than project B's 22 percent return.

Second, according to the NPV method, project B should be selected because it has a larger NPV.

Obviously, the two methods rank the two proposals differently. Which proposal is more beneficial? The answer may be found by using an incremental approach to evaluate the profitability of the incremental investment.

	Project B	*Project A*	*B – A*
Investment	–$42,960	–$26,350	–$16,610
Benefits (years 1–5)	15,000	10,000	5,000

Accordingly, investment B requires an additional (incremental) investment of $16,610 and results in additional annual benefits of $5,000 for 5 years.

Net present value of the incremental investment (at 10%)

= PV of benefits

= $5,000 × annuity value for 5 years at 10%

= $5,000 × 3.791 = $18,955

Less initial investment 16,610

Net present value = $ 2,345

The DCFR is the rate that coincides with a 3.322 present value for 5 years ($16,610 ÷ $5,000). This rate is between 15 and 16 percent (15.4 percent).

Therefore, the incremental investment produces a $2,345 NPV and a 15.4 percent DCFR. Since the DCFR on the incremental investment is higher than the cost of capital, the larger investment should be accepted. Unless the $16,610 incremental investment could be invested at a rate higher than 15.4 percent, it is better to accept project B than project A. Here, it seems that in ranking investments such as A and B, the decision based on the NPV gives the correct answer without resorting to the incremental analysis approach. Incidentally, the NPV method may be used under capital rationing to select from nonconflicting proposals by finding that combination of proposals that will give the highest total net present value for the same investment figure.

EXAMPLE

Two mutually exclusive projects are available to the WXY Corporation. The cost of capital to the corporation is 10 percent. The following information is given:

	Project A	*Project B*
Initial investment	$100,000	$100,000
Annual benefits (after taxes)	$55,066	$33,887
Economic life	3 years	6 years
Salvage	0	0
DCFR	30%	25%
NPV (at 10%)	$36,949	$47,578

Which project should be selected?

SOLUTION

According to the DCFR, project A should be selected because it has a higher DCFR. However, more careful analysis of the information reveals that project B may be more profitable than project A because of the unequal lives of the projects. If investment opportunities at higher rates will not be available, it is better to invest in the longer-lived investment B at 25 percent return than in the shorter-lived investment A. The DCFR method may mislead the decision maker in this case.

To elaborate, let us assume that the cash flows received are reinvested at 10 percent. Since the initial outlays for both investment A and investment B are the same ($100,000), let us see what would be the cumulative amount of cash flows at 10 percent return at the end of the 6 years for both project A and project B. The sum of the interest and principal is found by multiplying each amount (at 10 percent return) by 1.1 (1 + 0.10). A dollar invested at the beginning of a given year will be worth $1.10 at the end of that year if the interest rate is 10 percent. Accordingly, any amount at the beginning of each year may be multiplied by 1.10 to find the total of the interest and principal at the end of that year. See Tables 20 and 21 for these calculations.

Table 20. Calculations for project A.

	Sum of Principal and Interest at End of Year					
Cash Inflows	*Year 1*	*Year 2*	*Year 3*	*Year 4*	*Year 5*	*Year 6*
1st*	55,066	60,573	66,630	73,293	80,622	88,684
2nd		55,066	60,573	66,630	73,293	80,622
3rd			55,066	60,573	66,630	73,293
Total at end of 6th year						$242,599

*The $55,066 received at the end of the first year would be equal to $60,573 at the end of the second year ($55,066 × 1.10), and the $60,573 would be equal to $66,630 at the end of the third year ($60,573 × 1.10), and so on.

Table 21. Calculations for project B.

Cash Inflows	Sum of Principal and Interest at End of Year					
	Year 1	*Year 2*	*Year 3*	*Year 4*	*Year 5*	*Year 6*
1st	33,887	37,276	41,004	45,104	49,614	54,575
2nd		33,887	37,276	41,004	45,104	49,614
3rd			33,887	37,276	41,004	45,104
4th				33,887	37,276	41,004
5th					33,887	37,276
6th						33,887
Total at end of 6th year						$261,460

It is apparent that under these conditions the present value method gives a better measure of the ranking of proposed expenditures. This is true because under project B the $100,000 investment would result in the sum of $261,460 at the end of 6 years, whereas under project A the comparable figure is much smaller, $242,599.

Another Case for NPV

The DCFR method can be used only when the project has cash both in and out. When the project consists of one stream, either cash inflows or cash outflows, the DCFR cannot be used. In this case, the NPV method is superior to the DCFR method.

EXAMPLE

Two alternatives are available to the JKL Corporation for building an employee recreation center. The corporation's cost of capital is 15 percent, and the following information is available:

	Project A	*Project B*
Initial cash outlay	–$20,000	–$27,000
Maintenance, years 1 to 10	– 2,500	– 1,500

Which project should be selected?

SOLUTION

There is no DCFR for either project A or project B, because all cash flows are negative. Here, the DCFR method is not applicable.

The NPV may be computed for each project at the 15 percent cost of capital.

PROJECT A

		PV of $1 at 15%		*PV of Cash Flows*
Initial cash outlay	–$20,000	1.000	=	–$20,000
Maintenance	– 2,500	5.019	=	– 12,548
				–$32,548

PROJECT B

		PV of $1 at 15%		*PV of Cash Flows*
Initial cash outlay	–$27,000	1.000	=	–$27,000
Maintenance	– 1,500	5.019	=	– 7,529
				–$34,529

Although both NPV figures are negative, it is obviously better to select project A, since the cost will be minimized (a $32,548 cost for project A versus a $34,529 cost for project B). Here, the NPV can help to select the least expensive proposal, assuming that other features of the proposals are equally desirable.

NPV in Practice

In practice, the NPV method is not so commonly used as its competitor, the DCFR method. The NPV method is used by a small percentage of the responding firms. The present survey shows that for evaluating major projects it is used by 25 percent of the responding firms (49 of 197 firms). Fourteen of these respondents consider it the most important method of evaluation, 17 consider it second in importance, and the remaining 18 consider it third or lower.

The survey also shows that for "all other projects" the NPV method is used by 37 of 189 responding firms (20 percent). It is considered the most important method by 8 firms, second in importance by 16 firms, and third or lower by 13 firms.

As is the case with other methods, the NPV is seldom used by itself for evaluating capital expenditure proposals.

When the replies are classified by industry, it is found that for major projects the NPV method is used in 14 of the 17 industries. It is used by 56 percent of the respondents in the crude petroleum and natural gas industry versus 13 percent of the respondents in the office machines and other miscellaneous machines industry. The NPV method is used the most for evaluating major projects by the following five industries: crude petroleum and natural gas; petroleum refining; measuring, scientific and photographic; aircraft; and appliances, electronics.

The data for the "all other projects" category show that usage of the method ranges from 14 percent in the food and beverages industry to 40 percent in the petroleum refining industry. It is used the most for evaluating "all other projects" in the following five industries: petroleum refining; measuring, scientific and photographic; crude petroleum and natural gas; aircraft; and stone, clay, glass, and concrete products.

Advantages

The present survey shows four practical advantages (either great or slight advantage) to the NPV method. NPV considers the time value of money (90 percent of 63 responses), can be used for evaluating different types of investment proposals (76 percent), accurate (73 percent), and analyzes future data—not historical (67 percent). These four advantages are the same advantages checked by respondents for the DCFR method.

Weaknesses

From a practical viewpoint, 5 of 12 suggested weaknesses are found to be real weaknesses (at least 50 percent of the respondents regard them as major or minor weaknesses). They are: difficult to sell to operating personnel (75 percent of the 88 responses), difficult to compare with accounting data (70 percent), difficult to sell to top management (70 percent), unnecessarily complicated (66 percent), and imposes heavy demands on analysis staff personnel (65 percent).

These weaknesses were also frequently mentioned by the interviewees. It is important, when studying these weaknesses, to underline the fact that they represent roadblocks that often prevent increased use of advanced methods. It is not relevant whether these weaknesses are real or imaginary. If a respondent feels that a method has certain weaknesses, to him, until he is convinced to the contrary, they are weaknesses regardless of what others may think or believe.

These five weaknesses are easy to explain: The difficulty of selling the NPV method to operating personnel and to top management is due to their unfamiliarity with the method, the relatively recent usage of the NPV method by business firms to appraise their capital expenditure proposals, the difficulty associated with compound interest and the discounting process, the difficulty of interpreting the NPV figure, and the difficulty of determining the discount rate to be used in the computations.

The weakness of being difficult to compare with accounting data is due to the use of cash flows in the NPV computations and the fact that the evaluation is done on a project basis, whereas the books of accounts are usually kept on an annual basis.

The remaining two weaknesses, of being unnecessarily complicated and imposing heavy demands on analysis staff personnel, may be real when compared to the little work needed for the less sophisticated and informal methods. However, the complexity should be compared with the expected benefits from using a more dependable measure of profitability. In most cases, it will be found that the benefits will outweigh any inconvenience.

Familiarity with NPV

The limited use of the NPV method at the present time may be attributed in part to the relatively low degree of familiarity with this method. When asked if analysts, reviewers, and evaluators are familiar with NPV, the 200 respondents replied as shown below.

Response	*No. of Respondents*
Yes	109 (55%)
No	27 (14%)
Not sure	48 (24%)
No answer	16 (8%)

The total responses for yes (familiar) as a percentage of the yes, no, and not sure responses is 59 percent (109 of 184). The degree of familiarity with other methods (except MAPI) is usually higher than that of NPV.

Evaluation of NPV Performance

Although the NPV method is not as commonly used as the payback, ARR, or DCFR method, the majority of the respondents consider it satisfactory. Of 87 respondents who evaluated the NPV, 23 percent consider it very satisfactory; 52 percent, fairly satisfactory; 1 percent, unsatisfactory; and the remaining 24 percent have no opinion. Thus, 75 percent of the 87 respondents consider it satisfactory (either very satisfactory or fairly satisfactory). When compared with other methods, the NPV is placed fourth, preceded by DCFR, payback, and accountant rate of return, and it is considered the least unsatisfactory method.

Discontinued as Unsatisfactory

When asked if they had tried the NPV method and subsequently discontinued its use because of unsatisfactory results, 11 respondents indicate that their firms have done so. Those who discontinued its use, as a percentage of the possible replies (yes, no, and not sure), represent 8 percent (11 of 146), compared to 6 percent for discounted rate of return, 9 percent for MAPI, 13 percent for payback, and 20 percent for accountant rate of return. However, no definite conclusions can be reached because of the small number of responses.

Conclusion

The net present value (NPV) method of evaluating capital expenditure proposals is a theoretically advanced method. It uses cash flows in the analysis, and it considers the time value of money. When compared with the discounted rate of return (DCFR) method, it is usually credited with eliminating the trial-and-error process necessary to compute the DCFR and with being superior when evaluating investments of different lives and different sizes, and when selecting from among mutually exclusive proposals. The NPV method suffers, however, from the difficulty of determining the discount rate to be used in the computations and of interpreting the NPV figure. In practice, the NPV method is not so commonly used as the DCFR. However, there are indications that the NPV method will be used more often in the future, especially in combination with the DCFR method.

NOTES

1. Harold Bierman, Jr., and Seymour Smidt, *The Capital Budgeting Decision,* 3rd ed. (New York: Macmillan, 1971), pp. v–vi.
2. Franco Modigliani and Morton H. Miller, "The Cost of Capital, Corporation Finance, and the Theory of Investment," *American Economic Review,* Vol. 48 (June 1958), pp. 261–297.
3. Three highly recommended books are: Harold Bierman, Jr., and Seymour Smidt, *The Capital Budgeting Decision,* 3rd ed. (New York: Macmillan, 1971), Chapters 10, 11, 17, and 18; Robert W. Johnson, *Capital Budgeting* (Belmont, Calif.: Wadsworth, 1971), Chapters 4 and 5; and G. David Quirin, *The Capital Expenditure Decision* (Homewood, Ill.: Richard D. Irwin, 1967), Chapters 9 and 11.

7 / The MAPI Method

THE Machinery and Allied Products Institute (MAPI) method, also known as the MAPI formula, is one of the five basic methods of evaluating capital expenditure proposals. The MAPI formula should always be associated with its originator, George Terborgh, who, as early as 1949, developed this method and has continued developing it. His objective has been to make it more effective, more useful, and simpler to use in evaluating capital expenditures. Although one of his objectives was to make the analysis simpler, he was willing, at times, to sacrifice some simplicity for the sake of greater realism and comprehensiveness.

Terborgh was, until his recent retirement, the research director of the Machinery and Allied Products Institute and a significant contributor to the theory of investment analysis. He and his associates at the institute deserve all the credit for the origination and development of the MAPI method. The ideas in this chapter are summarized from the institute's publications.

It is not the purpose of this chapter to replace the literature on the MAPI method, for it would be impossible to accomplish such a task, but rather to introduce the reader to the method. It is hoped that the description of the method will encourage the interested reader to go directly to Terborgh's books to acquire more detailed information about the MAPI method. In other words, this chapter is concerned with the general rules; the exceptions are omitted.

The MAPI method is fascinating and has some appealing characteristics that make it a theoretically acceptable method. However, much confusion and misunderstanding surround the MAPI method in practice. During the course of collection of data for this book, it was found that, to the executives interviewed, the MAPI method is for the most part relatively unknown. Even among the few executives who know of the method, still fewer truly understand what the method is supposed to accomplish. Some executives willingly admitted that they simply do not understand it. Those executives familiar with the MAPI method seldom use it.

Of the 27 companies of different sizes at which interviews were conducted, only one uses the method extensively. In that one firm, the MAPI method is used almost exclusively for evaluating capital expenditures. It would not be surprising to find that the MAPI method is used more often by firms that are members of or are associated with the Machinery and Allied Products Institute.

It is intended that this chapter will provide a summary of the key aspects of the 1967 version (the third version) of the MAPI method, its strengths, and its limitations.[1]

What Is the MAPI Method?

The MAPI method may be regarded as a sophisticated rate-of-return method. It achieves the computation of an after-tax return, called the MAPI rate of return or MAPIR. This after-tax return is a measure of profitability. It measures the return on the average investment over the comparison period, most frequently one year. When a one-year comparison period is used, it measures the after-tax rate of return if the investment is undertaken now versus the alternative of waiting one more year before making the investment. Proposals may be ranked according to their rate of return. Also, the rate of return may be compared with the cost of capital to determine the attractiveness of a proposed investment.

The one-year comparison period is usually used for MAPIR calculations because the real choice is not, for example, between buying a new machine with a service life of, say, 20 years and keeping a 30-year-old machine for another 20 years, but between replacing the old machine now and replacing it later. (To base the analysis on a 20-year period is illogical, since an old machine cannot, or should not, be kept for that period.) Effective management of capital expenditures requires a periodic review (usually annually) of the facilities for determining the time that a replacement is needed. This means, in essence, that once a year the manager should ask himself the question: Is it advisable to replace each investment now or wait for another year and repeat the analysis then?

Another reason for using the one-year basis is that one year is the typical accounting period for financial reporting, and capital budgets are usually prepared annually. This means that if a different period is used by a company (for example, if capital expenditures are reviewed each two years), that period could be used as the comparison period for MAPI method calculations.

When comparison periods of longer than one year are used, the computations become more complicated. However, a shortcut method using simple averages may be used.

Like the accountant rate of return, the MAPI rate of return (which will be referred to as MAPIR) is found by dividing some form of benefits by an investment figure, thus:

$$\text{MAPIR} = \frac{\text{average benefits}}{\text{average investment}}$$

Although the end result of using the latest model (1967) of the MAPI method would be an after-tax rate of return on the average investment, more information could easily be derived. For example, it is easy to obtain from the form used the before-tax return and, with some manipulation, the payback period and the return on equity.

The MAPI method is designed for use in evaluating minor capital expenditure projects, or what may be called other projects or shop projects. It is not designed primarily for use in evaluating major capital expenditure projects (front-office projects). However, it could be used, with some modifications, as a supplementary measure or as an initial screening device for major projects.

Computation of MAPI

The 1967 MAPI rate of return concept may be expressed as follows:

$$\text{After-tax return} = \frac{a + b - c - d}{x}$$

where a = next-year or average operating advantage
b = next-year or average capital consumption avoided
c = next-year or average capital consumption incurred
d = next-year or average income tax adjustment
x = average net investment

For a one-year comparison period, the five components of the above formula may be described as follows:

(*a*) *Next-year operating advantage.* This is the sum of the increase in revenue and the reduction in operating costs resulting from the project, as compared, of course, with the operating results that would be obtained in its absence.

(*b*) *Next-year capital consumption avoided.* This is the difference between the initial investment (if any) in the alternative and the amount remaining at the end of the year.

(*c*) *Next-year capital consumption incurred.* Here we have the consumption of the project investment itself. It is the amount by which the remaining use value (or, as we shall call it, the "retention value") of the project at the end of the year is below its cost. In other words, it is the amount by which this value runs off during the year (the cost of the project being taken as the initial value).

(*d*) *Next-year income-tax adjustment.* It may seem at first glance that the after-tax return from a project is simply the pre-tax return reduced by the tax percentage. The matter is not so simple, however. A more complex calculation is necessary . . . . The adjustment itself is the *net increase* in income tax resulting from the project.

(*x*) *Average net investment.* This is the average of the net investment at the beginning and at the end of the year. The initial net investment is the installed cost of the project, less the initial investment in the alternative. The terminal net investment is the retention value of the project at the end of the year, less the disposal value of the alternative.[2]

The analysis of capital expenditures requires many working papers. To facilitate the computations of MAPIR, a summary form was developed. This form is reproduced as Figure 4.

At the top of the form a space is reserved for the project identification number. The first line, "project," is reserved for a brief verbal description of the project. The "alternative" entry is a reminder that for every course of action there is an alternative (there is always the alternative of doing nothing). The comparison period is usually a one-year period; however, it is possible, in this 1967 version, to accommodate longer comparison periods, in which case averages are used instead of first-year figures. "Assumed operating rate of project" is essentially the number of hours the project will be in operation over the comparison period, based on future expected use—not on past practices. This entry will depend upon the number of hours the project will be in operation per day and the number of operating days in a year. It could be as high as 6,000 hours for a three-shift company.

Part I of the form is concerned with the operating advantage and is divided into three parts. Part I-A is concerned with the effect of the project on revenue, because of the change in quality or volume of output. Part I-B pertains to the increase or decrease effect on operating costs. Part I-C is the combined effect of Parts A and B, which gives the annual operating advantage of the proposed investment.

Part II is divided into three parts. Part II-A is basically the installed cost of the project less the initial tax benefit from investment tax credit, where

Figure 4. MAPI summary form.

PROJECT NO.__________ SHEET I

MAPI SUMMARY FORM

(AVERAGING SHORTCUT)

PROJECT______________________________

ALTERNATIVE______________________________

COMPARISON PERIOD (YEARS) (P)__________

ASSUMED OPERATING RATE OF PROJECT (HOURS PER YEAR) __________

I. OPERATING ADVANTAGE

(NEXT-YEAR FOR A 1-YEAR COMPARISON PERIOD,* ANNUAL AVERAGES FOR LONGER PERIODS)

A. EFFECT OF PROJECT ON REVENUE

		INCREASE	DECREASE	
1	FROM CHANGE IN QUALITY OF PRODUCTS	$	$	1
2	FROM CHANGE IN VOLUME OF OUTPUT			2
3	TOTAL	$ X	$ Y	3

B. EFFECT ON OPERATING COSTS

4	DIRECT LABOR	$	$	4
5	INDIRECT LABOR			5
6	FRINGE BENEFITS			6
7	MAINTENANCE			7
8	TOOLING			8
9	MATERIALS AND SUPPLIES			9
10	INSPECTION			10
11	ASSEMBLY			11
12	SCRAP AND REWORK			12
13	DOWN TIME			13
14	POWER			14
15	FLOOR SPACE			15
16	PROPERTY TAXES AND INSURANCE			16
17	SUBCONTRACTING			17
18	INVENTORY			18
19	SAFETY			19
20	FLEXIBILITY			20
21	OTHER			21
22	TOTAL	$ Y	$ X	22

C. COMBINED EFFECT

23	NET INCREASE IN REVENUE (3X−3Y)	$	23
24	NET DECREASE IN OPERATING COSTS (22X−22Y)	$	24
25	ANNUAL OPERATING ADVANTAGE (23+24)	$	25

* Next year means the first year of project operation. For projects with a significant break-in period, use performance after break-in.

Copyright 1967, Machinery and Allied Products Institute

Source: Courtesy of the Machinery and Allied Products Institute.

Figure 4. MAPI summary form (continued).

SHEET 2

II. INVESTMENT AND RETURN

A. INITIAL INVESTMENT

26 INSTALLED COST OF PROJECT $______
MINUS INITIAL TAX BENEFIT OF $______ (Net Cost) $______ 26
27 INVESTMENT IN ALTERNATIVE
CAPITAL ADDITIONS MINUS INITIAL TAX BENEFIT $______
PLUS: DISPOSAL VALUE OF ASSETS RETIRED
BY PROJECT* $______ $______ 27
28 INITIAL NET INVESTMENT (26 − 27) $______ 28

B. TERMINAL INVESTMENT

29 RETENTION VALUE OF PROJECT AT END OF COMPARISON PERIOD
(ESTIMATE FOR ASSETS, IF ANY, THAT CANNOT BE DEPRECIATED OR EXPENSED. FOR OTHERS, ESTIMATE OR USE MAPI CHARTS.)

Item or Group	Installed Cost, Minus Initial Tax Benefit (Net Cost) A	Service Life (Years) B	Disposal Value, End of Life (Percent of Net Cost) C	MAPI Chart Number D	Chart Percent-age E	Retention Value $\left(\frac{A \times E}{100}\right)$ F
	$					$

ESTIMATED FROM CHARTS (TOTAL OF COL. F) $______
PLUS: OTHERWISE ESTIMATED $______ $______ 29
30 DISPOSAL VALUE OF ALTERNATIVE AT END OF PERIOD* $______ 30
31 TERMINAL NET INVESTMENT (29 − 30) $______ 31

C. RETURN

32 AVERAGE NET CAPITAL CONSUMPTION $\left(\frac{28-31}{P}\right)$ $______ 32
33 AVERAGE NET INVESTMENT $\left(\frac{28+31}{2}\right)$ $______ 33
34 BEFORE-TAX RETURN $\left(\frac{25-32}{33} \times 100\right)$ %______ 34
35 INCREASE IN DEPRECIATION AND INTEREST DEDUCTIONS $______ 35
36 TAXABLE OPERATING ADVANTAGE (25 − 35) $______ 36
37 INCREASE IN INCOME TAX (36 × TAX RATE) $______ 37
38 AFTER-TAX OPERATING ADVANTAGE (25 − 37) $______ 38
39 AVAILABLE FOR RETURN ON INVESTMENT (38 − 32) $______ 39
40 AFTER-TAX RETURN $\left(\frac{39}{33} \times 100\right)$ %______ 40

* After terminal tax adjustments.

Copyright 1967, Machinery and Allied Products Institute

Source: Courtesy of the Machinery and Allied Products Institute.

applicable, or other tax benefits (item 26), less item 27, which is the investment avoided by the project (net of tax benefits) plus the after-tax disposal value of the old investment retired. The end result of Part II–A is the amount of the initial net investment (item 28).

Part II–B, Terminal Investment, includes items 29, 30, and 31. Item 29 is the computation of the retention value of the project at the end of the comparison period, which is found from the charts (or estimated by the analyst).

The initial investment less the capital consumption allowance may be called the retention value of the project. For example, if a $10,000 investment will have $2,000 capital consumption allowance next year, the retention value at the end of one year is $8,000 ($10,000 - $2,000). MAPI charts (in the 1967 version) are available to provide the retention value as a percentage of the cost of the project if the following estimates are available: service life in years, salvage value at the end of life as a percentage of net cost of the asset, and the depreciation method used for tax purposes.

Eight MAPI retention value charts have been developed. These are:

Chart Number	*Description*
1A	One-year comparison period and sum-of-years-digits tax depreciation.
2A	One-year comparison period and double-declining-balance tax depreciation.
3A	One-year comparison period and straight-line tax depreciation.
4A	One-year comparison period and expensing.
1B	Longer than one-year comparison periods and sum-of-years-digits tax depreciation.
2B	Longer than one-year comparison periods and double-declining-balance tax depreciation.
3B	Longer than one-year comparison periods and straight-line tax depreciation.
4B	Longer than one-year comparison periods and expensing.

These charts (Figures 5, 6, and 7 are examples) are based on a prestructured set of assumptions. They are:

- Constant rate of obsolescence over the life of the investment.
- Equity capital of 75 percent and debt capital of 25 percent.
- Interest rate on the borrowed capital of 3 percent and an after-tax return of 10 percent on common equity.

Figure 5

MAPI CHART No. 1A

(ONE-YEAR COMPARISON PERIOD AND SUM-OF-DIGITS TAX DEPRECIATION)

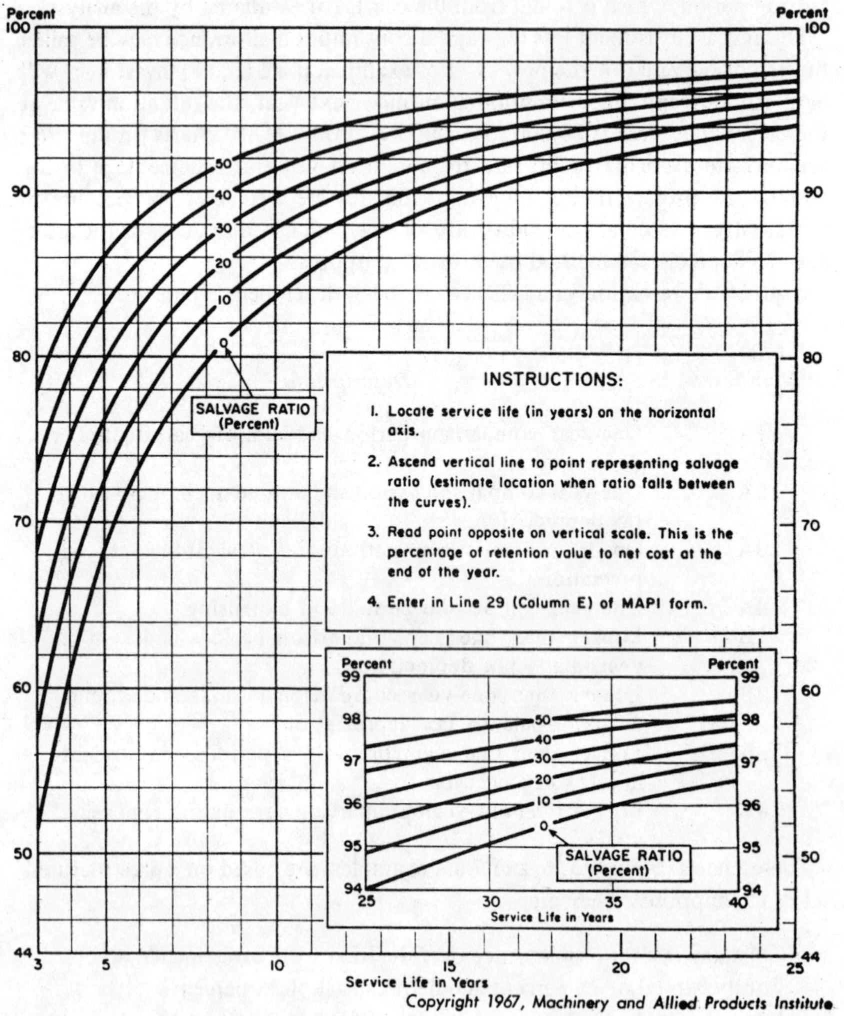

Source: Courtesy of the Machinery and Allied Products Institute.

Figure 6

MAPI CHART No. 1B

(LONGER THAN ONE-YEAR COMPARISON PERIODS AND SUM-OF-DIGITS TAX DEPRECIATION)

INSTRUCTIONS:

1. Locate on horizontal axis percentage which comparison period is of service life.
2. Ascend vertical line to point representing salvage ratio (estimate location when ratio falls between the curves).
3. Read point opposite on vertical scale. This is the percentage of retention value to net cost at end of comparison period.
4. Enter in line 29 (Column E) of MAPI form.

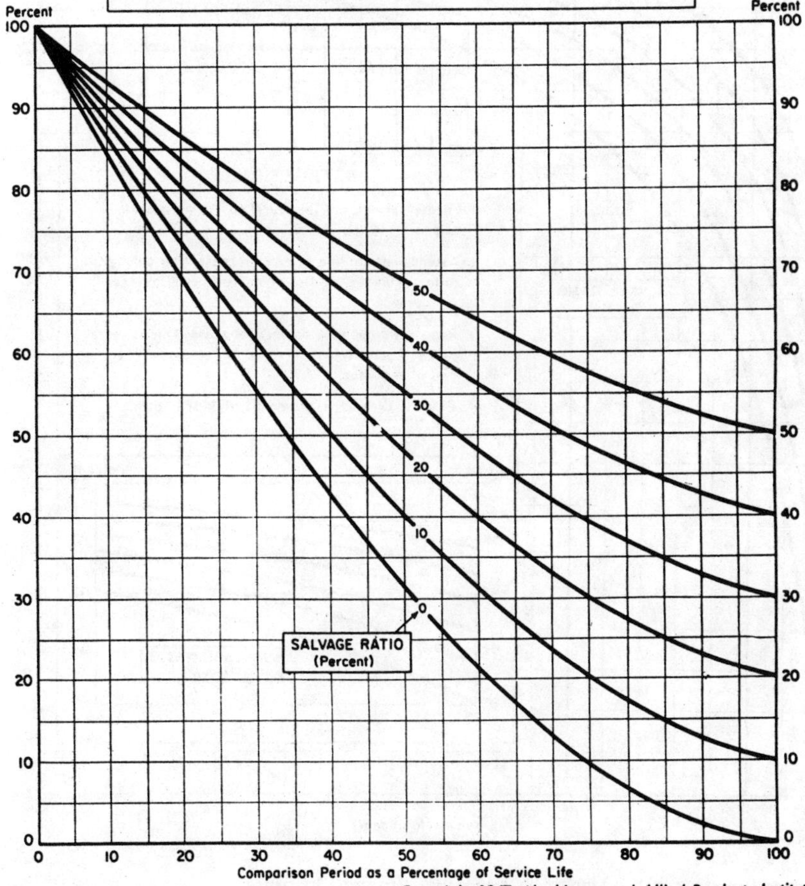

Copyright 1967, Machinery and Allied Products Institute

Source: Courtesy of the Machinery and Allied Products Institute.

Figure 7

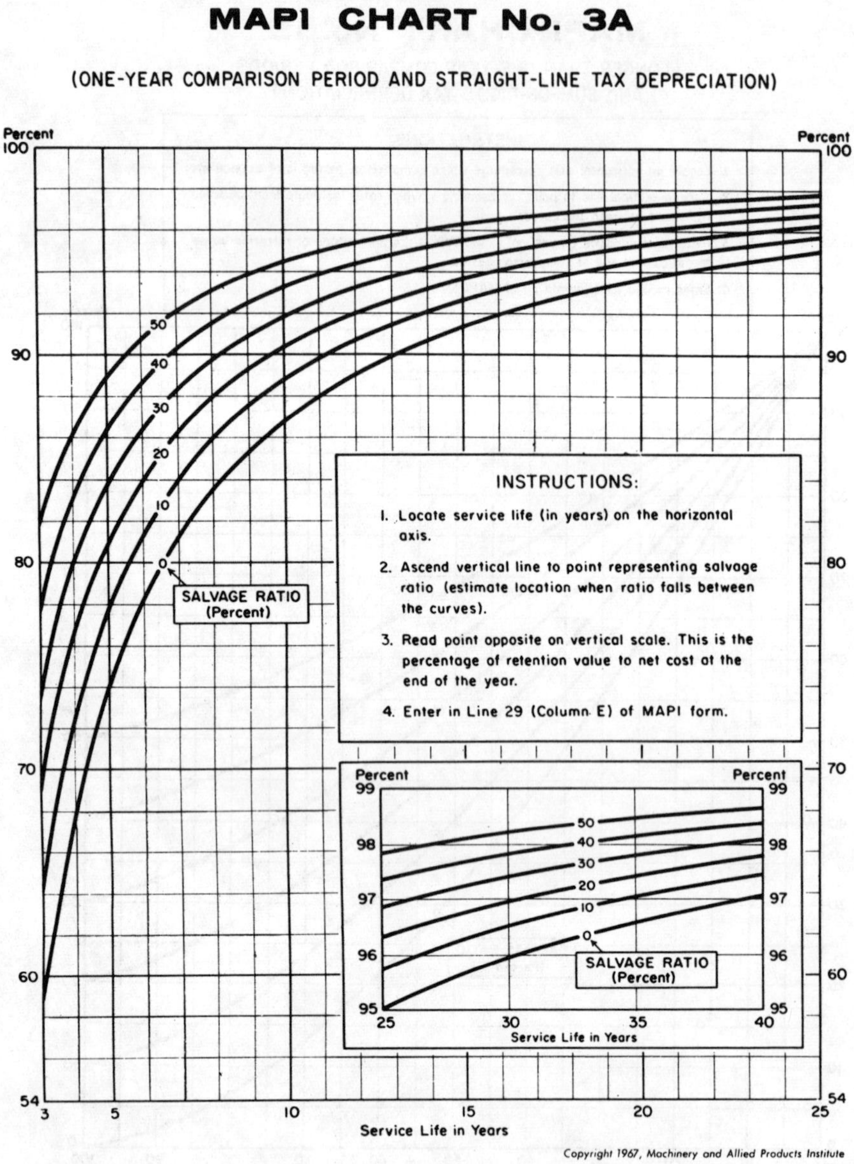

Source: Courtesy of the Machinery and Allied Products Institute.

The chart value may be called a formula solution since it is based on given assumptions. It should be noted, however, that it is possible for any firm to modify the assumptions and change the formula to suit its particular situation.

Item 30 is concerned with the disposal value of the alternative, if kept until the end of the period. Item 31, which is item 29 less item 30, gives the terminal net investment.

Part C, Return, is the final part and includes items 32 through 40. Item 32 is the average net capital consumption, which is the initial net investment minus the terminal net investment, divided by the comparison period. Item 33 is the average net investment, which is the initial net investment (item 28) plus the terminal net investment (item 31), divided by 2. Item 34, before-tax return, is the annual operating advantage (item 25) less average capital consumption (item 32), divided by the average net investment (item 33), with the result expressed as a percentage (multiplied by 100).

Item 35 is the increase in depreciation and interest deductions because of the project (represents the net tax shield). The depreciation figure depends on the methods used for tax purposes on project and alternative, and the interest deduction is the product of average net investment times debt ratio times the interest rate.

When item 35 is subtracted from the operating advantage (item 25), the taxable operating advantage results (item 36). Item 37 is the increase in income tax, which is item 36 times the firm's tax rate (50 percent is a commonly used figure because it is an easy number and very close to the actual rate in most cases). Item 38 is the operating advantage after tax. Item 39 is the amount available for return on investment (item 38 less item 32). Finally, item 40 is the after-tax return, which is the amount available for return on investment (item 39) divided by the average net investment (item 33) and multiplied by 100 to express the result as a percentage.

EXAMPLE

The production department in the Eastern plant of the ZYX Corporation submitted a proposal for the purchase of one fusion automatic brazing machine. This machine is expected to replace an old machine. The cost of the new machine, including installment and freight, is $12,300. The estimated life of the machine is 16 years, at the end of which the estimated salvage value is 5 percent of net cost. To simplify the analysis, assume that the assets to be retired have no disposal value; nor will there be capital additions required in the absence of the investment. The new machine is expected to result in an annual direct labor savings of $7,840, and a decrease in fringe benefits of $2,200.

In addition to the above information, the following stipulations are given:

Comparison period	1 year
Project operating rate	2,080 hours
Tax depreciation method	Straight-line
Tax rate	50 percent
Debt ratio	30 percent
Debt interest rate	5 percent

Compute the MAPI after-tax return.

The solution is given in the completed summary form, Figure 8.

EXPLANATION OF ENTRIES

Items 1 through 21 show the operating advantage resulting from a change in project revenue or operating costs. Item 22 is the total effect of operating costs resulting from savings in direct labor and fringe benefits. Since there are no other benefits, item 25 has the same total. Item 28 is the initial net investment, $12,300. Item 29 is the retention value from the charts (or estimated for items that are not covered by the charts, such as nondepreciable land). The retention value is found by using Chart 3A, one-year comparison period and straight-line tax depreciation (Figure 7), for a 16-year life of the machine, and 5 percent disposal value at end of life. The $11,390 value is the product of $12,300 times 92.6 percent.

Item 32, the average net capital consumption, is $12,300 (item 28) less $11,390 (item 31), which is $910 divided by 1 (for a one-year comparison period).

The $11,845 in item 33 is half of $23,690–the total of item 28 ($12,300) and item 29 ($11,390).

Item 34 is:

$$\frac{\$10{,}040 - \$910}{\$11{,}845} \times 100 = 77.08\%$$

Item 35 is $908. It is calculated by the method shown in Table 22 (p. 139).

Item 36 is:

Item 25	$10,040
Less item 35	908
	$ 9,132

Item 37 is:

Item 36 × tax rate = $9,132 × 0.5 = $4,566

Figure 8. Completed MAPI summary form, example 1

PROJECT NO. 1101J — SHEET 1

MAPI SUMMARY FORM

(AVERAGING SHORTCUT)

PROJECT Purchase of (1) Fusion Automatic Brazing Machine

ALTERNATIVE Continuing as is

COMPARISON PERIOD (YEARS) (P) One Year

ASSUMED OPERATING RATE OF PROJECT (HOURS PER YEAR) 2,080

I. OPERATING ADVANTAGE

(NEXT-YEAR FOR A 1-YEAR COMPARISON PERIOD,* ANNUAL AVERAGES FOR LONGER PERIODS)

A. EFFECT OF PROJECT ON REVENUE

		INCREASE	DECREASE	
1	FROM CHANGE IN QUALITY OF PRODUCTS	$	$	1
2	FROM CHANGE IN VOLUME OF OUTPUT			2
3	TOTAL	$ X	$ Y	3

B. EFFECT ON OPERATING COSTS

		INCREASE	DECREASE	
4	DIRECT LABOR	$	$ 7,840	4
5	INDIRECT LABOR			5
6	FRINGE BENEFITS		2,200	6
7	MAINTENANCE			7
8	TOOLING			8
9	MATERIALS AND SUPPLIES			9
10	INSPECTION			10
11	ASSEMBLY			11
12	SCRAP AND REWORK			12
13	DOWN TIME			13
14	POWER			14
15	FLOOR SPACE			15
16	PROPERTY TAXES AND INSURANCE			16
17	SUBCONTRACTING			17
18	INVENTORY			18
19	SAFETY			19
20	FLEXIBILITY			20
21	OTHER			21
22	TOTAL	$ Y	$ 10,040 X	22

C. COMBINED EFFECT

23	NET INCREASE IN REVENUE (3X−3Y)	$	23
24	NET DECREASE IN OPERATING COSTS (22X−22Y)	$ 10,040	24
25	ANNUAL OPERATING ADVANTAGE (23+24)	$ 10,040	25

* Next year means the first year of project operation. For projects with a significant break-in period, use performance after break-in.

Copyright 1967, Machinery and Allied Products Institute

Source: Courtesy of the Machinery and Allied Products Institute.

Figure 8. Completed MAPI summary form, example 1 (continued).

SHEET 2

II. INVESTMENT AND RETURN

A. INITIAL INVESTMENT

26	INSTALLED COST OF PROJECT	$			
	MINUS INITIAL TAX BENEFIT OF	$	(Net Cost)	$ 12,300	26
27	INVESTMENT IN ALTERNATIVE				
	CAPITAL ADDITIONS MINUS INITIAL TAX BENEFIT	$			
	PLUS: DISPOSAL VALUE OF ASSETS RETIRED BY PROJECT *	$		$	27
28	INITIAL NET INVESTMENT (26–27)			$ 12,300	28

B. TERMINAL INVESTMENT

29 RETENTION VALUE OF PROJECT AT END OF COMPARISON PERIOD
(ESTIMATE FOR ASSETS, IF ANY, THAT CANNOT BE DEPRECIATED OR EXPENSED. FOR OTHERS, ESTIMATE OR USE MAPI CHARTS.)

Item or Group	Installed Cost, Minus Initial Tax Benefit (Net Cost) A	Service Life (Years) B	Disposal Value, End of Life (Percent of Net Cost) C	MAPI Chart Number D	Chart Percentage E	Retention Value $\left(\frac{A \times E}{100}\right)$ F
One Fusion Auto. Brazing Machine	$ 12,300	16	5	3A	92.6	$ 11,390

	ESTIMATED FROM CHARTS (TOTAL OF COL. F)	$			
	PLUS: OTHERWISE ESTIMATED	$		$ 11,390	29
30	DISPOSAL VALUE OF ALTERNATIVE AT END OF PERIOD *			$	30
31	TERMINAL NET INVESTMENT (29–30)			$ 11,390	31

C. RETURN

32	AVERAGE NET CAPITAL CONSUMPTION $\left(\frac{28-31}{P}\right)$	$ 910	32
33	AVERAGE NET INVESTMENT $\left(\frac{28+31}{2}\right)$	$ 11,845	33
34	BEFORE-TAX RETURN $\left(\frac{25-32}{33} \times 100\right)$	% 77.08	34
35	INCREASE IN DEPRECIATION AND INTEREST DEDUCTIONS	$ 908	35
36	TAXABLE OPERATING ADVANTAGE (25–35)	$ 9,132	36
37	INCREASE IN INCOME TAX (36×TAX RATE)	$ 4,566	37
38	AFTER-TAX OPERATING ADVANTAGE (25–37)	$ 5,474	38
39	AVAILABLE FOR RETURN ON INVESTMENT (38–32)	$ 4,564	39
40	AFTER-TAX RETURN $\left(\frac{39}{33} \times 100\right)$	% 38.53	40

* After terminal tax adjustments.

Copyright 1967, Machinery and Allied Products Institute

Source: Courtesy of the Machinery and Allied Products Institute.

Table 22. Calculation of item 35.

Increase in depreciation:		
Cost		$12,300
Less salvage (5% of $12,300)		615
		$11,685
÷ Service life		16
= First-year depreciation		$730
Increase in interest charges:		
(a) Average net investment	$11,845	
(b) Debt ratio	30%	
(c) Debt interest rate	5%	
Interest = (a) × (b) × (c) $= \$11{,}845 \times \frac{30}{100} \times \frac{5}{100} =$		$178
Increase in depreciation and interest charges		$908

Item 38 is:

Item 25	$10,040
Less item 37	4,566
	$ 5,474

Item 39 is:

Item 38	$ 5,474
Less item 32	910
	$ 4,564

Item 40 is:

$$\frac{\text{Item 39}}{\text{Item 33}} \times 100 = \frac{4{,}564}{11{,}845} \times 100 = 38.53\%$$

EXAMPLE

The XYZ Corporation is considering the purchase of three ultramatic screw machines and attachments at an installed cost of $70,000. This project is expected to have the following annual results: $4,000 reduction of direct labor, $1,000 increase in indirect labor, $500 decrease in fringe benefits, $200 decrease in maintenance, $400 decrease in tooling, $100 decrease in supplies, $1,000 increase in scrap, $2,000 decrease in down time, $100 increase in power, $300 decrease in floor space, $1,500 increase in property taxes and insurance, $40,000 decrease in subcontracting, $1,000 increase in inventory carrying costs, and $300 each in safety and flexibility advantage. There will also be an annual increase in project revenue because of quality improvement, estimated at $400; and because of quantity increase, estimated at $600.

Comparison period	1 year
Project operating rate	4,000 hours
Service life	16 years
Terminal salvage value	0
Tax depreciation method	Straight-line
Tax rate	50 percent
Debt ratio	30 percent
Debt interest rate	5 percent

Compute the MAPI after-tax return.

The solution is given in the completed summary form, Figure 9.

EXPLANATION OF ENTRIES

(Dollar figures are rounded to the nearest dollar.)

Items 1 through 28 are self-explanatory.

Item 29, the retention value ($64,400), is found by multiplying item 26 ($70,000) by the 92 percent of Chart 3A (Figure 7), based on 16-year life, zero salvage, and straight-line depreciation.

Item 32 is:

$$\frac{\text{Item 28} - \text{item 31}}{1} = \frac{\$70{,}000 - \$64{,}400}{1} = \$5{,}600$$

Item 33 is:

$$\frac{\text{Item 28} + \text{item 31}}{2} = \frac{\$70{,}000 + \$64{,}400}{2} = \$67{,}200$$

Item 34 is:

$$\frac{\text{Item 25} - \text{item 32}}{\text{Item 33}} \times 100 = \frac{\$44{,}500 - \$5{,}600}{\$67{,}200} \times 100 = 57.89\%$$

Figure 9. Completed MAPI summary form, example 2.

PROJECT NO. 5501 SHEET 1

MAPI SUMMARY FORM

(AVERAGING SHORTCUT)

PROJECT 3 Ultramatic Screw Machines and Attachments

ALTERNATIVE Do nothing

COMPARISON PERIOD (YEARS) (P) One Year

ASSUMED OPERATING RATE OF PROJECT (HOURS PER YEAR) 4,000

I. OPERATING ADVANTAGE

(NEXT-YEAR FOR A 1-YEAR COMPARISON PERIOD,* ANNUAL AVERAGES FOR LONGER PERIODS)

A. EFFECT OF PROJECT ON REVENUE

		INCREASE	DECREASE	
1	FROM CHANGE IN QUALITY OF PRODUCTS	$ 400	$	1
2	FROM CHANGE IN VOLUME OF OUTPUT	600		2
3	TOTAL	$ 1,000 X	$ Y	3

B. EFFECT ON OPERATING COSTS

		INCREASE	DECREASE	
4	DIRECT LABOR	$	$ 4,000	4
5	INDIRECT LABOR	1,000		5
6	FRINGE BENEFITS		500	6
7	MAINTENANCE		200	7
8	TOOLING		400	8
9	MATERIALS AND SUPPLIES		100	9
10	INSPECTION			10
11	ASSEMBLY			11
12	SCRAP AND REWORK	1,000		12
13	DOWN TIME		2,000	13
14	POWER	100		14
15	FLOOR SPACE		300	15
16	PROPERTY TAXES AND INSURANCE	1,500		16
17	SUBCONTRACTING		40,000	17
18	INVENTORY	1,000		18
19	SAFETY		300	19
20	FLEXIBILITY		300	20
21	OTHER			21
22	TOTAL	$ 4,600 Y	$ 48,100 X	22

C. COMBINED EFFECT

23	NET INCREASE IN REVENUE (3X−3Y)	$ 1,000	23
24	NET DECREASE IN OPERATING COSTS (22X−22Y)	$ 43,500	24
25	ANNUAL OPERATING ADVANTAGE (23+24)	$ 44,500	25

* Next year means the first year of project operation. For projects with a significant break-in period, use performance after break-in.

Copyright 1967, Machinery and Allied Products Institute

Source: Courtesy of the Machinery and Allied Products Institute.

Figure 9. Completed MAPI summary form, example 2 (continued).

SHEET 2

II. INVESTMENT AND RETURN

A. INITIAL INVESTMENT

26 INSTALLED COST OF PROJECT $ 70,000
MINUS INITIAL TAX BENEFIT OF $ ______ (Net Cost) $ 70,000 26
27 INVESTMENT IN ALTERNATIVE
CAPITAL ADDITIONS MINUS INITIAL TAX BENEFIT $ ______
PLUS: DISPOSAL VALUE OF ASSETS RETIRED
BY PROJECT* $ ______ $ ______ 27
28 INITIAL NET INVESTMENT (26−27) $ 70,000 28

B. TERMINAL INVESTMENT

29 RETENTION VALUE OF PROJECT AT END OF COMPARISON PERIOD
(ESTIMATE FOR ASSETS, IF ANY, THAT CANNOT BE DEPRECIATED OR EXPENSED. FOR OTHERS, ESTIMATE OR USE MAPI CHARTS.)

Item or Group	Installed Cost, Minus Initial Tax Benefit (Net Cost) A	Service Life (Years) B	Disposal Value, End of Life (Percent of Net Cost) C	MAPI Chart Number D	Chart Percentage E	Retention Value $\left(\frac{A \times E}{100}\right)$ F
(3) Ultramatic Screw Machines and Attachments	$ 70,000	16	0	3A	92	$ 64,400

ESTIMATED FROM CHARTS (TOTAL OF COL. F) $ ______
PLUS: OTHERWISE ESTIMATED $ ______ $ 64,400 29
30 DISPOSAL VALUE OF ALTERNATIVE AT END OF PERIOD* $ ______ 30
31 TERMINAL NET INVESTMENT (29−30) $ 64,400 31

C. RETURN

32 AVERAGE NET CAPITAL CONSUMPTION $\left(\frac{28-31}{P}\right)$ $ 5,600 32
33 AVERAGE NET INVESTMENT $\left(\frac{28+31}{2}\right)$ $ 67,200 33
34 BEFORE-TAX RETURN $\left(\frac{25-32}{33} \times 100\right)$ % 57.89 34
35 INCREASE IN DEPRECIATION AND INTEREST DEDUCTIONS $ 5,383 35
36 TAXABLE OPERATING ADVANTAGE (25−35) $ 39,117 36
37 INCREASE IN INCOME TAX (36×TAX RATE) $ 19,559 37
38 AFTER-TAX OPERATING ADVANTAGE (25−37) $ 24,941 38
39 AVAILABLE FOR RETURN ON INVESTMENT (38−32) $ 19,341 39
40 AFTER-TAX RETURN $\left(\frac{39}{33} \times 100\right)$ % 28.8 40

* After terminal tax adjustments.

Copyright 1967, Machinery and Allied Products Institute

Source: Courtesy of the Machinery and Allied Products Institute.

Item 35 is:

$$\text{Depreciation} = \frac{\text{cost} - \text{salvage}}{\text{service life}} = \frac{\$70{,}000 - \$0}{16} = \$4{,}375$$

$$\text{Interest} = \text{item 33} \times \text{debt ratio} \times \text{interest rate}$$

$$= \$67{,}200 \times \frac{30}{100} \times \frac{5}{100} = \underline{1{,}008}$$

$$\text{Increase in depreciation and interest} = \$5{,}383$$

Item 36 is:

Item 25 less item 35 = \$44,500 - \$5,383 = \$39,117

Item 37 is:

Item 36 X tax rate = \$39,117 X 0.5 = \$19,559

Item 38 is:

Item 25 less item 37 = \$44,500 - \$19,559 = \$24,941

Item 39 is:

Item 38 less item 32 = \$24,941 - \$5,600 = \$19,341

Item 40 is:

$$\frac{\text{Item 39}}{\text{Item 33}} \times 100 = \frac{\$19{,}341}{\$67{,}200} \times 100 = 28.8\%$$

EXAMPLE

A capital expenditure proposal was submitted to the corporate headquarters of the OPQ Corporation. This proposal involves the purchase of thermal automatic electronic thermostat material heating equipment. The estimated cost of the machine is \$12,000. It is estimated that there will be a \$5,150 decrease in direct labor costs, a \$500 decrease in indirect labor costs, a \$200 increase in tooling, a \$300 decrease in maintenance, a cost increase of \$250 in floor space, an increase of \$300 in property taxes and insurance, an increase in power costs of \$200, a \$700 advantage in flexibility, a \$300 advantage of increased safety, and a \$1,000 decrease in subcontracting costs. In addition, the equipment will permit a reduction of \$2,000 in inventory investment.

In addition to the above information, the following stipulations are given:

Comparison period	1 year
Project operating rate	5,700 hours
Service life	10 years
Terminal salvage value	10 percent
Tax depreciation method	Sum-of-the-years-digits
Tax rate	50 percent
Debt ratio	30 percent
Debt interest rate	6 percent
Investment credit	10 percent

Compute the MAPI after-tax return.

The solution is given in the completed summary form, Figure 10.

EXPLANATION OF ENTRIES

Items 1 through 25 are self-explanatory.

Item 26 is the $12,000 cost, less 10 percent tax credit.

Item 27 is the reduction in inventory cost that would result from undertaking the project.

Item 29 is item 26 ($10,800) multiplied by the retention value of 86 percent (see Figure 5, Chart 1A) for a 10-year life with 10 percent salvage value.

Item 31 is the $9,288 in item 29, less the $2,000 investment in inventory at the end of the year if the project is not undertaken.

Item 32 is:

$$\frac{\text{Item 28} - \text{item 31}}{1} = \frac{\$8{,}800 - \$7{,}288}{1} = \$1{,}512$$

Item 33 is:

$$\frac{\text{Item 28} + \text{item 31}}{2} = \frac{\$8{,}800 + \$7{,}288}{2} = \$8{,}044$$

Item 34 is:

$$\frac{\text{Item 25} - \text{item 32}}{\text{item 33}} \times 100 = \frac{\$7{,}000 - \$1{,}512}{\$8{,}044} \times 100$$

$$= \frac{\$5{,}488}{\$8{,}044} \times 100 = 68.22\%$$

Figure 10. Completed MAPI summary form, example 3.

SHEET 1

PROJECT NO. 66–71

MAPI SUMMARY FORM

(AVERAGING SHORTCUT)

PROJECT Thermal Automatic Electronic Thermostat Material Heating Equipment

ALTERNATIVE Continuing as is

COMPARISON PERIOD (YEARS) (P) 1

ASSUMED OPERATING RATE OF PROJECT (HOURS PER YEAR) 5,700

I. OPERATING ADVANTAGE

(NEXT-YEAR FOR A 1-YEAR COMPARISON PERIOD,* ANNUAL AVERAGES FOR LONGER PERIODS)

A. EFFECT OF PROJECT ON REVENUE

		INCREASE	DECREASE	
1	FROM CHANGE IN QUALITY OF PRODUCTS	$	$	1
2	FROM CHANGE IN VOLUME OF OUTPUT			2
3	TOTAL	$ X	$ Y	3

B. EFFECT ON OPERATING COSTS

		INCREASE	DECREASE	
4	DIRECT LABOR	$	$ 5,150	4
5	INDIRECT LABOR		500	5
6	FRINGE BENEFITS			6
7	MAINTENANCE		300	7
8	TOOLING	200		8
9	MATERIALS AND SUPPLIES			9
10	INSPECTION			10
11	ASSEMBLY			11
12	SCRAP AND REWORK			12
13	DOWN TIME			13
14	POWER	200		14
15	FLOOR SPACE	250		15
16	PROPERTY TAXES AND INSURANCE	300		16
17	SUBCONTRACTING		1,000	17
18	INVENTORY			18
19	SAFETY		300	19
20	FLEXIBILITY		700	20
21	OTHER			21
22	TOTAL	$ 950 Y	$ 7,950 X	22

C. COMBINED EFFECT

23	NET INCREASE IN REVENUE (3X−3Y)	$	23
24	NET DECREASE IN OPERATING COSTS (22X−22Y)	$ 7,000	24
25	ANNUAL OPERATING ADVANTAGE (23+24)	$ 7,000	25

* Next year means the first year of project operation. For projects with a significant break-in period, use performance after break-in.

Copyright 1967, Machinery and Allied Products Institute

Source: Courtesy of the Machinery and Allied Products Institute.

Figure 10. Completed MAPI summary form, example 3 (continued).

SHEET 2

II. INVESTMENT AND RETURN

A. INITIAL INVESTMENT

26 INSTALLED COST OF PROJECT $ 12,000
MINUS INITIAL TAX BENEFIT OF $ 1,200 (Net Cost) $ 10,800 26
27 INVESTMENT IN ALTERNATIVE
CAPITAL ADDITIONS MINUS INITIAL TAX BENEFIT $
PLUS: DISPOSAL VALUE OF ASSETS RETIRED
BY PROJECT * $ 2,000 $ 2,000 27
28 INITIAL NET INVESTMENT (26–27) $ 8,800 28

B. TERMINAL INVESTMENT

29 RETENTION VALUE OF PROJECT AT END OF COMPARISON PERIOD
(ESTIMATE FOR ASSETS, IF ANY, THAT CANNOT BE DEPRECIATED OR EXPENSED. FOR OTHERS, ESTIMATE OR USE MAPI CHARTS.)

Item or Group	Installed Cost, Minus Initial Tax Benefit (Net Cost) A	Service Life (Years) B	Disposal Value, End of Life (Percent of Net Cost) C	MAPI Chart Number D	Chart Percentage E	Retention Value $\left(\frac{A \times E}{100}\right)$ F
Thermal Automatic Electronic Thermostat Material Heating Equipment	$ 10,800	10	10	1A	86	$ 9,288

ESTIMATED FROM CHARTS (TOTAL OF COL. F) $
PLUS: OTHERWISE ESTIMATED $ $ 9,288 29
30 DISPOSAL VALUE OF ALTERNATIVE AT END OF PERIOD * $ 2,000 30
31 TERMINAL NET INVESTMENT (29–30) $ 7,288 31

C. RETURN

32 AVERAGE NET CAPITAL CONSUMPTION $\left(\frac{28-31}{P}\right)$ $ 1,512 32
33 AVERAGE NET INVESTMENT $\left(\frac{28+31}{2}\right)$ $ 8,044 33
34 BEFORE-TAX RETURN $\left(\frac{25-32}{33} \times 100\right)$ % 68.22 34
35 INCREASE IN DEPRECIATION AND INTEREST DEDUCTIONS $ 2,109 35
36 TAXABLE OPERATING ADVANTAGE (25–35) $ 4,891 36
37 INCREASE IN INCOME TAX (36×TAX RATE) $ 2,446 37
38 AFTER-TAX OPERATING ADVANTAGE (25–37) $ 4,554 38
39 AVAILABLE FOR RETURN ON INVESTMENT (38–32) $ 3,042 39
40 AFTER-TAX RETURN $\left(\frac{39}{33} \times 100\right)$ % 37.82 40

* After terminal tax adjustments.

Copyright 1967, Machinery and Allied Products Institute

Source: Courtesy of the Machinery and Allied Products Institute.

Item 35 is:

Installed cost	\$12,000
Less salvage (10%)	1,200
	\$10,800

First-year depreciation using sum-of-the-years-digits

$$= \frac{10}{10+9+8+7+6+5+4+3+2+1} = \frac{10}{55}$$

$$\text{Depreciation} = \$10{,}800 \times \frac{10}{55} = \$1{,}964$$

$$\text{Interest} = \text{average investment} \times \text{debt ratio}$$

$$\times \text{ interest rate} = \$8{,}044 \times \frac{30}{100} \times \frac{6}{100} = \underline{\quad 145}$$

$$\text{Increase in interest and depreciation} = \$1{,}964 + \$145 = \$2{,}109$$

Item 36 is:

Item 25 – item 35 = \$7,000 – \$2,109 = \$4,891

Item 37 is:

Item 36 × tax rate = \$4,891 × 0.5 = \$2,446

Item 38 is:

Item 25 – item 37 = \$7,000 – \$2,446 = \$4,554

Item 39 is:

Item 38 – item 32 = \$4,554 – \$1,512 = \$3,042

Item 40 is:

$$\frac{\text{Item 39}}{\text{Item 33}} \times 100 = \frac{\$3{,}042}{\$8{,}044} \times 100 = 37.82\%$$

Additional Information That Could Easily Be Obtained

The 1967 version of the MAPI summary form offers a variety of useful information.

Here are some examples, using the last figures as a basis:

1. Dollar amount of net gain: The dollar amount of the net gain from the investment, as opposed to the alternative, may be obtained directly from item 39. In the previous example, it is \$3,042. This is the after-tax incremental profit if the project is undertaken.

2. Return on equity investment: The return on equity, if desired, may be obtained by using the information from item 33 and item 39. From item 33,

Average net investment is	$8,044
Deduct 30% debt capital	2,413
Equity portion is	$5,631

Item 39, less interest charges,* equals the benefits after interest:

$$\$3{,}042 - \$73 = \$2{,}969$$

The return on equity equals the amount available for equity divided by equity capital:

$$\frac{\$2{,}969}{\$5{,}631} \times 100 = 52.73\%$$

3. Cash throwoff and payback period: The cash throwoff, the amount of investment that will be recovered in cash annually, may be obtained as follows:

$$\text{Item 25} - \text{item 37} = \$7{,}000 - \$2{,}446 = \$4{,}554$$

The payback period may be obtained by dividing item 28 by the cash throwoff obtained previously:

$$\frac{\$8{,}800}{\$4{,}554} = 1.93 \text{ years}$$

The user may think of other information that could be obtained from the form.

Key Characteristics

Some of the key characteristics of the MAPI method are discussed here briefly. (The discussion will relate to the latest version of MAPI, published in 1967.)

Measure of Profitability

The MAPI method is a measure of profitability. It measures the rate of return on the average investment over the comparison period.

*Because interest is deductible for tax purposes, the after-tax cost is found by multiplying interest times (1 - tax rate). Accordingly, $145 (1 - 0.5) = $73. The reason for using $73 rather than $145 in the equation is that the $3,042 is computed after taxes.

Time Value of Money

The MAPI method is a comparison-period rate of return. Nothing in the computations allows for the time value of money (except with regard to the retention value as derived from the charts). The return is practically identical with the time-adjusted result (continuous-functions basis) for a one-year comparison period, but diverges for longer periods.

The MAPIR can be criticized for not taking the time value of money into consideration. However, this may not be critical, for the following reasons: (1) The appropriate comparison period is usually much shorter than the life of the project, thus reducing the importance of discounting. (2) The most common comparison period is one year, for which the return, as noted, is almost identical with the correct result. (3) Even for multi-year comparison periods up to eight years, the returns computed by the MAPIR averaging method are acceptably close to those computed by the discounted cash flow method. This is particularly true when the operating advantage over the period is fairly stable, and when the after-tax rate of return is less than 15 percent.

This means that other methods such as discounted cash flow should be used when analyzing major projects when the study period is long, when benefits vary significantly from one period to another, and when refined analysis is warranted.

Treatment of Obsolescence

A key characteristic of the MAPI method is that it takes into consideration the factor of obsolescence in equipment. This is done through the retention value and the retention value charts. Accordingly, the MAPI system is often credited with what is called "establishing a more objective basis for determining the influence of obsolescence on the rate of return.[3]

More Complete Analysis

The MAPI system aspires to provide a more complete analysis of capital expenditures than that provided by payback and accountant rate of return methods. The two parts of the latest MAPI form provide a rather complete list of items that compose the operating advantage of the investment. Part A lists items that affect project revenue through change in quality and quantity. Part B shows the effect on operating costs of changes in direct labor, indirect labor, fringe benefits, maintenance, tooling, materials and supplies, inspection, assembly, scrap and rework, down time, power, floor space, property taxes and insurance, subcontracting, inventory, safety, flexibility, and other factors. This last category in Part B is reserved for any operating cost advantage that does not fall in the list provided. It is added as a reminder to include all operating cost adjustments.

The MAPI system advocates using an estimate for all benefits (negative or positive) whenever it is possible, including both the easy-to-quantify adjustments and those that are estimated by "educated guess." The premise is that it is better to include a value based on judgment than to leave it out, since leaving an item out results in treating it as of zero value or, in a less explicit way, as a qualitative statement. Whenever it is possible, a dollar value should be assigned to all effects of the project and included.

Terborgh's *Business Investment Management* (cited in note 1) includes, in its delineation of the MAPI system, more than a description of a measure of profitability. It is a study of the total system, including such items as policy and policy questions; forms and procedures; screening, justifying, selecting, and postauditing capital expenditures; special problems of cost of capital, inflation, and different types of decisions; and a variety of illustrative cases.

No Bias Toward Immediate Purchase of Equipment

Although the MAPI method was developed by Terborgh and his associates at the Machinery and Allied Products Institute, the method is *not* generally considered biased toward immediate purchase of equipment.

MAPI Method in Practice

Very little is found in the capital expenditure analysis literature on the use of the MAPI method. In addition, it seems that the method is not very popular. Of the 48 firms studied by Istvan in 1959, only 2 firms (4 percent) used the MAPI method for evaluating capital expenditure proposals.[4] Eight years later, a study by the National Association of Accountants showed that only one of 28 firms surveyed (4 percent) used the MAPI method for evaluating capital expenditure proposals.[5]

This lack of popularity of the MAPI method is confirmed by the present study. For evaluating major projects, the survey indicates that 9 percent of the respondents (18 of 197 respondents) use the MAPI method. Of those that use the method, one firm considers it the most important method, 6 firms consider it second in importance, and the remaining 11 firms consider it third or lower.

For "all other projects," the MAPI formula is used by 8 percent (16 of 189 responding firms). It is considered first in importance by 3 firms, second by 4 firms, and third or lower by 9 firms.

The MAPI method is seldom used exclusively for evaluating any type of capital expenditure proposal by the responding firms.

When the replies are classified by industry, it is found that the MAPI method is used for major projects in 9 of the 17 industries. It is used most in metal manufacturing.

As indicated by the respondents, the MAPI method is not used for major projects by any of the following industries: mining; textiles; paper and allied products; rubber; stone, clay, glass, and concrete products; metal products; motor vehicles and trucks; and measuring, scientific, and photographic.

For "all other projects," the replies indicated that the MAPI method is used the most in the aircraft, petroleum refining, and metal manufacturing industries.

Advantages

The present survey shows that the MAPI method is considered to have only two practical advantages: it is accurate (68 percent of the 19 respondents to the question) and analyzes future data–not historical (58 percent).

Weaknesses

The respondents feel that the MAPI method has the following weaknesses:

1. Difficult to sell to operating personnel (81 percent of 40 respondents)
2. Unnecessarily complicated (78 percent)
3. Imposes heavy demands on analysis staff personnel (78 percent)
4. Difficult to sell to top management (73 percent)
5. Difficult to compare with accounting data (71 percent)
6. Places too much emphasis on estimates (53 percent)

The practical weakness of being unnecessarily complicated deserves some explanation. The MAPI method, when studied for the first time, does seem rather complicated. This complexity is apparent rather than real; however, it is a primary reason why the method is not well known and not commonly used.

Familiarity with MAPI

When compared with the other four methods (payback, accountant rate of return, DCFR, and net present value), the MAPI method is the least familiar.

When asked if their analysts, reviewers, and evaluators were familiar with MAPI, the 200 respondents replied as shown below.

Response	*No. of Respondents*	*Percentage*
Yes	39	20
No	68	34
Not sure	70	35
No answer	23	12

Only about 20 percent of the respondents are familiar with the MAPI method. This is undoubtedly a major reason for its unpopularity.

Evaluation of MAPI Performance

When asked to evaluate the performance of the MAPI method, only 20 did so. Of those 20, 4 consider it very satisfactory, 11 consider it fairly satisfactory, and 5 consider it unsatisfactory. This means that the MAPI method is placed last in terms of satisfaction with the results (as compared with the other four methods previously discussed). However, no definite conclusions can be reached because of the small number of responses.

Discontinued as Unsatisfactory

When asked to indicate whether his company had used any of the selected methods and subsequently discontinued its use because of unsatisfactory results, 14 respondents checked yes. "No" answers were given by 103, "not sure" by 33, and 50 did not respond.

This discontinuance rate places the MAPI method as the third most discontinued method, preceded by accountant rate of return and payback and followed by net present value and discounted cash flow rate of return. However, no definite conclusions can be reached because of the small number of responses.

Typical Comments

"I have never heard of it." "We do not have any need for it." "We do not use it." "I do not understand it, only engineers do." "It is too complicated." "It is designed for tool manufacturers only." These statements are representative of what a person would hear if he asked financial officers about the MAPI method. For the most part, they reflect common unfamiliarity and often lack of understanding of the method.

The manager of capital planning of a large electronics firm stated that MAPI is difficult to understand and is not applicable to projects reviewed at the corporate level.

The controller of a successful firm that uses MAPI as the primary evaluation method indicated that he was generally pleased with the method and did not have any major complaints about it. However, these are some of his observations:

- The preparation of estimates and data needed for the MAPI method imposes heavy demands on involved personnel.
- Postauditing of projects is a problem, especially when major differences exist between the planned and the actual project operating rates.
- Some of the operating personnel do not fully understand the MAPI method.
- It is possible at times for top management personnel mistakenly to treat the MAPI urgency rating as some form of payback period.

Because the MAPI method is described in a comprehensive manual, some firms use it in lieu of their own manual for capital expenditures.

Another correspondent, the president of a manufacturer of orthopedic, prosthetic, and surgical appliances and supplies, indicated that his firm is in the proccss of rewriting its procedures manual and that the "... new procedure is patterned along the lines of the Machinery and Allied Products Institute's Capital Expenditure Plan. . . ."

Comments by Terborgh, the originator of the MAPI method, in a personal interview provide some valuable insight for the utilization of MAPI for capital expenditure analysis. They may be summarized as follows:

1. A major contribution of the MAPI formula is that it forces management to think over investment ideas thoroughly.

2. The MAPI method is designed mainly for shop or minor projects and not for front-office or major projects, except on a supplementary basis.

3. It is not surprising to find that the MAPI method is not used extensively in practice. It is estimated that even among members of the Machinery and Allied Products Institute the MAPI method is used by about 20 to 25 percent. The rather low percentage may be due in part to the lack of any major campaign by the institute to promote use of the MAPI method. It is left to be adopted on its own merits.

4. In many cases, a one-year comparison period is the most important, representative, and practical approach to appraising minor projects.

5. The MAPI charts are based on given assumptions. If needed, special charts may be drawn to fit the particulars of a given firm. In most cases, however, the present MAPI charts are adequate, even when the actual situation is slightly different from the assumptions on which the charts are based.

6. What is done as the final step in an analysis to derive the justification indicator is less important than the preceding processes of the analysis itself.

7. The main difference between the MAPI method and accountant rate of return lies in the computations of capital consumption allowance and retention value. The accounting rate of return method usually uses straight-line depreciation.

8. The MAPI method is often blamed unjustly for complicating analysis. Estimates are needed, regardless of what method is used. The MAPI method only points out the need for such estimates; it does not make the evaluation process more difficult than it actually is.

Conclusion

The MAPI method is a rather sophisticated average-rate-of-return method. Its inclusion of important factors in the analysis makes it one of the theoretically acceptable methods of evaluating capital expenditure proposals. Its place in theory is above the payback and accountant rate of return and below discounted cash flow. MAPI can be used as a major method for minor projects and as a supplementary measure for evaluating major projects. Before using the method in practice, the reader should consult Terborgh's *Business Investment Management* for detailed instructions.

The MAPI method has not obtained its rightful place in practice because it is relatively less well known than other methods and because it appears complicated. If the MAPI method and its assumptions are fully understood, it is flexible enough to allow tailoring to suit the particular needs of the user.

NOTES

1. For more complete information about the latest version of the MAPI method, the reader should consult George Terborgh's *Business Investment Management* (Washington, D.C.: Machinery and Allied Products Institute, 1967).
2. Terborgh, op. cit., p. 81.
3. Richard L. Smith, "Capital Expenditures: Control Today for Profit Tomorrow," *N.A.A. Bulletin* (November 1957), p. 29.

4. Donald F. Istvan, "The Capital-Expenditure Decision-Making Process in Forty-eight Large Corporations" (D.B.A. dissertation, Indiana University School of Business, 1959), p. 177.
5. *Financial Analysis to Guide Capital Expenditure Decisions*, N.A.A. Research Report 43 (New York: National Association of Accountants, 1967), p. 66.

8 / The Methods Combined

IN the previous chapters, five methods of evaluating capital expenditure proposals were individually discussed: payback, accountant rate of return (ARR), discounted cash flow rate of return (DCFR), net present value (NPV), and the Machinery and Allied Products Institute rate of return (MAPIR). It is time now to summarize briefly the key characteristics of these methods. Also, since the majority of firms use combinations of these methods rather than one method exclusively, more information is provided here regarding the usual combinations of methods used by the firms surveyed. This discussion is followed by quick reference to the dominance of rate of return methods, the extent of usage of theoretically efficient (DCFR, NPV, and MAPIR) versus theoretically inefficient methods (ARR and payback), and five other methods of evaluation. Finally, some selected comments are cited.

The Five Methods in Theory

The differences among the five methods may be best summarized by the following questions:

1. Does the method measure profitability? Four of the five methods provide some measure of profitability. They are: ARR, DCFR, NPV, and MAPIR. The payback method does not measure profitability.

2. Does the method use cash flows (instead of accounting income) in the analysis? The payback, DCFR, and NPV usually use cash flows in the analysis. Although some firms compute payback from accounting income, the preferred and theoretically correct practice requires using cash flows. The accountant rate of return and MAPIR usually use some form of accounting income (instead of cash flows) in the analysis.

3. Does the method consider the time value of money? Two of the five methods explicitly consider the time value of money: DCFR and NPV. This is one reason for treating these two methods as theoretically superior to the other methods.

4. Is the method theoretically acceptable? Of the five methods, two are considered generally acceptable from a theoretical viewpoint: NPV and DCFR. MAPIR is also acceptable when it is used for evaluating shop projects ("all other projects") and when the assumptions on which the method is based are satisfied. The payback and ARR methods are not considered theoretically acceptable as primary methods for evaluating capital expenditure proposals.

5. How do the methods rank in terms of being theoretically acceptable? The methods may be ranked as follows:

Ranking	*Method*
1st or 2nd	DCFR
1st or 2nd	NPV
3rd	MAPIR
4th	ARR
5th	Payback

The NPV and DCFR compete for first place. Those who prefer NPV argue that it is easier to compute and does not create problems with respect to the reinvestment assumption or multiple yields, and that it is the best suited (with modifications) for selecting among projects of different lives and among mutually exclusive proposals. Those who favor DCFR argue that it is easier to interpret, that it is more familiar to businessmen, that it allows proposals to be ranked according to their rates of return, and that the arguments against it are unfounded.

6. Does the method measure risk? None of the five methods fully measures risk. Risk is related to the certainty and distribution of cash flows. The pinpoint approach (using one estimate for each item) used in the computations so far does not provide for a full measurement of risk. The payback method provides some indication of risk, but it does not measure risk. The payback period may be regarded as the period during which capital would be invested with risk.

7. Is the end result of the computations a unique figure? There are several ways of computing the ARR, and each could result in a different measure of the worth of an investment. When the payback method is used, differences may be found depending on whether the payback period is determined by division or by subtraction. There are three MAPI systems, each leading to a different result. However, by using a given MAPI system and following the instructions provided in the MAPI manual, the end result is unique. When the DCFR is used, the resulting return is usually unique, except in the rare case of unconventional cash flows, when more than one return could be computed from the same data. Once the discount rate is selected, the end result

of the NPV method is a unique figure. Accordingly, the NPV is placed first in terms of providing a single answer from the computations.

8. Is the method easy to compute? The payback method is easy to compute. The ARR is also easy to compute once a decision is made regarding the version of the method to be used. The trial-and-error process of computing the DCFR makes it relatively difficult to calculate; however, available short-cuts and computer programs reduce the difficulties. Once a discount rate is determined, the NPV computation is very simple. Finally, the MAPIR, which seems to be complicated, is not difficult if the instructions are followed and the method is well understood.

The Five Methods in Practice

The five methods may be best compared by the responses to the evaluation questionnaire with respect to use, importance in decision making, advantages, weaknesses, familiarity with the methods, evaluation of their performance, and discontinuance as unsatisfactory.

Comparison in Terms of Use

According to the extent of use of the five methods for evaluating major projects, they may be ranked as follows:

Rank	*Method*	*Percentage of Users*
1	Payback	80
2	DCFR	69
3	ARR	57
4	NPV	25
5	MAPIR	9

"All other projects" may be ranked as follows:

Rank	*Method*	*Percentage of Users*
1	Payback	80
2	ARR	56
3	DCFR	54
4	NPV	20
5	MAPIR	8

Relative Importance in the Evaluation

When the five methods are ranked according to the number of respondents who consider them the *most important* for capital expenditure evaluation, and expressed as a percentage of total users of that method, the following results for major projects are obtained:

Method	*No. of Firms*	*Percentage of Users*
1. DCFR	93	68
2. ARR	58	51
3. NPV	14	29
4. Payback	45	28
5. MAPIR	1	6

For "all other projects" the following results are obtained:

Method	*No. of Firms*	*Percentage of Users*
1. ARR	56	53
2. DCFR	53	52
3. Payback	57	38
4. NPV	8	22
5. MAPIR	3	19

The above results suggest that DCFR is considered the most important method (using the percentage column as a basis) for evaluating major projects, with the accountant rate of return considered the most important for evaluating "all other projects." Although payback is the most commonly used method, it is placed fourth in importance for evaluating major projects and third for evaluating "all other projects." The NPV and MAPIR methods are considered less important for evaluating capital expenditure proposals than the DCFR or ARR methods.

Advantages of the Methods

The common advantages of the five methods, ***as viewed by the respondents,*** are summarized in Table 23.

Table 23. Advantages of methods as viewed by respondents.

Advantage	Payback	ARR	DCFR	NPV	MAPIR
1. Low in cost	√	√			
2. Simple in use	√	√			
3. Accurate			√	√	√
4. Well known	√	√			
5. Easy to understand	√	√			
6. Requires few assumptions	√				
7. Analyzes future data—not historical		√	√	√	√
8. Can be used for evaluating different types of investment proposals	√	√	√	√	
9. Considers the time value of money			√	√	
10. Easy to postaudit	√	√			
11. Easy to sell to top management	√	√			
12. Easy to sell to operating personnel	√	√			

Weaknesses of the Methods

The responses indicate that none of the 12 suggested weaknesses are considered real drawbacks of the payback or accountant rate of return methods. However, the DCFR and NPV have the same five common weaknesses. These are:

1. Unnecessarily complicated.
2. Imposes heavy demands on analysis staff personnel.
3. Difficult to compare with accounting data.
4. Difficult to sell to top management.
5. Difficult to sell to operating personnel.

The MAPIR has the five common weaknesses cited above plus the additional weakness of placing too much emphasis on estimates.

Familiarity with the Methods

In terms of familiarity of analysts, reviewers, and decision makers with the methods, the five methods may be ranked as follows:

Rank	*Method*	*Percentage of Respondents**
1	Payback	99
2	ARR	91
3	DCFR	77
4	NPV	59
5	MAPIR	22

Evaluation of the Methods' Performance

The respondents appraised the performance of the methods as follows. (The totals of the percentages do not add up to 100 percent because of rounding.)

Method	*Total Answers*	*Very Satis-factory*	*Fairly Satis-factory*	*Unsatis-factory*	*No Opinion*
DCFR	137	46%	47%	2%	4%
Payback	159	24	65	9	2
ARR	143	20	58	15	7
NPV	87	23	52	1	24
MAPIR	67	6	16	7	70

Methods Discontinued as Unsatisfactory

Each respondent was asked to indicate whether his company had used any of the methods within the last five years and subsequently discontinued its use because of unsatisfactory results. The replies may be summarized as:

	No. of Respondents			
Method	*Yes*	*No*	*Not Sure*	*No Opinion*
ARR	28	106	7	59
Payback	17	112	6	65
MAPIR	14	103	33	50
NPV	11	123	12	54
DCFR	9	129	9	53

*This percentage is found by dividing the total responses for yes (familiar) by the total of yes, no, and not sure responses for each method.

The yes answers, as a percentage of yes, no, and not sure, indicate that the ranking of the methods according to their discontinuance as unsatisfactory is ARR, payback, MAPIR, NPV, and DCFR. Therefore, the NPV and DCFR methods seem to have been discontinued less frequently than the other three.

Combinations of Methods

Previous studies have indicated that business firms seem to realize that each method answers a different question about a proposal and that it is often desirable to use more than one method for evaluating capital expenditure proposals.[1] This conclusion is endorsed by the present study.

The replies from responding firms indicate that *very few* firms use one method alone for evaluating capital expenditure proposals. The number of firms using various combinations of methods are summarized in Table 24.

Table 24. Number of methods used simultaneously.

No. of Methods in Combination	*For Major Projects*	*For All Other Projects*
1	26	37
2	90	87
3	65	45
4	7	5
5	9	9
Totals	197	183

The overwhelming majority of corporations use a combination of methods for evaluating capital expenditures rather than one method exclusively. Considering the five basic methods, 26 firms use only one for major projects, and 37 firms use only one for "all other projects." Also, 9 firms use all five methods for evaluating major projects, and 9 firms use all five for evaluating "all other projects." It is apparent that a majority of the respondents use a two-method combination. Table 25 shows the number of firms that use only a single method.

Table 25. Number of firms that use a single method.

Method	*For Major Projects*	*For All Other Projects*
DCFR	12	7
NPV	3	1
MAPIR	0	1
ARR	4	8
Payback	7	20
Totals	26	37

The most common combinations for both major projects and "all other projects" in each of the following categories are:

No. of Methods	*Most Common Combination*
2	DCFR and payback and/or ARR and payback
3	DCFR, ARR, and payback
4	DCFR, NPV, ARR, and payback

Dominance of Rate of Return Methods

An observation from previous studies, confirmed by this study, is the dominant use of rate of return methods (time-adjusted and/or not time-adjusted) by firms in evaluating their capital expenditure proposals. The present survey indicates that, for major projects, 183 of 197 firms (93 percent) use the DCFR and/or the ARR method, and the remaining 14 firms (7 percent) use neither of these two methods.

For "all other projects," 157 of 189 firms (83 percent) use the DCFR method and/or the ARR method, and the other 32 firms (17 percent) use neither.

Efficient and Inefficient Methods

For the purpose of presentation here, three methods (DCFR, NPV, and MAPIR) are defined as efficient or theoretically sound, and the remaining two methods (payback and ARR) as inefficient or theoretically unsound.

Using the above definition, the present survey indicates that 149 of 197 responding firms (76 percent) use efficient methods for evaluating major projects, and the remaining 48 firms (24 percent) use inefficient methods.

For evaluating "all other projects," 116 of 189 responding firms (61 percent) use efficient methods, and the remaining 73 firms (39 percent) use inefficient methods.

When these results are compared with practices of ten years ago, a definite conclusion is reached: Large corporations are presently making more use of the advanced, or theoretically sound, methods of evaluating capital expenditure proposals than was the case a decade ago.

However, it is also evident that there is still room for improvement. The use of advanced methods by large corporations is far from reaching the ideal 100 percent level.

The picture is different for small and medium-size corporations. None of the five small firms interviewed for the study use any of the three advanced methods. They use intuition, rule of thumb, subjective judgment, and, occasionally, payback and ARR.

On the basis of data collected from the 27 interviews with representatives of different-size corporations, a direct relationship seems to exist between the size of a company and the degree of sophistication of methods employed. The larger the company, the more sophisticated the method or combination of methods used.

Small companies are usually less formal in evaluating their capital expenditures, and accept–reject decisions are in the hands of the top manager. In a small company, the top manager is very close to what is happening in his firm and may weigh all the factors in his head without resorting to other methods of evaluation. Also, managers of small firms usually spend a large percentage of their time on day-to-day operations, with little time left for long-term planning. In addition, it may be argued that no sophisticated methods are needed because the capital expenditure budget for a small firm is very small.

To give some idea of how small companies evaluate their capital expenditures, here are some examples:

A paper manufacturing company with a small capital expenditure budget uses need as the basis for approving capital expenditures. Capital expenditure proposals are submitted to the board of directors for approval, and projects are grouped into categories according to the degree of need. The justification for this practice is that the company is small and closely managed, and most of the proposed capital expenditure items are required to improve the quality of output. The firm does not have a manual or any written policy and does not use any standard forms for evaluating capital expenditures.

A small manufacturer of aluminum sports products uses subjective judgment only; it does not use any other method of evaluating capital expenditures. A machine was recently acquired, and the controller was not even aware of the purchase until a shipping invoice was received. The controller stated that most of the company's capital expenditures are made on what amounts to impulse buying. When the controller was asked to indicate how his firm determines the time when machines have to be replaced, he stated simply that they are kept until they are beyond repair. The mechanic is considered the final judge of whether the machine should be repaired or scrapped.

Intuition, hunch, and occasionally payback are the only methods used by a small metal foil manufacturer.

Despite all the justifications for using less sophisticated methods of evaluating capital expenditures in small companies, these arguments are not very convincing. Small firms would undoubtedly benefit a great deal from using some combination of the five common methods for evaluating their capital expenditures. Although the capital expenditure budget of a small company is small in dollar terms, it is often large when compared to the size of the firm. A $10,000 mistake in a capital expenditure, of little significance in a large corporation, may result in the bankruptcy of a small firm.

A possible fringe benefit for a small firm using any one of the methods of evaluation of capital expenditures discussed previously is more readily obtainable financing. Bankers generally prefer theoretically sound methods.

Other Methods

The five methods discussed previously are not the only methods of evaluating capital expenditures, though they are the most commonly used ones. Although the following discussion is not intended to provide a comprehensive list of methods of evaluating capital expenditure proposals, five additional methods are described briefly because of frequent references to them in practice. These methods are: discounted payback, necessity, postponability, rule of thumb, and subjective judgment.

Discounted Payback

The discounted payback method combines the appealing characteristics of payback (the time required to recover the investment) and the discounted cash flow (consideration of the time value of money). Simply, it is the time required to recover the investment, with the time value of money considered. The computation may be made by first finding the payback period and then inspecting the entries in a present-value table (e.g., Table 11) at the required discount rate. The value that coincides with the payback period is identified (if it falls between two rows in the table, an interpolation process is needed) and the corresponding value in the years column is the discounted payback period.

EXAMPLE

An investment requires a capital outlay of \$4,355 and is expected to result in an annual cash flow after taxes of \$1,000 per year for 10 years. What is the discounted payback period if the required return is 10 percent?

SOLUTION

$$\text{Regular payback period} = \frac{\text{investment}}{\text{annual cash flow}}$$

$$= \frac{\$4{,}355}{\$1{,}000} = 4.355 \text{ years}$$

Since the required return is 10 percent, the column for the present value of \$1 received annually at 10 percent is searched to find the value \$4.355. By inspection, it is found that this value is the sixth entry in this column, which corresponds to 6 years. Therefore, the discounted payback period is 6 years.

EXAMPLE

A capital expenditure of \$5,441 is expected to result in an annual cash flow of \$1,000 per year for 17 years. What is the discounted payback period if the required return is 10 percent?

SOLUTION

$$\text{Regular payback period} = \frac{\$5{,}441}{\$1{,}000} = 5.441 \text{ years}$$

An inspection of the entries in the 10 percent column of the present value of an annuity of \$1 shows that 5.441 falls between years 8 and 9. An interpolation process is needed to get the answer.

	Present Value of \$1 Annuity at 10%
Year 8	5.335
Discounted payback	5.441
Year 9	5.759

$$\text{Discounted payback period} = 8 + \frac{5.441 - \text{year } 8}{\text{year } 9 - \text{year } 8}$$

$$= 8 + \frac{5.441 - 5.335}{5.759 - 5.335}$$

$$= 8 + \frac{0.106}{0.424} = 8 + 0.25$$

$$= 8.25 \text{ years}$$

Although the discounted payback does not ignore the time value of money, it is still unacceptable because it ignores the proceeds after payback. The discounted payback is not a measure of profitability and should not be used exclusively. As a supplementary measure of evaluating capital expenditure proposals it provides a useful input. It is superior to the regular payback method.

Necessity

Necessity means extreme need for the capital expenditure. For example, a spare part necessary to operate a machine is a must if production is to continue. Necessity is not a general method of evaluation because it is highly subjective. Project evaluation should be based on the degree of profitability. If carried to an extreme, necessity as a method would lead to inefficient allocation of resources and using obsolete facilities.

Postponability

According to the postponability method, proposals are ranked according to how long they can be delayed. It is not a generally acceptable method of evaluating capital expenditures. There is no direct relationship between profitability and postponability, and, when used, this method could lead to the misallocation of resources and the maintaining of obsolete facilities. Projects should be ranked according to their degree of profitability, not their postponability.

Rule of Thumb

The *American College Dictionary* defines a rule of thumb as "a rule based on experience or practice rather than on scientific knowledge," and "a rough, practical method of procedure."

A rule of thumb is, therefore: (1) a rough rule that is used to make quick decisions, (2) a tool with no basis of scientific knowledge and therefore of questionable value, (3) a rule mainly dependent on experience and practice.

Rules of thumb are helpful for getting quick answers, and they may save the cost of elaborate analyses. However, rules of thumb are not designed for solving difficult problems or for making decisions that have many variables to be considered. By necessity, rules of thumb must oversimplify the practical situation, and it is a dangerous practice to use them by themselves in the vital area of capital investment analysis.

The rule of thumb is not recognized academically as an acceptable method of evaluating capital expenditure proposals. Examples of rules of thumb are many. Joel Dean has listed five that were used in making replacement decisions regarding motor vehicles. They are:

1. Replace every X years or Y miles.
2. Replace when the vehicle is fully depreciated.
3. Replace when the maintenance cost of the old vehicle exceeds the new vehicle's depreciation charge and maintenance.
4. Replace when the unit cost of the old vehicle is lowest.
5. Replace when the vehicle is "worn out beyond repair."[2]

Rules of thumb are sometimes used by corporations for evaluating their capital expenditure proposals; however, the present survey shows that rules of thumb are used by only 11 percent of the respondents for major projects and 14 percent for "all other projects," and that they are *not* used by themselves for these evaluations.

Subjective Judgment

No evaluation tool ever developed can claim to replace or eliminate the need for subjective judgment in any managerial decision. Until management becomes an exact science, where everything is subject to precise measurement, subjective judgment must remain an important element in decision making.

It is implicitly assumed that subjective judgment is exercised to some extent in evaluating any capital expenditure proposal. However, the question to be considered here is whether it is unaided judgment or enlightened judgment that is used.

For major projects, the evaluation questionnaire shows that of 87 firms in which subjective judgment is reported to be used, none use this method exclusively; 62 of the 87 firms (71 percent) use it in combination with at least one of the three theoretically sound methods (DCFR, NPV, and MAPIR). The remaining 25 firms (29 percent) use subjective judgment with one or more of the following theoretically unsound methods: payback, accountant rate of return, and rule of thumb.

For "all other projects," of 97 firms that reported they use subjective judgment for evaluating this type of capital expenditure proposal, 3 firms (3 percent) use it exclusively, 55 firms (57 percent) use it with one or more of the three theoretically sound methods (DCFR, NPV, and MAPIR), and 39 firms (40 percent) use it to supplement at least one of the three theoretically unsound methods (payback, ARR, and rule of thumb).

The majority of the companies surveyed use subjective judgment, not by itself, but rather to supplement other methods—the superior approach. The availability and increasing recognition and acceptance of theoretically sound methods of capital expenditure analysis (such as DCFR, NPV, or MAPIR) apparently have reduced the emphasis on unaided judgment and increased the use of enlightened judgment that is based on as much objective data as possible.

Typical Comments

What is considered the best method depends on many factors, such as the type of business, its size, the amount of capital expenditures, and the type of management it has. The supervisor of a plant of a large chemical company, who assumes a large role in evaluating capital expenditures at the plant level, indicated that the ideal method is one that will result in maximizing profits, particularly dollars, and is easy to understand.

The majority of the companies surveyed, as indicated previously, use a combination of methods. For a better understanding of the reasons and advantages of such practices, selected comments are presented.

A questionnaire respondent had this to say about using a combination of methods:

> Our company does not consider any one method of evaluating a capital expenditure proposal . . . as the sole or primary criteria for accepting or rejecting the request for expenditure. The various methods of evaluation are used as tools to aid and assist management in making the ultimate decision. The discounted rate of return, annual profit contribution, cash payback (both from date of first expenditure and from on-stream date) and return on the additional capital employed, along with subjective judgment as to risk, need and relationship to short range and long range plans are all incorporated to arrive at the final accept or reject decision.

The president of a large corporation stated some of the key criteria used for analyzing capital expenditures in his corporation. They are:

> 1. The conventional payout calculation specifying the years of project life necessary for the cash earnings (total income less operating cost and taxes) to return the capital invested in the project.
>
> 2. Actuarial rate of return, that is, discounted cash flow analysis where the percent rate of return is the discount factor applied to the positive and negative annual cash flows to discount them to zero at some point in time—most frequently start of operation.

> 3. Discounted profitability index where the ratio of cash earnings discounted at [a given rate] to investment discounted at [a given rate] is calculated.
>
> 4. For all major projects the book rate of return for the first five or ten years of the project's operation is also determined defined as book profit divided by average capital employed during each year.
>
> 5. Other suitable indicators are frequently used, such as present worth cost plots as a function of value of money to compare alternative methods of accomplishing a given objective. . . .
>
> Minimum standards for each of the first three methods outlined above are set annually and vary from category to category of investment opportunities depending on the relative risk and relationship to overall corporate objectives. These minimum levels for discretionary investment opportunities are above our company's average return on capital employed to recognize that certain operating necessity expenditures will have no net earnings and that there is some possibility of failure in any given project.

The treasurer of a large metal stampings manufacturing company wrote:

> Each year is evaluated by our management before the end of the preceding year and our capital expenditures plan is developed at that time based on a number of factors such as (1) payment period, (2) profit improvement, (3) technological improvement of facilities, and last but not least (4) funds available.

In a large conglomerate corporation, a correspondent highlighted his capital expenditure analysis procedure as follows:

> After line personnel and field executives have submitted appropriation requests, the Corporate Controller's office and the Office of the President review the proposals. Sophisticated financial analysis utilizing payback period and discounted cash flow plays a major role in capital expenditure decisions. Executive expectations concerning the future viability of specific industries and producer lines also enter into the decision process.

One correspondent stated that his firm's approach to the evaluation of capital expenditures and the expected returns may be explained as follows:

> 1. The following financial computations are usually prepared for major capital expenditure proposals: return on average investment, payback, net present value, internal rate of return [DCFR].

2. The required rate of return will vary, depending on the type of capital investment that is involved. (For example, the return required on a field office building would differ from the expected return on production equipment.)

3. All returns are calculated on an after-tax basis.

4. In certain instances, when a project does not meet the rate of return acceptable to [the company], approval may still be granted, based on non-financial [factors], e.g., governmental regulations, safety, personnel considerations, etc.

Another correspondent outlined his procedure as follows:

In any investment decision, we attempt to determine whether the particular investment is an effective use of the Company's resources and whether there is an alternative investment that is more attractive. The principal measure that we use to answer these questions is the long-term after-tax return on the proposed investment. This return is calculated by dividing the average annual profits that are realized over the economic life of the facility by the average investment level (including any associated changes in cash, inventories, or receivables). This return is then compared with the returns for the alternative investments and with the Company's cost of capital to evaluate the desirability of making the investment.

In evaluating investment proposals, we also take into consideration the time period required to pay back the investment. The payback period is, of course, the time required for the cash flows generated by the investment (profits after taxes plus non-cash charges such as depreciation) to equal the original cash outlay. The payback period is used to choose between alternative investments that have the same returns and to ensure that the investment is repaid before product changes or obsolescence causes us to have to replace the facility.

As a guide in evaluating certain investment proposals, we also determine the time-adjusted rate of return or the present value of the cash flows to take into account the time value of money. These procedures are somewhat more complicated than the average return and payback methods described above, and for the majority of our many investment decisions the additional effort is not justified because it would not result in a different decision. Discounted cash flows are always used, however, to supplement the basic analysis in evaluating lease-versus-buy proposals and in cases where the cash flows are so irregular that the average return method could be misleading.

One correspondent ably described his procedure in the following manner:

> [The firm] operates under formal capital plan procedures whereby prospective projects exceeding $100,000 each are included in capital plans reviewed at six-month intervals. The capital plan format requires that each division and subsidiary company rank their projects according to the primary objectives of increased profitability and return on assets. However, the ranking must also consider so-called "must" projects for the abatement or control of water or atmospheric pollution, safety standards, maintenance, etc. After review by the executive managements of divisions and subsidiaries, and by the corporate executives, during which some projects are rescheduled or eliminated, a plan is presented to the corporate Board of Directors listing those projects which executive management judges to be the most vital for the corporation to undertake. After approval of the overall plan by the Board, detailed appropriations for each project are presented for evaluation.
>
> Several methods are employed for evaluating economics supporting proposed appropriations for capital expenditures:
>
> 1. *Payback plus an objective rate of return*—A calculation is made on a cash-flow basis to determine the period of time required to recover the total investment, *plus* an established annual rate of return on the unrecovered portion of the investment at the end of each year. This method informs management of the prospects for recovering the investment during the life of the product, which in many cases is fairly short. Investments in products frequently include substantial amounts of jigs, dies, and fixtures peculiar to a particular product. Therefore, the time required to recover the investment in such tooling plus an objective return can be related to the estimated life of the product and a measurement of the risk in the investment reasonably established.
>
> 2. *Internal rate of return*—The payback method requires a supplemental evaluation when the product or project life is forecasted to be longer than the payback period. The internal rate of return is computed under the conventional discounted cash-flow methods. An additional use for this method is the ability where applicable to rank projects or alternatives.
>
> 3. *Other methods*—In other situations, e.g., lease vs. buy, the present value method may be used applying rates appropriate for the particular circumstances. All presentations display pre-tax and post-tax profit differentials. Depreciation on a straight-line basis is included in published financial statements, but, accelerated depreciation is used for tax purposes and is reflected in cash-flow calculations.

Conclusion

Methods of evaluating capital expenditure proposals are usually used in combination and not individually. Businessmen prefer a rate of return measure over other methods that do not provide a rate of return figure.

NOTES

1. *Financial Analysis to Guide Capital Expenditure Decisions.* N.A.A. Research Report 43 (New York: National Association of Accountants, 1967), p. 4; and Elly Vassilatou-Thanopoulos, *Financial Analysis Techniques for Equipment Replacement Decisions,* N.A.A. Research Monograph 1 (New York: National Association of Accountants, 1965), p. 12.
2. Joel Dean, *Capital Budgeting* (New York: Columbia University Press, 1951), p. 110.

9 / Evaluation Techniques

THERE appear to be four stages of sophistication in the evaluation of capital expenditures: rules of thumb and simple methods, advanced methods, combinations of methods, and techniques. In the first stage (rules of thumb and simple methods), the evaluation of capital expenditures is based mainly on intuition and judgment of the evaluator, supplemented by simple rules of thumb (such as investing an amount equal to depreciation, replacing an asset every ten years, or replacing an asset when it is completely worn out) and simple methods such as payback or accountant rate of return.

In the second stage (advanced methods) old rules of thumb and simple methods are disregarded in favor of one of the advanced methods. In this stage, the decision maker's judgment is aided by *one* of the advanced methods, such as net present value (NPV) or discounted cash flow rate of return (DCFR).

In the third stage (combinations of methods), the decision maker realizes that each method measures something and that no method is altogether good or altogether bad. In this stage, a combination of methods is used for the evaluation of capital expenditures. The underlying assumption is that there are many facets to an investment, and a combination of methods would provide a better basis for decisions than the single-method approach.

Finally, in the fourth stage (techniques), the methods are supplemented by techniques. The use of quantitative techniques may be regarded as an extension to or a refinement of the evaluation methods. When the NPV method is used, for example, one set of estimates of cash outlays and cash inflows is used. Quantitative techniques may be used to accommodate the fact that there are several possible outcomes besides the one used in computing the NPV. Some of these techniques show what change would occur in the NPV

Note: The author wishes to thank his colleague and friend Dr. Glenn H. Gilbreath, assistant professor of quantitative management at Virginia Commonwealth University, for reading drafts of this chapter and offering many helpful suggestions.

(or the measure of profitability used) as a result of given changes in the values of some of the elements forming the cash outlays or cash inflows (benefits). Modern quantitative techniques used in capital expenditure analysis may help to provide answers to such questions as:

- What is the effect of a given change in construction costs, wages, price of product, quantity sold, and other key factors on the profitability (rate of return) of the proposed investment?
- What are the possible consequences of certain proposed investments?
- What is the probability distribution of various profitability levels of a proposed investment?
- What is the ideal mix of proposals that will maximize the benefits derived from limited resources?

These questions and many others can be answered, at least partially, through the use of quantitative techniques.

The four stages of sophistication are not necessarily evolutionary in the sense that every business firm moves from stage 1 to stage 2, to stage 3, and finally to stage 4. It is possible for a firm to move to any stage in any order. However, the *overall* pattern of American businesses seems to follow a general movement from 1 to 2, to 3, to 4. Since the first three stages have been explored in previous chapters, the emphasis here will be on *selected* techniques for capital expenditure analysis. Although a detailed discussion of these techniques is beyond the scope of this book, each technique will be described so that the potential user can identify situations to which each technique is applicable. He may then consult experts in that area or books that contain a more advanced treatment of the subject.

Generally speaking, quantitative methods and their applications are receiving increasing attention from both business firms and academic institutions. Various terms—such as management science, operations research, and decision theory—are used to reflect the trend toward more quantitative analysis and less emphasis on intuition and rule-of-thumb approaches, which are ill-equipped to handle the problems of the present technology.

The management science approach to decision making is not aimed at usurping the manager's authority by replacing his judgment with formulas and mathematical models. These quantitative methods are designed to help the manager obtain additional information for assisting him in making better decisions. The output of these techniques is precisely described by Hanssmann when he says: "The output of operations research is not decisions but information. . . ."[1]

It should be pointed out that although most of these quantitative techniques have been known for some time, their application in the capital expenditure decision-making process is relatively new.

In theory, quantitative techniques have a good potential for use in the evaluation of capital expenditure proposals.

The objective of this chapter is to identify six selected techniques and the number of responding firms using them in the evaluation of their capital expenditure proposals. The following techniques are examined: the computer, sensitivity analysis, simulation and models, risk analysis, linear programming, and program evaluation and review technique (PERT).

The six techniques selected in the chapter are not mutually exclusive. Any combination of them is possible, and the line of demarcation between them is not always clear-cut. Although it is not strictly a technique in itself, the computer is included as one of the six techniques because it is becoming an increasingly essential tool in the implementation of capital expenditure evaluation techniques.

The Computer

Computers have achieved wonders by providing rapid computational facilities for masses of data that would have taken years to process otherwise. Computers are frequently blamed for eliminating some jobs and for creating an uneasy atmosphere and promoting resistance to change by hundreds of people who could not cope with the required change, or who underestimated the power of computers and treated them as simple calculators. On the whole, computers deserve full recognition for enabling us to reach beyond our dreams.

There are many indications that the "thinking computer" is not very far away. An article in *Business Week* predicts that this may be achieved even before 1980:

> The "thinking" machines are coming. Some of them will make diagnoses from X-ray negatives. Others will fight fires, mine coal, or handle explosives. Still others will write computer programs, read books and store information from them, and even scan blueprints to figure out how to make simple products. It sounds like the 21st Century, but "intelligent" machines may be around before 1980.[2]

The use of computers in evaluating capital expenditure proposals is becoming more practical and more popular. A number of factors are responsible for this trend. Among them are[3]:

1. The costs of special purpose computers have been reduced and their availability increased.

2. Standard programs developed by the principal computer manufacturers are now available.

3. Discounted cash flow calculations that are often considered difficult and time consuming can be done faster and more efficiently with the computer. It is also possible, with the aid of the computer, to obtain additional information about the attractiveness of a proposal, when using such measures as accountant rate of return, net present value, profitability index, payback, and discounted payback periods, at a nominal additional cost.

4. The use of computers has made it possible to accommodate the more sophisticated and more realistic mathematical models. Furthermore, such techniques as sensitivity analysis, linear programming, and simulations are made more practical and feasible through the use of high-speed computers.

5. It is becoming increasingly possible to use a remote-access time-sharing plan to reduce the costs of using computers and to make using them more convenient.

The Computer in Practice

Respondents were asked to check each of the techniques currently used by their company in evaluating capital expenditure proposals. Of 154 respondents that answered this part of the question (by checking yes, no, or not sure), 93 firms (60 percent) use a computer, 55 (36 percent) do not use one, and the remaining 6 respondents (4 percent) are not sure (a computer being used very rarely or in the introductory stages).

The vice-president of finance of a large electronics firm warned against excessive reliance on computers. He advised that although computers can help with routine calculations and other steps in the analysis of capital expenditures, they (so far) cannot think. Computers aid but cannot replace the judgment of a manager who knows his business well.

Sensitivity Analysis

In the early stages of sophistication of methods of evaluating capital expenditure proposals, estimates based on one possible outcome were acceptable. For example, when evaluating a capital expenditure proposal, one set of figures was used—one value for cost of investment, one value for first-year benefits, one value for second-year benefits, and so on.

As the analysis of capital expenditure proposals becomes more refined, it becomes apparent that single estimates of cash flows and single estimates of the profitability of the proposed investment are usually unrealistic. The practice of using one estimate for each item of cost or benefit results in a single estimate of the profitability of a capital expenditure proposal. For example, using a single set of values for cash inflows and cash outflows and computing the discounted cash flow rate of return (DCFR), a capital expenditure proposal may be estimated to produce a 15 percent return on the investment.

In reality, many of the estimates used to compute the DCFR are subject to error. The expected error may be small or large, depending upon the items being estimated (for example, repetitive expense items are usually easier to estimate than volume of sales or the price of a new product) and the method of estimation used (guess versus refined forecasting approaches).

This possibility of error in estimation is due to the simple fact that we are dealing with future values which are uncertain or unknown. The lack of knowledge regarding future values is commonly known as the uncertainties surrounding the estimates. Some individuals differentiate between risk and uncertainty; however, for the purpose of this book, the two terms are used synonymously.

Returning to our proposal with 15 percent DCFR, a study of the estimates for the proposal may reveal that if everything goes as expected, the proposed investment will have a 15 percent return. However, it is possible, because of changes in the values of some elements that constitute the cash flows, to get as low as a 10 percent return if the benefits are not fully realized or as high as a 20 percent return if benefits are better than expected. In other words, the 15 percent DCFR computed in the conventional analysis is the most likely value, but it is only a single value out of a range of possible values between 10 and 20 percent. These three estimates–10, 15, and 20 percent–may be called pessimistic, most likely, and optimistic.

Two investments, A and B, each with an expected return of 15 percent, are not equally desirable if it is known that, for example, investment A is expected to result in a return between 10 percent and 20 percent whereas investment B is expected to result in a return between -5 percent and 35 percent. Although the most likely return in each case, based on single estimates, is 15 percent, the two projects are not of equal risk. Investment A has a profitability range of 10 percent (the range is defined as the highest less the lowest value; in this case it is 20 percent less 10 percent = 10 percent), and investment B has a profitability range of 40 percent (35 percent less -5 percent = 35 percent + 5 percent = 40 percent). Investment B is generally considered more risky than investment A because it has a wider profitability range, which is also known as dispersion or variation. Other things being equal, the project with the smallest profitability range is considered to have the least risk.

The expected degree of dispersion in the profitability of an investment proposal is one measure of risk. The range was used here to measure dispersion whereas in more refined analysis the standard deviation (defined as the square root of the average of the squared deviations from the mean) may be used instead. In still more refined analysis the coefficient of variation, the standard deviation divided by the mean, may be used to compare the dispersion of one group with another when the two means are not similar.

Another example may help illustrate the idea of using a single estimate versus a range of values. A single estimate of $20,000 for first-year benefits of an investment represents the most likely value but does not tell the whole story. A more careful study of this estimate may reveal that there are several possible values, not just a single value. We may be able to provide a list of possible values and the chances of their occurrence. It may look as follows:

Possible Value of Benefits	*Chance of Occurrence*
8,000	0.05
12,000	0.10
16,000	0.15
20,000	0.40
24,000	0.15
28,000	0.10
32,000	0.05

Treatment of uncertainties regarding the estimates of key factors in the conventional analysis of capital expenditure proposals is often haphazard, leaving much to be desired. Many times, these uncertainties are ignored or delayed until the profitability of a proposal is established, and then they are considered through subjective judgment aided by descriptive statements that indicate the nature of the project and the likelihood of changes in the profitability of a project.

More recently, the techniques of sensitivity analysis and risk analysis have been used to provide an organized and refined way of explicitly dealing with uncertainties surrounding the estimates.

What Is Sensitivity Analysis?

Sensitivity analysis is a technique designed to measure the response or change in the profitability of a project as a result of changes in the key factors that affect a project's cash inflows and cash outflows. The first step in the use of sensitivity analysis is to identify the key factors. The second step is to initiate some change in one key factor at a time and measure the effect of this change on the profitability of the investment. Profitability is measured by using one of the methods of evaluation discussed in previous chapters. The third and final step is to summarize the findings in either tabular or graphic form.

Thus, sensitivity analysis is not competing with the methods discussed earlier—discounted cash flow rate of return (DCFR), net present value (NPV), payback, accountant rate of return, and MAPI. Sensitivity analysis is, in essence, a supplement to these methods and is usually used in association with advanced methods of evaluation, in particular DCFR or NPV.

One type of information that might be obtained through sensitivity analysis would be to find out what happens to the DCFR (or the measure of profitability used) if sales decrease by 10 percent. Or, what happens to the DCFR if production costs increase by 5 percent, or 10 percent; or if there is a sudden change in market acceptance of the product; or if maintenance costs increase by 5 percent or 10 percent?

A key factor common to sensitivity studies is price-level changes. Some authors suggest that price changes and the sensitivity of different proposals to these changes should be investigated whenever there is a possibility of such changes in the future.[4]

If a small change in one estimate of a given item results in a major change in the profitability of the proposal, the capital expenditure project is considered sensitive to the estimate of this item. If this small change could result in changing the decision to accept the proposal, the project is considered especially risky. But if a small change in the estimate of the factor does not change the decision, the project is not considered sensitive to that factor.

Sensitivity analysis can help the capital expenditure analysis decision maker in at least two ways. First, it can warn him of very risky proposals where a small change in key elements would have a large effect on the profitability of these proposals. This may help when selecting from among proposals competing for limited funds. Second, it can help to identify areas where additional information is needed to improve the estimates of selected items.

Sensitivity analysis, however, is not a precise technique. It does not usually consider the effect of a *combination of changes* in various items or factors on the profitability of a proposal and does not normally provide information on the probability that these changes may occur. Its main contribution lies in providing useful information about how sensitive the project is to changes in different factors. Other things being equal, less sensitive projects are preferred over more sensitive projects since a small change in any factor would have a significant effect on the sensitive project and might change the estimated profits from the project to losses.

Two methods are suggested in the literature for measuring the sensitivity of a capital expenditure proposal to a particular factor. The first is by calculating the change in the measure of profitability (for example, discounted rate of return or DCFR) as a result of a given change in a factor (for example, 1 percent or 5 percent). If a small change in a factor (for example, 2 percent) results in a much larger change in the DCFR (for example, 10 percent), then the project is considered especially sensitive (risky).

Sensitivity may also be measured by finding the needed percentage of change in the factor to change the DCFR by a given percentage, such as 1 percent.[5] For example, if a 5 percent change in the factor is required to produce a 1 percent change in the DCFR, that factor is judged less sensitive than if a 0.01 percent change in it is required to produce a 1 percent change in the DCFR.

William C. House studied the effects of errors in estimates of selected factors on the profitability of eight capital expenditure proposals (as measured by the discounted cash flow rate of return or DCFR) in the area of wholesale distribution of natural gas. The selected errors in these factors included: a 5 percent decrease in sales volume, a 5 percent decrease in sales price, a 5 percent increase in purchase price, a 5 percent increase in operating expense, a 5 percent increase in taxes other than federal, a 5 percent increase in capital investment, and a 5-year decrease in the project's economic life.

It was found that these proposals were generally more sensitive (that is, small changes in the factors resulted in large changes in the DCFR) to changes in sales price, sales volume, and project life of the proposal. They were not significantly sensitive to changes in purchase price, operating expense, other taxes, and capital investment.[6]

Sensitivity Analysis in Practice

Of 150 responding firms, sensitivity analysis is used by 70 firms (47 percent), not used by 68 firms (45 percent), and the remaining 12 are not sure.

Simulation and Models

Simulation, a process of imitation or duplication, has wide application in business. It allows the decision maker in business firms to experiment with the variables affecting a decision and to learn more about the possible outcomes before actually making a decision. Simulation also has a useful role to play in investment analysis: it allows the decision maker to study an investment and to learn more about the consequences of such an investment before actually investing any money.

Two things are needed for simulations: a mathematical model to represent a real-world situation and a mechanism through which numbers are produced at random. These essential requirements may be referred to as a model and a random-number generator.

A model is a representation of something; it may be physical, conceptual, or mathematical. An example of a physical model is a model of a city, used in city planning. A conceptual model is a concept formed in a person's mind when he talks about a certain subject. Mathematical models are usually more well defined and expressed in quantitative terms. For example, if gross profit (P) is 40 percent of net sales (S), the mathematical model expressing this relationship may be written as $P = 0.4S$.

Because models, by necessity, emphasize the important aspects of what they represent and ignore unimportant details, they have limitations. The question that should be asked when using a mathematical model is: Is the model sufficiently representative of what it is intended to describe? A model should not be too elaborate, for it would be too difficult to study; nor should it be so simple that essential variables are omitted. Thus, a model should be as simple as possible, yet detailed enough to be representative of what it was set up to describe.

Let us consider as an example a familiar model, that of flipping a coin. The probability distribution (a listing of all possible outcomes and their probabilities) of flipping a coin once is:

Possible Outcome	*Probability*
0 head (tail shows)	0.50
1 head	0.50
	1.00

Our model indicates that each time a fair coin is tossed, there is a 50 percent chance that a head will show face up. In practice, each time a coin is tossed, either a head or a tail must occur. Over the long run of a series of tosses, we should get the same number of heads as tails. Knowing this probability distribution for heads and tails, how can we simulate the occurrence of a head or a tail on a given toss?

To simulate the above model, we need a random-number generator. As was mentioned above, this refers to a way of producing numbers at random which conform to some specified probability distribution. A simple form of random-number generator for the above problem is that of writing each number from 1 through 10 on small pieces of paper, folding these papers and mixing them well in a box, then selecting one paper at a time, replacing each paper and mixing again before the next draw, and repeating the process as many times as needed. Since in flipping a fair coin there is a 50 percent chance each time of getting heads and a 50 percent chance of getting tails, we may use half the values to represent heads (1, 2, 3, 4, 5) and half the values to represent tails (6, 7, 8, 9, 10). Accordingly, we have the following key:

No.	*Outcome*	*No.*	*Outcome*
1	Heads	6	Tails
2	Heads	7	Tails
3	Heads	8	Tails
4	Heads	9	Tails
5	Heads	10	Tails

Now, mix the pieces of paper and select one. Suppose the first piece of paper selected is 10. Looking back at our key, a 10 stands for a tail. Our model has simulated the tossing of a coin and the outcome of a tail on the toss. Now, fold the paper and put it back into the box, mix the papers, and repeat the selection process again and again. Suppose the following values are found, 10, 9, 8, 2, 2, 7. This means: tails, tails, tails, heads, heads, and tails. Thus, in six simulated tosses, we have observed four tails and two heads.

What we are doing is simulating the probability distribution of flipping a coin *without* actually flipping the coin. Tables of random numbers and computers may also be used to generate random numbers, rather than writing values on pieces of paper.

The probability distribution illustrated is a discrete distribution because only whole numbers can occur. For example, in flipping coins you can get only one head, or two, or three, but never one and one-half heads or two and three-fourths. The probability distribution of some of the key variables in a capital expenditure proposal follows a continuous distribution where values other than whole numbers can occur, necessitating some adjustment in the process. However, the idea is still basically the same.

Simulations may be used in several business areas. For example, simulation may be used in determining the optimum inventory level, the economic order quantity, the reorder point, and the ideal number of checkout booths to have at different times in a supermarket. In some financial management classes, business simulation games are used to give the student a chance to apply basic business concepts by making decisions and learning from mistakes without actually risking real money. These simulation games are based on the same premise as the previous illustration, a mathematical model and a random-number generator.

Likewise, for capital expenditure analysis, the simulation technique gives the decision maker in a business firm a chance to experiment with different proposals and to evaluate the possible consequences of different courses of action before actually investing any money. The technique is as valid for business as is flying a plane in a wind tunnel so that an aerospace engineer can observe the plane's reaction to many different flight conditions before releasing it for actual flight. The following discussion of risk analysis will include additional material with reference to simulation.

The main limitations of the simulation technique lie in the development of a representative model and in the fact that simulations are usually more complex and more expensive to use than the conventional approaches. Elaborate simulations cannot be made without the aid of a computer. Often, specially designed computer programs are needed to account for the specific characteristics of a firm and the particular capital expenditure projects being considered.

Part of the complication of simulations is due to the need for forming mathematical models. Models are not very popular with businessmen. Executives are usually skeptical of mathematical models because they are frequently hard to understand. Operations research personnel frequently use sophisticated mathematical symbolism that is not usually a part of the businessman's vocabulary. Too often no attempt is made to explain the models in language that the average businessman can understand.

Analysts should not expect a hard-working businessman to go back to school for several years to learn to understand the models proposed by the operations research department; nor should he be expected to accept such models without understanding the underlying assumptions, relationships, and implications. Progress in this area will be enhanced if models are explained in language that management can understand.

Time and time again, during the collection of the data for this book, businessmen indicated that they simply do not understand all those sophisticated models proposed in the literature. They also indicated that they cannot accept such models blindly since their future depends upon the outcome of their decisions.

Simulation and Models in Practice

Of 152 responding firms, simulation and models are used by 65 firms (43 percent), not used by 80 firms (53 percent), and the remaining 7 are not sure.

Risk Analysis

Risk analysis may be regarded as an extension of sensitivity analysis. Sensitivity analysis points out what would happen to the profitability of a proposal if some changes in the estimates of key factors occurred. It does not address itself to the question of the probability of occurrence of such changes. Risk analysis, on the other hand, includes probability. In other words, risk analysis is an extension of sensitivity analysis that explicitly takes into consideration the probability of changes in the estimates of key factors and the combined effect of these changes.

A simple form of risk analysis has been used by many companies for some time without being referred to as risk analysis. In estimating profits from certain projects, the practice of showing three possible figures for profit—high, low, and middle—is an example of such a simple form of risk analysis. Informal and haphazard methods of allowing for different levels of risk associated with proposals, such as raising the minimum rate of return requirements, may lead to the undesirable practice of continuously accepting high-risk, high-return proposals at the expense of other, possibly better, low-risk, low-return proposals.

Because of the many variables associated with risk analysis, it is unlikely that informal and intuitive approaches can lead to the right conclusions about the prospects of different proposals.

Risk analysis as applied to capital expenditure analysis was best described in a *Harvard Business Review* article by David B. Hertz.[7] Hertz's article, when combined with John F. Magee's two articles[8] on decision trees and their use in capital investment, provides an excellent description of risk analysis. The following description, benefiting from ideas in these articles, is designed to show what is involved in risk analysis.

Since probability is used with risk analysis, a description of this concept is needed. The probability of something is an expression of the chances or the likelihood of its occurrence. For example, the probability of getting a head when a fair coin is tossed once is 0.50. The value 0.50 is the ratio of the number of ways of getting a head in one toss divided by all possible outcomes (a head or a tail).

Probability may be defined in three ways. The coin example uses the theoretical approach to probability since it is based on the fact that one face out of two is a head, and that both faces are equally likely to occur. The second approach may be called empirical or experimental. Here, by experiment or observation, the probability is determined. For example, if we toss a coin 5,000 times and get 2,000 heads, on the basis of this experiment we can say that the probability of getting heads is 0.4 (2,000 divided by 5,000). The first and second approaches (both are also known as the objective approach to probability) do not always help with business applications. Most business situations do not repeat themselves; seldom are two situations exactly alike.

The third probability approach, most applicable to business situations, is called the subjective approach. The probability here is determined on the basis of the strength of belief of the decision maker. For example, when the sales manager says he thinks there is a 60 percent chance of next year's sales being $10 million, this 60 percent is not based on the theoretical approach; nor is it based on the empirical approach (it does not make sense to say that if you try 5,000 times then $10 million sales would occur 60 percent of the time). It is based on an opinion, an educated guess–the subjective approach.

EXAMPLE

Two mutually exclusive investment proposals are being considered. The following information is available:

	Investment A	*Investment B*
Cost of the project	$12,000	$12,000
Life of the project	2 years	2 years
Cash inflows in each year of project life	$ 8,000	$ 8,000
Salvage	0	0

Upon further study of these estimates, assume that it was found that the cost of the project is a certain amount, and so is the life of each project. However, the possible cash inflows each year for project A are distributed as follows:

Possible Outcome	*Probability*
$ 4,000	0.2
8,000	0.6
12,000	0.2
	1.0

The possible cash inflows each year for project B are distributed as follows:

Possible Outcome	*Probability*
$ 7,000	0.2
8,000	0.6
9,000	0.2
	1.0

Use a simple form of risk analysis to show the consequences of selecting each investment and to indicate which proposal should be selected. Assume the cost of capital is 10 percent.

SOLUTION

Under conventional analysis, A and B are equally desirable projects since each has the same figures for cash inflows and cash outflows.

At 10 percent cost of capital, the NPV of each project is:

PV of first year	= 8,000 × 0.909 =	$ 7,272
PV of second year	= 8,000 × 0.826 =	6,608
		$13,880
Less initial outlays		12,000
Net present value		$ 1,880

When one looks at the distribution of cash inflows for each project, it becomes apparent that project A is more risky than project B, since the range of values is wider for A than for B. Under these extremely simple conditions, an examination of the data would lead to the choice of B (assuming managers are usually averse to risk), without any need for risk analysis. However, even in this simple example, risk analysis provides an organized way of examining the possible investments and also provides additional information. Of course, when more realistic figures with additional and complicated distributions are used, a mere examination of the figures cannot provide reliable answers.

The tree diagrams or decision trees of Figures 11 and 12 show each project in our simplified example.

The tree diagrams show that there are nine possible outcomes, each represented by a branch or path. For project A (Figure 11), the first branch may be read as follows: cost of the investment is $12,000, first-year cash inflows are $4,000, and second-year cash inflows are $4,000. The values written above or below the branches represent probabilities. The combined probabilities column is the product of the two probability values for each path, which signifies the probability of getting the first and the second values. This column total adds to one, signifying that all possible outcomes are accounted for.

Figure 11. Decision tree for project A.

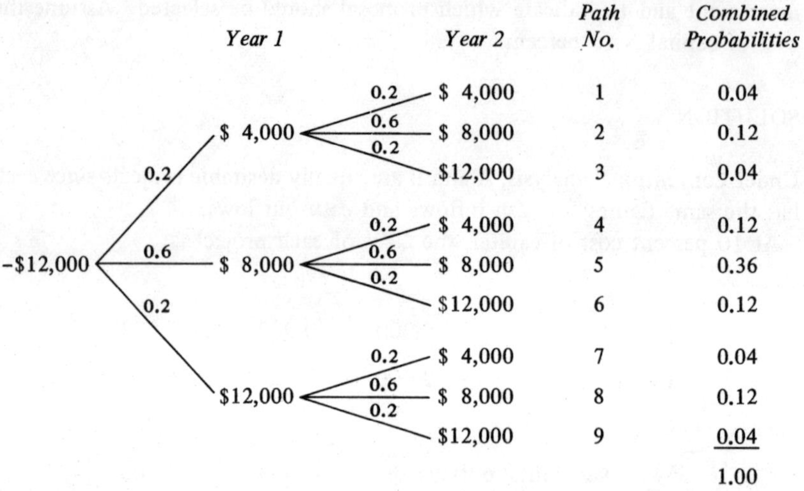

NPV of each path:

Path 1: $-\$12{,}000(1) + \$4{,}000(0.909) + \$4{,}000(0.826)$
$= -\$12{,}000 + \$3{,}636 + \$3{,}304 = -\$5{,}060$

Path 2: $-\$12{,}000(1) + \$4{,}000(0.909) + \$8{,}000(0.826)$
$= -\$12{,}000 + \$3{,}636 + \$6{,}608 = -\$1{,}756$

Path 3: $-\$12{,}000(1) + \$4{,}000(0.909) + \$12{,}000(0.826)$
$= -\$12{,}000 + \$3{,}636 + \$9{,}912 = \$1{,}548$

Path 4: $-\$12{,}000(1) + \$8{,}000(0.909) + \$4{,}000(0.826)$
$= -\$12{,}000 + \$7{,}272 + \$3{,}304 = -\$1{,}424$

Path 5: $-\$12{,}000(1) + \$8{,}000(0.909) + \$8{,}000(0.826)$
$= -\$12{,}000 + \$7{,}272 + \$6{,}608 = \$1{,}880$

Path 6: $-\$12{,}000(1) + \$8{,}000(0.909) + \$12{,}000(0.826)$
$= -\$12{,}000 + \$7{,}272 + \$9{,}912 = \$5{,}184$

Path 7: $-\$12{,}000(1) + \$12{,}000(0.909) + \$4{,}000(0.826)$
$= -\$12{,}000 + \$10{,}908 + \$3{,}304 = \$2{,}212$

Path 8: $-\$12{,}000(1) + \$12{,}000(0.909) + \$8{,}000(0.826)$
$= -\$12{,}000 + \$10{,}908 + \$6{,}608 = \$5{,}516$

Path 9: $-\$12{,}000(1) + \$12{,}000(0.909) + \$12{,}000(0.826)$
$= -\$12{,}000 + \$10{,}908 + \$9{,}912 = \$8{,}820$

Figure 12. Decision tree for project B.

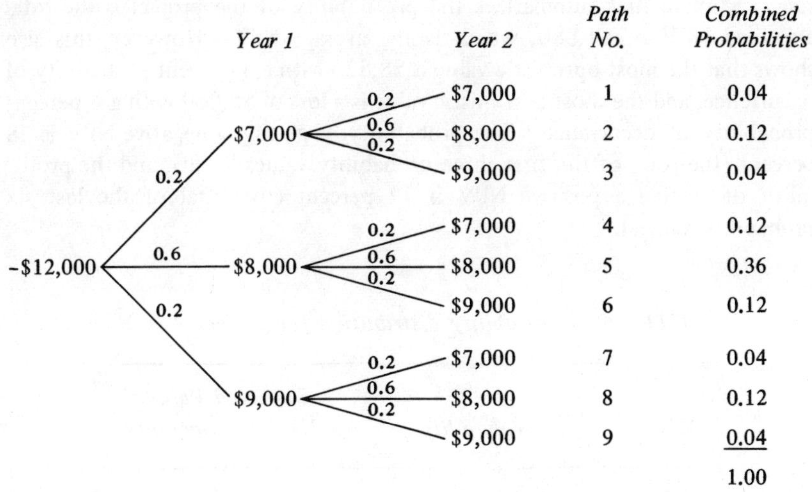

NPV of each path:

Path 1: $-\$12{,}000(1) + \$7{,}000(0.909) + \$7{,}000(0.826)$
$= -\$12{,}000 + \$6{,}363 + \$5{,}782 = \$145$

Path 2: $-\$12{,}000(1) + \$7{,}000(0.909) + \$8{,}000(0.826)$
$= -\$12{,}000 + \$6{,}363 + \$6{,}608 = \$971$

Path 3: $-\$12{,}000(1) + \$7{,}000(0.909) + \$9{,}000(0.826)$
$= -\$12{,}000 + \$6{,}363 + \$7{,}434 = \$1{,}797$

Path 4: $-\$12{,}000(1) + \$8{,}000(0.909) + \$7{,}000(0.826)$
$= -\$12{,}000 + \$7{,}272 + \$5{,}782 = \$1{,}054$

Path 5: $-\$12{,}000(1) + \$8{,}000(0.909) + \$8{,}000(0.826)$
$= -\$12{,}000 + \$7{,}272 + \$6{,}608 = \$1{,}880$

Path 6: $-\$12{,}000(1) + \$8{,}000(0.909) + \$9{,}000(0.826)$
$= -\$12{,}000 + \$7{,}272 + \$7{,}434 = \$2{,}706$

Path 7: $-\$12{,}000(1) + \$9{,}000(0.909) + \$7{,}000(0.826)$
$= -\$12{,}000 + \$8{,}181 + \$5{,}782 = \$1{,}963$

Path 8: $-\$12{,}000(1) + \$9{,}000(0.909) + \$8{,}000(0.826)$
$= -\$12{,}000 + \$8{,}181 + \$6{,}608 = \$2{,}789$

Path 9: $-\$12{,}000(1) + \$9{,}000(0.909) + \$9{,}000(0.826)$
$= -\$12{,}000 + \$8{,}181 + \$7{,}434 = \$3{,}615$

The profitability distribution for project A is summarized in Table 26. The single estimate that summarizes the profitability of the project is the total expected NPV of $1,880, which is the average NPV. However, this also shows that the most optimistic value is $8,820 with a 4 percent probability of occurrence, and the most pessimistic value is a loss of $5,060 with a 4 percent probability of occurrence. The probability of getting a negative NPV is 28 percent (the total of the first three probability values listed), and the probability of getting a positive NPV is 72 percent (the total of the last six probability values).

Table 26. Profitability distribution for project A.

NPV	*Probability*	*Expected Value = NPV X Probability*
$ -5,060	0.04	$ -202.40
-1,756	0.12	-210.72
-1,424	0.12	-170.88
1,548	0.04	61.92
1,880	0.36	676.80
2,212	0.04	88.48
5,184	0.12	622.08
5,516	0.12	661.92
8,820	0.04	352.80
	1.00	$1,880.00

The profitability distribution for project B is summarized in Table 27. The single estimate that summarizes the profitability of the project is the total expected NPV of $1,880. However, this also shows that the most optimistic value is $3,615 with a 4 percent probability of occurrence, and the most pessimistic value is $145 (still positive) with a 4 percent probability of occurrence. It also shows that the probability of getting a negative NPV is zero. Thus, project B is certain to yield a positive NPV.

Table 27. Profitability distribution for project B.

NPV	*Probability*	*Expected value = NPV X Probability*
$ 145	0.04	$ 5.80
971	0.12	116.52
1,054	0.12	126.48
1,797	0.04	71.88
1,880	0.36	676.80
1,963	0.04	78.52
2,706	0.12	324.72
2,789	0.12	334.68
3,615	0.04	144.60
	1.00	$1,880.00

The above information for both project A and project B is summarized in Table 28. Which project should be selected? This is a difficult question to answer because the answer depends upon the type of individual making the decision. Some managers are more averse to risk than others. Preference profiles could be made to help portray the attitudes of top management toward risk. It is possible to quantify the preference profile as a utility function and use utility analysis as a basis for selecting between alternatives. However, this is beyond the scope of the present discussion. The key contribution of risk analysis is to provide the decision maker with more information. Which project to select is the decision maker's privilege and ultimate responsibility.

Table 28. Comparison of values for projects A and B.

	A	*B*
Expected value of NPV	$ 1,880	$1,880
Optimistic NPV	8,820	3,615
Pessimistic NPV	-5,060	145
Probability of a positive NPV	72%	100%
Probability of a negative NPV	28%	0%

The following example compares the three approaches to investment analysis: conventional approach, sensitivity analysis, and risk analysis.

EXAMPLE

A single investment proposal is being considered. The cost of the project is $10,000. The life of the project is 2 years. It is expected to generate cash inflows after taxes of $7,000 in the first year and $8,000 in the second year. The cost of capital is 10 percent. Upon further study of these estimates, it was found that these values are from estimates based on what seems to be most likely to occur. The detailed figures and their associated probabilities are as follows:

Cost of Project	*Probability of Occurrence*
$10,000	0.6
12,000	0.4

First-year cash inflows:

Amount	*Probability*
$ 2,000	0.3
7,000	0.7

If first-year cash inflows are $7,000, second-year cash inflows are:

Cash Inflows	*Probability*
$ 6,000	0.4
8,000	0.6

If first-year cash inflows are $2,000, second-year cash inflows are:

Cash Inflows	*Probability*
$ 3,000	0.3
4,000	0.4
5,000	0.3

What is the net present value of the proposed investment?

SOLUTIONS

(a) Solution by conventional analysis is given in Table 29. According to this analysis, the net present value is positive and the proposal is profitable.

Table 29. Calculations for solution (a).

Year (1)	*Cash Inflows* (2)	*Present Value of $1 at 10%* (3)	*Present Value of Cash Flows (2 X 3)* (4)
1	$7,000	0.909	$ 6,363
2	8,000	0.826	6,608
	Present value of cash inflows		$12,971
	Less initial investment		10,000
	Net present value (NPV)		$ 2,971

(b) Solution by using a simple form of sensitivity analysis: The NPV is computed as usual to be $2,971. Then, additional information is provided on the basis of asking such questions as: What is the NPV if the cost of the project is increased by 10 percent, or the first-year cash inflows are decreased by 10 percent, or the second-year cash inflows are decreased by 10 percent? Thus, the sensitivity of NPV to each of the three changes will be examined.

If the cost of the project is increased by 10 percent to $11,000 (a $1,000 increase) and other things remain unchanged, the NPV will be:

Present value of cash inflows (as computed earlier)	$12,971
Less initial investment	11,000
NPV	$ 1,971

Thus, an increase in the cost of the project of 10 percent would result in a decrease in the NPV (profitability measure) of 34 percent ($1,000 ÷ $2,971).

If first-year cash inflows are decreased by 10 percent to $6,300 (a $700 decrease), and other things remain unchanged, the NPV will be decreased by $636, as calculated in Table 30. Thus, a decrease in first-year cash inflows of 10 percent would result in a 21 percent decrease in the NPV ($636 ÷ $2,971).

Table 30. Solution (b), calculations for 10 percent decrease in first-year cash inflows.

Year (1)	*Cash Inflows* (2)	*Present Value of $1 at 10%* (3)	*Present Value of Cash Flows (2 X 3)* (4)
1	$6,300	0.909	$ 5,727
2	8,000	0.826	6,608
	Present value of cash inflows		$12,335
	Less initial investment		10,000
	NPV		$ 2,335

If the second-year cash inflows are decreased by 10 percent to $7,200 (an $800 decrease), and other things remain unchanged, the NPV will be decreased by $661, as calculated in Table 31. Thus, a decrease in second-year cash inflows of 10 percent would result in a decrease in the NPV of 22 percent ($661 ÷ $2,971).

Table 31. Solution (b), calculations for 10 percent decrease in second-year cash inflows.

Year (1)	*Cash Inflows* (2)	*Present Value of $1 at 10%* (3)	*Present Value of Cash Flows (2 X 3)* (4)
1	$7,000	0.909	$ 6,363
2	7,200	0.826	5,947
	Present value of cash inflows		$12,310
	Less initial investment		10,000
	NPV		$ 2,310

The above results may be summarized as follows:

Item	*Percentage Change*	*NPV*	*Percentage Change in NPV*
No change	0	$2,971	0
Cost of project	+10	1,971	-34
First-year cash inflows	-10	2,335	-21
Second-year cash inflows	-10	2,310	-22

This analysis suggests that the project is very sensitive to all three factors. A 10 percent change in any factor could result in a much higher change in the profitability measure. It also shows that, in terms of sensitivity to different items, the project is most sensitive to estimates of its cost, followed by estimates of second-year cash inflows, and least sensitive to estimates of first-year cash inflows (34, 22, and 21 percent change in NPV as shown above for a 10 percent change in the item). It also shows that a change of 10 percent in any one of these estimates would not result in a negative NPV, which is one of the favorable aspects of this project.

This simplified analysis could be extended to detailed estimates of elements that resulted in the cash flows, and also to the usually longer life of a typical investment, with added considerations of salvage values and working capital. However, the idea is still the same: sensitivity analysis usually stops short of measuring the effect of a combination of changes in these factors and of estimating the probability of occurrence of changes in each item or in a combination of items.

(c) Solution using a simple form of risk analysis: First a simple tree diagram or decision tree is needed to illustrate the problem.

Figure 13 shows ten possible outcomes, each represented by a branch or path. The branch with the highest probability is the first branch, which may be read as cost of the investment, \$10,000; first-year cash inflows, \$7,000; and second-year cash inflows, \$8,000. The values written above and below the branches represent probabilities. The probability column is the product of the three probability values for each path; it signifies the probability of getting the first, second, and third values. This column total adds to 1, signifying that all possible outcomes are accounted for.

The above information may be summarized as shown in Table 32. (Figures are rounded to the nearest dollar.)

Accordingly, the project's expected return is a negative net present value of \$645, which signifies an unprofitable investment. The previous analysis provides more information than the conventional analysis. It reveals that the outcome with the highest probability value is an NPV of \$2,971, and that there is a 0.036 probability that the project could result in a negative present value of \$7,704.

In the preceding analysis all the possible outcomes were listed and depicted in a tree diagram. In a realistic investment situation, many variables enter into the analysis. If we assume, for example, that the cost of the investment is dependent upon the cost of 10 factors, and each of these 10 factors has 10 possible values, we find that there are 10 billion possible outcomes (10^{10})

Figure 13. Tree diagram for risk analysis problem.

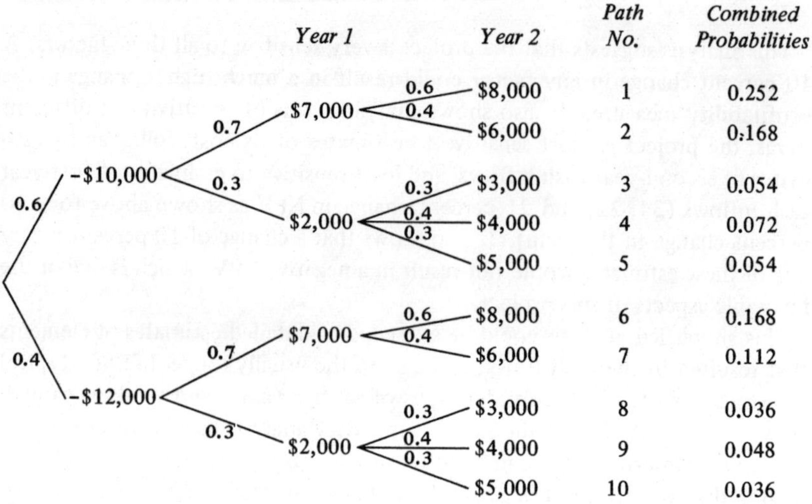

NPV of each path at 10%.

Path 1: -$10,000(1) + $7,000(0.909) + $8,000(0.826)
= -$10,000 + $6,363 + $6,608 = $2,971

Path 2: -$10,000(1) + $7,000(0.909) + $6,000(0.826)
= -$10,000 + $6,363 + $4,956 = $1,319

Path 3: -$10,000(1) + $2,000(0.909) + $3,000(0.826)
= -$10,000 + $1,818 + $2,478 = -$5,704

Path 4: -$10,000(1) + $2,000(0.909) + $4,000(0.826)
= -$10,000 + $1,818 + $3,304 = -$4,878

Path 5: -$10,000(1) + $2,000(0.909) + $5,000(0.826)
= -$10,000 + $1,818 + $4,130 = -$4,052

Path 6: -$12,000(1) + $7,000(0.909) + $8,000(0.826)
= -$12,000 + $6,363 + $6,608 = $971

Path 7: -$12,000(1) + $7,000(0.909) + $6,000(0.826)
= -$12,000 + $6,363 + $4,956 = -$681

Path 8: -$12,000(1) + $2,000(0.909) + $3,000(0.826)
= -$12,000 + $1,818 + $2,478 = -$7,704

Path 9: -$12,000(1) + $2,000(0.909) + $4,000(0.826)
= -$12,000 + $1,818 + $3,304 = -$6,878

Path 10: -$12,000(1) + $2,000(0.909) + $5,000(0.826)
= -$12,000 + $1,818 + $4,130 = -$6,052

Table 32. Profitability distribution for the project.

Path No. (1)	NPV (2)	Probability (3)	Expected Value (2 X 3) (4)
1	$2,971	0.252	$749
2	1,319	0.168	222
6	971	0.168	163
7	-681	0.112	-76
5	-4,052	0.054	-219
4	-4,878	0.072	-351
3	-5,704	0.054	-308
10	-6,052	0.036	-218
9	-6,878	0.048	-330
8	-7,704	0.036	-277
		1.000	-$645

with regard to the cost of the investment alone. If we add to this the factors that affect the possible cash inflows each year for the life of an investment of 10 years, we have such a tremendous number of possibilities that it would be impossible to list them. Also, if we consider the fact that the probability of some estimates follows a continuous distribution, an even greater problem of enumeration of the possible outcomes is presented.

Because of the number of possibilities associated with the investment analysis of major projects, simulation techniques using a computer are needed. First, a list of the key factors that affect cash inflows and cash outflows is made. Second, a probability distribution for each of these factors is formed. Third, these probability distributions are fed into the computer, and the computer is programmed to generate random numbers according to these distributions (as models). Fourth, a trial run is made; in each trial run the computer selects at random one value for each of the factors according to their distribution and combines all these values to compute a net present value for the project. Fifth, this process is repeated for a large number of trials. Finally, the results of such trials are summarized in the form of a distribution of the possible values of NPV.

Some computer programs provide a graph of the NPV distribution. From such a profile, the needed information–such as the expected NPV based on these trial runs, the lowest and highest NPV, and the probability distribution of possible NPV for the proposal–is collected.

On the basis of the information collected through risk analysis, the decision maker would have three options: (1) accept the proposal, (2) reject the proposal, or (3) collect additional information. The latter option would eventually lead to rejection or acceptance of the proposal. It is possible to compute the value of this additional information by using the Bayesian probability approach, as found in the literature on decision making under uncertainty, and a computer is usually necessary to carry out the calculations needed for the complete analysis.

The risk analysis technique, by collecting information that helps to reveal the risks involved in different capital expenditure proposals, can aid in classifying proposals according to their risk. Then, proposals of similar risks may be grouped together and evaluated accordingly. When the DCFR method is used, the decision maker can use different cutoff points for projects in different risk classes, or he can compare proposals with proper information regarding the risks inherent in those proposals.

Because realistic applications of risk analysis require simulation of the probability distributions of the various factors that affect the profitability of the investment proposal, risk analysis may be considered a simulation technique.

Extensive use of risk analysis seems to be limited to large corporations. Even in large corporations, its use is usually confined to major projects during the latter stages of their approval. Risk analysis is undoubtedly more complicated than conventional means of dealing with risk. It requires collection of additional information about each project and the estimation of probabilities which are not easy to obtain in the early stages of project evaluation. Some businessmen do not feel at ease with probability estimates, and the application of risk analysis may require hiring specialists in simulation and the extensive use of computers.

Despite all the difficulties, risk analysis is finding its way into the manuals of large industrial corporations, and it is expected to have more extensive usage in investment analysis in the years to come.

Risk Analysis in Practice

Of 162 responding firms, risk analysis is used by 87 firms (54 percent), not used by 70 firms (43 percent), and the remaining 5 are not sure.

Linear Programming

Linear programming may be regarded as a planning technique. It is designed to achieve the most efficient use of limited resources by effectively allocating them among competing demands where the decisions are interrelated. The limited resources may be expressed in linear equations or inequalities, called constraints. A linear equation is an equation in which the exponents or powers of the variables are all 1's. One such example is: $x + y = 10$. The exponent of x is 1 and of y is 1.* The equation says that x and y may vary so long as their total is 10. An inequality such as $x + y \leqslant 10$ means that the total of x and y must be less than or equal to 10. The inequality $x + y \geqslant 10$ means that the total of x and y must be greater than or equal to 10. (The mathematical symbol "<" reads "less than," and ">" reads "greater than.")[9]

Constraints are exemplified by the plant size, the number of hours that the plant can operate in a day, the time of top management personnel, the upper limit for the capital expenditure budget that management does not want to exceed, the maximum production that could be stored within the present storage facilities, and the maximum production that could be handled within the present channels of distribution.

Linear programming may be used in investment analysis to help in selecting the best mix of proposals that will maximize the total profit (or minimize costs) for a firm over a given period of time. In other words, linear programming aspires to answer the following question: What is the ideal mix of proposals that would maximize the benefits derived from limited resources?

The solution to the linear programming problem may be obtained after developing the inequalities and determining the objective function. A graphic method may be used to solve simple problems. However, one of the most widely known techniques used in solving linear programming problems is the simplex method (which is not as simple as the name may imply). Computer programs are available, and a computer is usually used to solve realistic linear programming problems.

One drawback to linear programming occasionally voiced is that real-world situations cannot always be expressed in the form of linear equations. However, the linear programming technique may be used when the relationships are approximately linear, or when they are so over what is called "the relevant range." Of course, if the actual relationships cannot be approximated by linear equations, other mathematical programming approaches should be used instead.

A simple example will help to illustrate the linear programming approach using the graphic method.

*By convention, the exponent 1 is not shown as it is for higher exponents (x^2, x^3, and so on).

EXAMPLE

The ZZZ Corporation has two types of projects to select from: X and Y. Each X project results in a $2,000 net present value (NPV), and each Y project results in a $3,000 NPV. Top management wants to limit the capital budget to $100,000. The president of the company wants to limit the time spent by him to manage these projects to 200 hours per year. Each unit of project X requires a $10,000 investment and 50 hours of the president's time, whereas each unit of project Y requires $20,000 cash investment and 25 hours of the president's time. Management does not desire any more than three units of porject X. Find the optimal mix of X and Y projects that will maximize the total NPV.

SOLUTION

In this simple linear programming problem two limited resources, cash and the president's time, are available and it is desired to maximize the benefits, as represented by the NPV of these limited resources. The objective function is to maximize $2{,}000X + 3{,}000Y$, subject to the following constraints:

Cash: $\$10{,}000X + \$20{,}000Y \leqslant \$100{,}000$
President's time: $50X + 25Y \leqslant 200$
Three or fewer units of X: that is, $X \leqslant 3$
Both X and Y are positive values.

The solution to this simple problem may be found by a graphic method or by solving the three inequalities simultaneously. The results of graphing the problem are shown in Figure 14.

The shaded area represents the feasible region. The optimal solution is at one of the five corners:

Corner	*X*	*Y*	*NPV*
1	0	0	0
2	3	0	6,000
3	3	2	12,000
4	2	4	16,000
5	0	5	15,000

The highest NPV is achieved by selecting 2 units of X and 4 units of Y.

The main limitations of linear programming are that many relationships in business are not strictly linear, and that these studies often require the use of outside consultants or specialized personnel and are consequently expensive. However, financial analysts may be trained to recognize situations to which linear programming studies are applicable. Also, like other quantitative

Figure 14. Graphical representation of constraints and the feasible region.

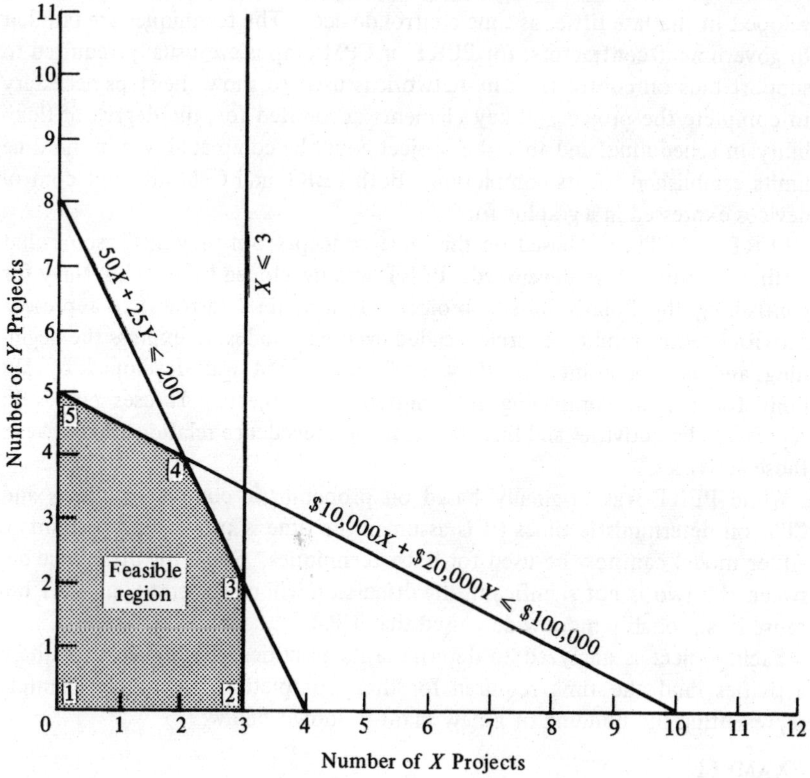

studies, these studies do not account for qualitative information important to decision making. However, despite all criticisms, linear programming is undoubtedly a useful technique with a promising potential for capital expenditure analysis.

Linear Programming in Practice

Of 149 responding firms, linear programming is used by 43 firms (29 percent), not used by 100 firms (67 percent), and the remaining 6 are not sure.

PERT/CPM

The program evaluation and review technique (PERT) and the critical path method (CPM) are network planning techniques.* PERT and CPM were developed in the late fifties as time control devices. The techniques are familiar to government contractors, for PERT or CPM graphs are usually required to support bids on contracts. The network is used to show the steps necessary to complete the project, all key elements accounted for, the degree of flexibility in scheduling, and that the project could be completed within the time limits established for its completion. Both PERT and CPM are time control devices expressed in a graphic form.[10]

PERT and CPM are based on the same concepts, but they differ somewhat in the way they were developed. PERT was developed by the U.S. Navy for controlling the Polaris missile project. It uses lines (arrows) to represent activities, with numbered circles, called events or nodes, to express the beginning and ending points for these activities. CPM was developed by Du Pont for use in controlling its maintenance projects. It uses circles to represent the activities and lines to show the precedence relationship between those activities.

While PERT was originally based on probabilistic completion times and CPM on deterministic times (it is assumed the time is known with certainty), either model can now be used for both techniques. Since the difference between the two is not significant, the discussion will concentrate on PERT because it is probably more widely used than CPM.

Each project is analyzed to determine its activities, the sequence of these activities, and the time required for their completion. A simple example representing the building of a new plant is shown below.

EXAMPLE

Top management of the XYZ Corporation is considering the construction of a new plant. One capital expenditure proposal seems to provide the maximum quantitative benefits. However, before final approval, the president asked that a PERT graph be made to provide information regarding the expected completion time of the project and scheduling flexibility.

It is extremely important to have the plant ready within 85 weeks to benefit from an expected seasonal increase in demand at that time. After studying the project, management made available the information shown in Table 33.

*The author wishes to thank his colleague and friend Dr. John A. Bachmann, assistant professor of management at Virginia Commonwealth University, for reading the draft of this section and offering helpful suggestions.

Table 33. Summary of activities required and proposed timing.

Activity Number	*Description*	*Immediate Predecessors*	*Expected Time (Weeks)*
A	Develop blueprints and plans	–	12
B	Dig foundation	A	4
C	Construct foundation	B	12
D	Building frame	C	18
E	Plumbing	D	10
F	Electricity	D	11
G	Heat and air conditioning	E	6
H	Complete interior building work	F, G	10
I	Complete exterior building work	F, G	7
J	Ordering equipment lead time	A	28
K	Installing equipment	H, J	4
L	Landscaping	I	2
M	Final inspection	K, L	1

The first column is used for the activity number, the second column for a brief description of the activity. The third column shows the activities that must be completed before the activity listed can begin. Finally, the expected time column shows the time required to complete each activity. (To simplify the example, the activities were kept to a minimum, and the deterministic model of using one time estimate was used rather than the three time estimates usually associated with PERT. Also, cost information was not included for the same reason.)

Prepare a PERT and a CPM network.

SOLUTION

A PERT network for the simplified project at hand may look like Figure 15. Analysis of all possible paths in the network shows that the most critical path (the longest path) is that identified by heavy lines: A, B, C, D, E, G, H, K, M. It takes 77 weeks to complete the project. Accordingly, the project would be finished within the desired 85 weeks.

A CPM diagram (Figure 16) is shown for comparison purposes. Whereas PERT is usually more difficult to graph than CPM, it is easier to interpret.

Under PERT, three estimates of time can be made for every activity: a pessimistic, an optimistic, and a most likely time. A commonly known

Figure 15. PERT network.

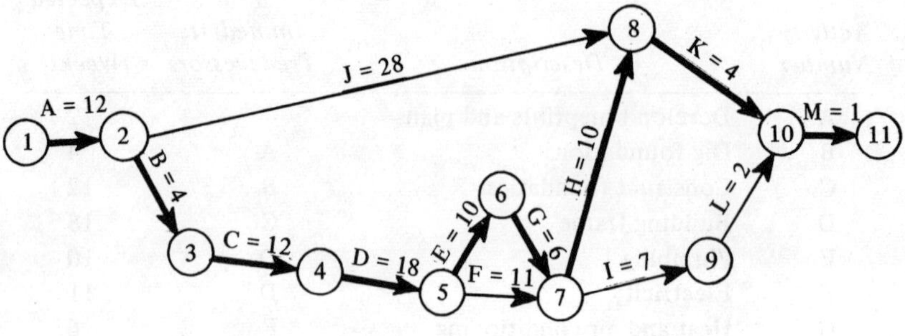

formula used to compute the expected time from these three time estimates, which is a weighted average of the three, is:

$$\text{Expected time} = \frac{\text{optimistic} + 4\,(\text{most likely}) + \text{pessimistic}}{6}$$

For example, if the estimates of time necessary to complete a given task are 5, 7, and 11 weeks, the expected time would be:

$$\frac{5 + 4(7) + 11}{6} = \frac{44}{6} = 7.33 \text{ weeks}$$

Figure 16. CPM network.

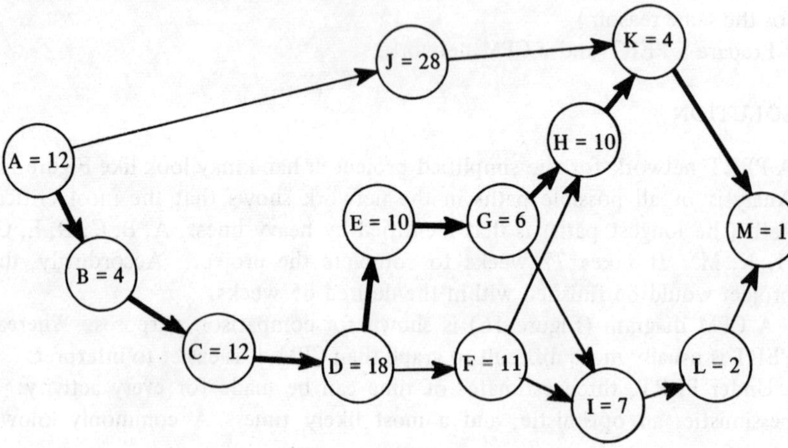

Time estimates and the variance of these estimates may be used to compute the probability of completing the project on schedule.

One of the important concepts in PERT is the critical path. This path, the longest through the network, is critical because any delay in that path means a delay in the whole project. Careful study of the network can help identify trouble areas in advance. Then, through follow-up reports, potential trouble areas could be watched closely, and, if needed, corrective action may be taken at the proper time. Also, a study of the critical path may reveal schedule flexibility and ways of speeding up the completion date through investment in improvements.

There are several variations of PERT, ranging from a simple network with time estimates to more sophisticated networks and follow-up reports. Some applications of PERT introduce cost estimates in the analysis and provide different cost estimates for the project under varying options. These can help select the best option, especially when probability factors are included.

Elaborate applications of PERT use the simulation technique and the computer in developing the required data. A computer is usually needed to determine the critical path in cases where there are large numbers of events that make it infeasible to diagram manually.

PERT has a significant role to play in evaluating capital expenditures. It can help provide information regarding the time dimension. It can also help in showing the steps necessary to complete the project, the sequence of events, the interdependence among the events, and the possible trouble areas. Given the choice between various projects, PERT can help to identify better or more flexible projects and can indicate the probability of meeting deadlines for these various projects.

Thus, PERT can provide additional information for better decisions, especially with regard to the uncertainties surrounding the time estimates of a capital expenditure proposal.

The more typical use of PERT, however, is at the execution stage after the project is accepted. Through PERT charts, progress over time can be measured for medium- and large-size projects that usually take a long time to complete. PERT helps in identifying trouble areas and in recording achievements through progress reports.

PERT/CPM in Practice

Project time and cost estimating, using the critical path method (CPM) and/or program evaluation review technique (PERT), are reported to be used by 63 (43 percent) of 145 responding firms, not used by 73 firms (50 percent), and the remaining 9 are not sure.

The Techniques Combined

It was found that some techniques are more popular than others, as shown in Table 34. The ranking shows that the computer is the most-used technique. This is not unexpected since a computer is required in the use of other techniques. According to the responses, a computer is used with other techniques by 82 of the 93 responding firms that reported using the computer. The computer has a definite place in capital investment analysis because it can relieve people of detailed work and can provide needed information accurately and quickly.

The least-used technique, as shown above, is linear programming. Its lack of popularity may be explained by the fact that expert help from outside the firm is usually needed. However, the data are not sufficient to warrant definite conclusions in this respect.

Table 34. Techniques ranked in order of their relative use.

Rank	*Technique*	*No. of Using Firms*	*Total Answers*	*Users as a Percentage of Total Answers*
1	The computer	93	154	60.4
2	Risk analysis	87	162	53.7
3	Sensitivity analysis	70	150	46.7
4	PERT/CPM	63	145	43.4
5	Simulation and models	65	152	42.8
6	Linear programming	43	149	28.9

Different techniques are used simultaneously. Of 136 responding firms, 32 use one technique by itself and 104 firms use more than one technique simultaneously. The number of techniques used and the number of respondents who reported using them are provided in Table 35.

Table 35. Number of techniques used simultaneously.

No. of Techniques Used	*No. of Firms*
1	32
2	27
3	18
4	28
5	17
6	14
Total	136

The most common combinations of techniques in each of the following categories are:

No. of Techniques	*Most Common Combination*
2	Sensitivity analysis and risk analysis.
3	Risk analysis, PERT/CPM, and the computer.
4	Sensitivity analysis, risk analysis, simulation and models, and the computer; or sensitivity analysis, simulation and models, PERT/CPM, and the computer.
5	Sensitivity analysis, risk analysis, simulation and models, linear programming, and the computer; or risk analysis, simulation and models, linear programming, PERT/CPM, and the computer.

An analysis of the replies by industry indicates at least two differences in usage of the techniques. First, some industries reported more overall extensive use of the techniques than other industries. For example, mining, crude petroleum and natural gas, textiles, and petroleum refining industries have generally made more extensive use of the six techniques than industries such as metal products or foods and beverages.

Second, certain techniques appear better suited to particular industries. For example, on the basis of the responses given, sensitivity analysis is popular in the crude petroleum and natural gas industry and not so popular in the motor vehicle industry. The risk analysis technique is used most in the textile industry and least in the metal products industry. The third technique, simulation and models, is used more in the petroleum refining industry than in the metal products or rubber industries. Linear programming is popular in the crude petroleum and natural gas, petroleum refining, and paper and allied products industries. PERT is most popular in mining and in paper and allied products industries. Finally, the computer is used most extensively in the petroleum refining industry.

Conclusion

Management science techniques have much to contribute to capital expenditure analysis. Although many questions remain unanswered regarding the extent to which they are used and their success or failure in practice, two conclusions based on the responses to the evaluation questionnaire may be drawn. They are:

1. Large corporations are still experimenting and in the process of increasingly adopting these techniques for capital expenditure evaluation.

2. Some techniques are less popular than others. Their lack of popularity may be due to their recent introduction, which may imply additional use in the future. Another possibility is that some techniques are better suited to capital expenditure analysis than others. Still another possibility is that these techniques are in the experimental stage and have not yet proved themselves.

NOTES

1. Fred Hanssmann, *Operations Research Techniques for Capital Investment* (New York: John Wiley & Sons, 1968), p. 13.
2. "The Age of Thinking Machines," *Business Week* (October 30, 1971), p. 91.
3. The following list is based on *Financial Analysis to Guide Capital Expenditure Decisions,* N.A.A. Research Report 43 (New York: National Association of Accountants, 1967), p. 163.
4. Eugene L. Grant and William G. Ireson, *Principles of Engineering Economy,* 4th ed. (New York: Ronald Press, 1960), p. 257.
5. H. C. Thorne, W. W. Twaddle, and E. R. Grahi, "How to Evaluate Chemical Projects," *Petroleum Refiner,* Vol. 40, No. 3 (March 1961), p. 175.
6. William C. House, Jr., *Sensitivity Analysis in Making Capital Investment Decisions,* Research Monograph 3 (New York: National Association of Accountants, 1968), pp. 75–76.
7. David B. Hertz, "Risk Analysis in Capital Investment," *Harvard Business Review* (January–February 1964).
8. John F. Magee, "Decision Trees for Decision Making," *Harvard Business Review* (July–August 1964); and "How to Use Decision Trees in Capital Investment," *Harvard Business Review* (September–October 1964).
9. For more detailed information, see Richard I. Levin and Rudolph P. Lamone, *Linear Programming for Management Decisions* (Homewood, Ill.: Richard D. Irwin, 1969).
10. For more detailed information, see Jerome D. Wiest and F. K. Levy, *A Management Guide to PERT/CPM* (Englewood Cliffs, N.J.: Prentice-Hall, 1969).

10 / Common Problem Areas

THE literature regarding capital expenditure analysis is frequently criticized. It is often said that the emphasis given methods and their routine application gives the false impression that the primary problem is the selection of a method for evaluating capital expenditure proposals. Nevertheless, some key problems stand in the way of achieving maximum efficiency of any capital expenditure evaluation program. Unfortunately, these problems have received little attention in the literature.

The purpose of this chapter is to point out some of these key problem areas and to determine how the survey participants evaluate the role played by these problems in their firms. These problem areas were selected because of repeated reference to them by interviewees during the preliminary stages of the study, or because of repeated reference to them in the literature on capital expenditure evaluation.

Some of the purposes served by a study of the problem areas with regard to capital expenditure analysis are:

1. Identification of key problems helps to direct the attention of both practitioners and theoreticians to the areas that need their efforts the most.
2. By knowing what problems face similar firms, an individual manager may be relieved to find that he is not facing these problems alone. He can prepare for those potential problems that others have faced but that have not yet reached significant magnitude in his own firm.
3. If possible, a measurement of the extent of these problems in a firm may be made and compared with like measurements over time, as an indicator of the progress made in attacking these problems.
4. Identifying the key problems is prerequisite to their solution.

The following pages give a quick bird's-eye view of the responses to the part of the questionnaire regarding problem areas. A list of the suggested problem areas is included, followed by an identification of common problems and an indication of their role as measured by the index of importance. Second, each of the sixteen problem areas is discussed. Finally, the problem areas are viewed collectively once again.

Sixteen Problem Areas

Respondents were asked to appraise the role of sixteen problem areas as experienced by their corporations in the evaluation of capital expenditure proposals. They were asked to check whether the role assumed by the problem area is that of a major problem, a minor problem, or no problem; once with respect to major projects, and again with regard to "all other projects."

No attempt was made to impose a specific definition of major or minor problem, since it is an objective of the study to report such evaluation by the participants. Therefore, if the participant responded that a particular problem area is a major problem in his firm, it is in fact a major problem for that respondent regardless of what others might decide or respond.

The sixteen problem areas are:

1. Disclosure of alternatives.
2. Forecasting in general.
3. Underestimation of costs.
4. Overestimation of costs.
5. Underestimation of benefits.
6. Overestimation of benefits.
7. Qualitative information not subject to quantitative analysis.
8. Inability of operating personnel to understand logic behind evaluation.
9. Shortage of well-qualified analysts and reviewers.
10. Background and interests of top management.
11. Background and interests of the board of directors.
12. Price-level changes.
13. Lack of standardization in methods and assumptions used by analysts and evaluators.
14. Inability of the accounting department at a later date to confirm or disprove the accuracy of cash flows in the original capital expenditure projection.
15. Lack of unified and consistent treatment of the topic in the literature.
16. Shortage of time on the part of top management to keep up with developments in the field.

Common Problems

To identify common problems and to differentiate between them and other problems that are less common, a decision was made that for a problem to qualify as a common problem at least half the respondents (those who checked problem areas as major, minor, or no problem) should consider it a problem of some sort (that is, either a major or a minor problem). Using this 50 percent rule, the responses indicated that of the 16 problem areas, 11 are common problems with respect to evaluating major projects. These are:

1. Disclosure of alternatives.
2. Forecasting in general.
3. Underestimation of costs.
6. Overestimation of benefits.
7. Qualitative information not subject to quantitative analysis.
8. Inability of operating personnel to understand logic behind evaluation.
9. Shortage of well-qualified analysts and reviewers.
12. Price-level changes.
13. Lack of standardization in methods and assumptions used by analysts and evaluators.
14. Inability of the accounting department at a later date to confirm or disprove the accuracy of cash flows in the original capital expenditure projection.
16. Shortage of time on the part of top management to keep up with developments in the field.

Again, using the same definition of common problems for "all other projects," it was found that there are ten common problems. They are the same problems as those with respect to major projects, except for shortage of time on the part of top management to keep up with the developments in the field. Thus, the latter problem is not a common problem in the evaluation of "all other projects."

Index of Importance

In addition to identifying whether or not a problem area is a common problem, a measure of the role assumed by every common problem is needed to place it in its proper relative standing with respect to other common problems. For this purpose, the "index of importance" is computed in the following manner. First, common problems are identified for major projects and for "all other projects," as described previously. Second, for each common problem, the number of respondents that consider it a major problem is multiplied by 2 (to give the major classification twice as much weight as the minor classification), and the results are added to the number of respondents who consider it a minor problem. Finally, the total from the previous step is divided by the total number of answers for that part to determine the index of importance.

The computations are made twice, once for major projects and another time for "all other projects." The index varies between 0.0 and 2.0. It is practically impossible to achieve either extreme, for two reasons. First, for the index to be exactly 0.0, every respondent would have to rate the problem area as no problem, a very unlikely assumption. On the other hand, for the index to be 2.0, every respondent would have to rate the problem as a major problem, also a very unlikely assumption. It is felt that an index value of 1 or more indicates that the problem area is a critical problem. The reason is that an index of 1 means either that half of the responding firms consider the problem area a major problem or that all the responding firms consider the problem area a minor problem. A problem of such magnitude is considered a critical problem.

Table 36 shows the index of importance of the common problems and their ranking by the index.

Table 36. Index of importance of the common problems.

	Major Projects		*All Other Projects*	
*Problem Area** (1)	*Index* (2)	*Rank* (3)	*Index* (4)	*Rank* (5)
1	1.06	5	0.93	3
2	1.33	1	1.03	1
3	1.09	3	0.82	6
6	1.10	2	0.92	4
7	1.08	4	0.87	5
8	0.75	10	0.67	10
9	0.88	8	0.74	7
12	1.00	7	0.74	7
13	0.78	9	0.73	9
14	1.05	6	0.95	2
16	0.69	11	–	–

*See text for detailed list.

The results show that in every case the index is higher for major projects than for "all other projects." This can be interpreted to mean that the problems assume a stronger role with respect to major projects in the responding firms.

For major projects, problem areas 1, 2, 3, 6, 7, 12, and 14 are critical problems (index value of 1 or more). What is of special significance is the fact that forecasting in general (problem area 2) is the only problem that has an index value of 1 or more for "all other projects." Forecasting is considered the primary problem for both major projects and "all other projects." Therefore, it is the only problem that is critical for all projects. This seems to indicate that the writers of the last decade have not yet succeeded in solving the persistent problem of forecasting.

Problem Area 1: Disclosure of Alternatives

Wise capital expenditure decisions are assured when relevant alternative courses of action are recognized and studied. Every situation offers at least two alternatives: either go on with the proposed investment or do nothing.

In replacing equipment, for example, Elly Vassilatou-Thanopoulos suggested six major alternatives that could be considered.

1. To remodel the present equipment.
2. To lease another one.
3. To buy a used one.
4. To buy a new one.
5. To continue with the old one.
6. To discontinue the procedure altogether.[1]

Writers on capital expenditure management indicate three reasons for considering alternatives. They are:

1. The chances of overlooking possible superior alternatives are reduced.
2. Overlooking some alternatives might often lead to the wrong decision.
3. To collect relevant estimates of costs and benefits of proposals for incremental analysis, alternatives should be identified.

A problem of disclosure of alternatives would exist if the party sponsoring the proposal declined to specify the alternatives for the proposed investment regardless of whether this reluctance was intentional or unintentional.

To assure consideration and proper treatment of alternatives, some firms require, when a proposal is submitted, the inclusion of a narrative description of the alternatives studied and an explanation as to why they were disregarded.

The Problem in Practice. With regard to major projects, 52 respondents indicate that disclosure of alternatives is a major problem, 77 consider it a minor problem, 41 consider it no problem, and 30 did not answer. Therefore, 129 of the 170 respondents (76 percent) consider disclosure of alternatives a problem for major projects.

Of the 151 firms that answered the question with regard to "all other projects," 38 indicate that disclosure is a major problem; 65, a minor problem; and 48, no problem. Therefore, disclosure of alternatives is considered a problem for 103 of 151 respondents (68 percent) for "all other projects."

Since more than half of the respondents consider that disclosure of alternatives is a problem, it is considered a common problem. The index of importance ranks this problem fifth for major projects and third for "all other projects."

Problem Area 2: Forecasting in General

Estimates of costs and benefits are needed for capital expenditure analysis. The quality of the capital expenditure decisions is greatly dependent upon the quality of the estimates. The sophistication of the methods used in determining the economic worth of capital expenditure proposals is no cure for poor estimates. As one of the interviewees stated, if the estimates are not very reliable it is hard to accept the idea that by discounting them (that is, using the DCFR or NPV method) a more useful figure will be produced.

Is forecasting a problem? The answer is undoubtedly positive. Forecasting involves estimates or predictions of future values. The future is hard, and often impossible, to predict. Although much has been realized in the area of forecasting, perfection is not yet achieved, and deviation from estimates is the rule rather than the exception. A respondent to the evaluation questionnaire indicated that the available methods and techniques of capital expenditure analysis are adequate, but "the problem is really in the area of obtaining better input data estimates."

Is forecasting impossible? The answer is no. Although no method has been found that will always produce a 100 percent accurate estimate, forecasts within a range of plus or minus 5 percent are frequently achieved by large corporations. As managers gain experience in forecasting and learn from studying deviations and the reasons for their occurrence, better estimates can be achieved. Most of the financial executives of the large industrial corporations interviewed in the study indicated that estimates are often realized within a 5 to 10 percent range.

The problem of forecasting is too often used as an excuse for inefficient methods of handling capital expenditure analysis. The argument is that since one is dealing with estimates, it does not make any difference whether the payback or the DCFR method is used. This argument is erroneous. Although a forecasting error is bound to exist each time the future is estimated, the use of inefficient methods of handling estimates compounds any error by introducing others. An unavoidable error in forecasting due to inability to foresee the future does not justify the additional, *avoidable* error of using an inefficient method of measuring the profitability of a capital expenditure proposal based on questionable estimates.

Although the use of efficient methods of evaluating capital expenditures may not result in the right decision in a particular situation, it is bound to produce better decisions in the majority of cases.

The Problem in Practice. For major projects, 80 respondents indicate that forecasting is a major problem, 70 consider it a minor problem, 23 consider it no problem, and 27 did not answer. Therefore, 150 of the 173 respondents (87 percent) consider forecasting a problem for major projects.

For "all other projects," 48 respondents classify forecasting as a major problem; 64, a minor problem; 43, no problem; and 45 did not answer. Therefore, 112 of 155 respondents (72 percent) consider forecasting a problem for "all other projects."

Forecasting in general qualifies as a common problem for major projects and for "all other projects." The index of importance ranks this problem first for evaluating all projects.

Problem Areas 3 and 4: Underestimation and Overestimation of Costs

The key estimates needed for the evaluation of any capital expenditure proposal may be conveniently divided into estimates of costs and estimates of benefits. Estimation of costs is an essential part of any investment analysis. The advisability of a proposal can be determined by comparing its costs and benefits. Therefore, either overestimation or underestimation of costs can lead to a wrong decision.

Underestimation of costs is more likely to occur than overestimation. Underestimation may be due to failure to consider such extra costs associated with capital expenditure projects as costs created by the savings from replacing labor with machines (for example, costs due to severance pay, possible law suits, retraining programs, and effect on morale of other employees), maintenance costs, and costs of machine trial runs and debugging.

An underestimation of costs problem exists if analysis of completed projects reveals that the actual costs exceed the estimates in the majority of cases. Small differences between actual and forecasted costs are expected, but persistently large deviations in the form of underestimation of costs is a problem.

Underestimates may be due to the inability to forecast the future accurately because of lack of experience, changing conditions, or the nature of the investment project (wide distribution of cash flows). Underestimation may be intentional or unintentional.

If there is a pattern in cost underestimation, it may be necessary in the future to adjust the estimates made by certain individuals to accommodate their patterns of deviation. Profiles of reliability of estimates provided by various individuals and different departments over the years could be developed.

The Problems in Practice. With regard to major projects, underestimation of costs is considered a major problem by 41 responding firms, a minor problem by 105 firms, and no problem by 25 firms; 29 firms did not answer the question. Therefore, it is considered a problem in 146 (85 percent) of 171 firms.

For "all other projects," underestimation of costs is a major problem in 22 responding firms, a minor problem in 82 firms, and no problem in 49. Therefore, it is considered a problem in 104 (68 percent) of 153 firms.

Overestimation of costs for major projects is considered a major problem in 6 responding firms, a minor problem in 62 firms, and no problem in 96 firms. Of 164 responding firms, 68 (41 percent) consider overestimation a problem for major projects.

For "all other projects," overestimation of costs is a major problem in 5 responding firms, a minor problem in 47 firms, and no problem in 95 firms. Thus, of 147 responding firms, 52 (35 percent) consider overestimation of costs a problem for "all other projects."

The above results indicate that, among the firms surveyed, underestimation of costs is a greater problem than overestimation.

Underestimation of costs qualifies as a common problem for both major projects and "all other projects." The index of importance ranks it third for major projects and sixth for "all other projects."

Overestimation of costs is not a common problem in the firms that responded to the survey.

Problem Areas 5 and 6: Underestimation and Overestimation of Benefits

Estimates of benefits, like estimates of costs, are essential to capital expenditure evaluation. Weston and Brigham maintain that in the entire capital budgeting process probably nothing is more important than a reliable estimate of benefits.[2]

One difficulty in estimating the benefits is that sometimes the proposed investment is not the only factor that influences expected benefits. An example is a proposed long-term sales-promotion program. In such a case, the estimated sales figure should be separated into two parts: the normal consequence of a secular rise in demand, and increases attributed to the proposed promotional investment.

Benefits are generally more difficult to estimate than costs, because benefits are not always expressed in quantitative terms. Benefits are also subject to underestimation and overestimation, either of which could pose a problem in evaluating capital expenditure proposals.

The Problems in Practice. For major projects, underestimation of benefits is a major problem in 10 responding firms, a minor problem in 59 firms, and no problem in 98 firms. Therefore, it is considered a problem in 69 (41 percent) of 167 firms.

For "all other projects," underestimation of benefits is a major problem in 8 responding firms, a minor problem in 43 firms, and no problem in 99 firms. Therefore, of the 150 firms, 51 (34 percent) consider it a problem.

Overestimation of benefits for major projects is a major problem in 43 responding firms, a minor problem in 104 firms, and no problem in 26 firms. Of 173 responding firms, 147 (85 percent) consider it a problem.

For "all other projects," overestimation of benefits is a major problem in 26 responding firms, a minor problem in 90 firms, and no problem in 39 firms. Therefore, of 155 responding firms, 116 (75 percent) consider it a problem.

The results indicate that, unlike costs, overestimation of benefits is a greater problem than underestimation among the responding firms.

Overestimation of benefits qualifies as a common problem for both major projects and "all other projects." The index of importance ranks overestimation of benefits second for major projects and fourth for "all other projects."

Underestimation of benefits is not a common problem in the responding firms.

Problem Area 7: Qualitative Information Not Subject to Quantitative Analysis

During the course of evaluating capital expenditure proposals, their advantages and disadvantages are sometimes best described in qualitative terms. Some benefits are difficult to measure in quantitative terms, and to force a quantitative analysis on such proposals would be meaningless. The responses to the question about qualitative information not subject to quantitative analysis show either the frequency with which this is a problem or the extent of the problem posed by such qualitative information.

Methods of handling qualitative information may differ from one company to another. However, it would seem that the consensus is to state in narrative terms the qualitative aspects of a proposal and to leave to the decision maker's judgment the emphasis or weight that should be given to such information.

The Problem in Practice. For major projects, qualitative information not subject to quantitative analysis is a major problem in 47 firms, a minor problem in 86 firms, and no problem in 33 firms. Thus, it is considered a problem in 133 (80 percent) of the 166 responding firms.

For "all other projects," it is a major problem in 30 responding firms, a minor problem in 68 firms, and no problem in 49 firms. Thus, it is considered a problem in 98 (67 percent) of 147 responding firms.

Qualitative information is a common problem for both major projects and "all other projects." The index of importance ranks it fourth for major projects and fifth for "all other projects."

Problem Area 8: Inability of Operating Personnel to Understand Logic Behind Evaluation

The success of any capital investment program depends on the contribution and support of operating personnel. Since their understanding can earn this support, the inability of operating personnel to understand the logic behind evaluation is included among the selected problem areas.

An interviewee indicated that one of his problems in implementing a capital expenditure analysis program is that the operating people down the line do not understand the logic behind the evaluation. He said that, in many instances, they thought analysts and reviewers created unnecessary restrictions.

Perhaps the importance of explaining the logic behind capital expenditure evaluation to operating personnel is a result of the current thinking with regard to management's prerogatives. Operating personnel have the right to know why one proposal is rejected while another is accepted, they have the right to question the evaluation process, and they need to understand the logic behind capital expenditure evaluation if their full support of the firm's program is to be obtained.

The Problem in Practice. For major projects, the inability of operating personnel to understand the logic behind evaluation is a major problem in 26 firms, a minor problem in 75 firms, and no problem in 68 firms. Thus, of the 169 responding firms, it is considered a problem in 101 firms (60 percent).

For "all other projects," inability of operating personnel to understand the logic behind evaluation is a major problem in 18 firms, a minor problem in 65, and no problem in 68. It is considered a problem in 83 (55 percent) of the 151 responding firms.

Inability of operating personnel to understand the logic behind evaluation qualifies as a common problem for both major projects and "all other projects." The index of importance ranks this problem tenth for all projects.

Problem Area 9: Shortage of Well-Qualified Analysts and Reviewers

Well-qualified analysts and reviewers of capital expenditure proposals can make the difference between the success and failure of any investment analysis. Therefore, whether finding well-qualified analysts and reviewers is a problem is included in the study.

The problem, as described by one interviewee, lies not in *finding* analysts and reviewers, but in finding *good* analysts and reviewers. It is hard to find good analysts and reviewers who know one's business, understand the theory, apply the theory whenever it is appropriate, and, most of all, raise the right questions about investment proposals.

Another interviewee, the director of resources planning and analysis of a large food and beverages manufacturer, advised that there is a shortage of a special kind of analyst: the skilled, mature analyst who really knows what is happening and is able to deal with the heart of capital budgeting and quantification of ideas. It is these analysts, and those who are also able to separate the significant from the insignificant data, who are hard to find.

The Problem in Practice. For major projects, the shortage of well-qualified analysts and reviewers is a major problem in 37 responding firms, a minor problem in 77, and no problem in 57. Thus, it is a problem in 114 (67 percent) of the 171 responding firms.

For "all other projects," the shortage of well-qualified analysts and reviewers is a major problem in 24 responding firms, a minor problem in 65 firms, and no problem in 64 firms. Thus, it is a problem in 89 (58 percent) of the 153 responding firms.

The shortage of well-qualified analysts and reviewers is a common problem for both major projects and "all other projects." The index of importance ranks it eighth for major projects and seventh for "all other projects."

Problem Area 10: Background and Interests of Top Management

Top management plays a vital role in capital expenditure analysis; it is the final authority for acceptance or rejection of proposals. Since management is composed of a number of people with varied backgrounds and interests, and all new methods and techniques must be approved by top management, the backgrounds and interests of top management represent a potential problem area.

Some of the financial executives interviewed explained that they are still using the payback and accountant rate of return methods, although they personally prefer the discounted cash flow rate of return method, because top management asks for such methods. Until top management personnel are sold on the advanced methods and techniques of capital expenditure evaluation, and until they understand these methods and techniques, capital expenditure decisions will be based on old and inefficient methods.

The Problem in Practice. For major projects, the background and interests of top management is a major problem in 20 responding firms, a minor problem in 40 firms, and no problem in 108 firms. Therefore, it is considered a problem in 60 (36 percent) of the 168 firms that responded to the survey.

For "all other projects," background and interests of top management is a major problem in 12 responding firms, a minor problem in 35, and no problem in 104. Thus, it is considered a problem in 47 (31 percent) of the 151 respondent firms.

Background and interests of top management is not a common problem in the responding firms.

Problem Area 11: Background and Interests of the Board of Directors

The board of directors is involved in the decision-making process on capital expenditures, though the degree of involvement differs from company to company. In some companies, only a few major proposals are reviewed by the board of directors, while in others the board must approve any expenditure above a certain minimum dollar figure.

The potential problem of different backgrounds and interests exists with members of the board of directors as well as with top management. Therefore, the problem of different backgrounds and interests of the board of directors is included among the key problem areas.

The Problem in Practice. For major projects, the question of the background and interests of the board of directors is a major problem in 17 responding firms, a minor problem in 28, and no problem in 121. Thus, of the 166 firms, 45 (27 percent) consider it a problem.

For "all other projects," the question of the background and interests of the board of directors is a major problem in 12 firms, a minor problem in 21 firms, and no problem in 117 firms. Thus, of the 150 responding firms, 33 (22 percent) consider it a problem.

Background and interests of the board of directors fails to qualify as a common problem in the responding firms.

Problem Area 12: Price-Level Changes

The problem of price-level changes and the need for considering it is recognized in the accounting literature. Eldon S. Hendriksen's statement is typical.

> Historical dollar reporting serves a useful purpose in providing accountability for stewardship of cash funds, for cash flow analysis, and in tracing dollars through the business processes. For most other purposes, neglecting price-level changes results in serious errors in reporting. Under the concepts of income based on either the maintenance of capital or the matching of expenses and revenues, adjustments must be made for price-level changes in order to provide better information for measuring efficiency, to provide a basis for prediction of future income, and for managerial decision making.[3]

Much progress has been realized in the area of price-level changes and how to take them into consideration for financial reporting. However, a standard reporting practice has yet to gain full acceptance.

Since the problem of price-level changes is not fully resolved for financial reporting, which is concerned with past events, it is evident that these changes are even more difficult for capital expenditure evaluation, which must rely on forecasts of future changes.[4]

One interviewee indicated that, in practice, price-level changes and the future worth of the dollar are unpredictable, and it is not feasible or practicable to include them in the analysis.

The Problem in Practice. For major projects, the question of price-level changes is a major problem in 42 responding firms, a minor problem in 85, and no problem in 42. Thus, it is considered a problem in 127 (75 percent) of the 169 responding firms.

For "all other projects," price-level changes is a major problem in 20 firms, a minor problem in 72 firms, and no problem in 60 firms. Thus, it is considered a problem in 92 (61 percent) of the 152 responding firms.

Price-level changes qualify as a common problem for both major projects and "all other projects." The index of importance ranks price-level changes seventh for all projects.

Problem Area 13: Lack of Standardization in Methods and Assumptions

Several answers can be obtained from the same information, if handled in different ways. In analyzing capital investment proposals, several assumptions have to be made. The possible combinations of differences in the assumptions and methods of handling the data often pose a problem.

The Problem in Practice. For major projects, 32 firms find that the lack of standardization in methods and assumptions used by analysts and reviewers is a major problem, 68 firms consider it a minor problem, and 69 firms consider it no problem. Thus, 100 companies (59 percent) of the 169 responding firms consider it a problem.

For "all other projects," it is considered a major problem by 28 firms, a minor problem by 55 firms, and no problem by 69 firms. Thus, it is considered a problem by 83 (55 percent) of the 152 firms that responded to the survey.

Lack of standardization in methods and assumptions used by analysts and evaluators is a common problem for both major projects and "all other projects." The index of importance ranks this problem ninth for all projects.

Problem Area 14: Contemporary Accounting

Dr. John W. Coughlan, a former professor of accounting at The George Washington University and a certified public accountant, superbly describes contemporary accounting when he says:

> Within the confines of mercantile [contemporary] accounting it is quite impossible to prove that an accountant is wrong. Turn fifty different accountants (all highly skilled) loose on the same business and ask them to measure its income. They will all use different combinations of inventory-pricing and depreciation methods, and they will all come up with different figures. Which of the fifty different (in some cases diametrically different) income statements is correct? They are all correct, says the mercantile accountant. To disprove the mercantile accountant it is necessary to prove that a particular method of inventory-pricing or of depreciation accounting is best. But all these methods are conventions. The best depreciation method does not exist. Accordingly, one must accept the absurd proposition that all fifty figures are correct and that a business really has fifty different net incomes! An accounting that cannot be wrong cannot be right. . . .[5]

Financial accounting is far from being perfect for reporting the present and the past. It is therefore difficult to obtain perfect figures when it is necessary to adjust the figures for capital expenditure analysis purposes. The difficulty stems from some inherent accountant characteristics outlined previously and summarized here:

1. Accounting is mainly concerned with reporting for a specific operating year or parts of that year. Thus, isolation of data by project is not typical. Cash flows needed for capital investment follow-up and analysis are related to specific projects and therefore cannot be easily obtained from the regular accounting records.

2. Accounting books are usually kept on an accrual basis, whereas project estimates are usually needed on a cash basis.

3. The time value of money is usually taken into consideration in capital expenditure analysis, whereas it is not usually accounted for in contemporary accounting.

4. Opportunity cost of investments is considered in capital expenditure evaluation systems, whereas opportunity cost is usually ignored in financial accounting.

The Problem in Practice. For major projects, the inability of the accounting department to confirm or disprove at a later date the accuracy of cash flows in capital expenditure projections is considered a major problem in 51 responding firms, a minor problem in 74 firms, and no problem in 43 firms. Thus, it is considered a problem in 125 (74 percent) of the 168 responding firms.

For "all other projects," it is considered a major problem in 39 responding firms, a minor problem in 67, and no problem in 46. Thus, it is considered a problem in 106 (70 percent) of 152 responding firms.

This problem qualifies as a common problem for both major projects and "all other projects." The index of importance ranks it sixth for major projects and second for "all other projects."

In a large industrial corporation in which the availability of sufficient data on individual projects for postaudits was a problem, the controller has tried to solve this problem in an interesting manner. Before any authorization for a capital expenditure is granted, the head of the department requesting such authorization must sign this statement: "Provision has been made for record keeping sufficient to postaudit the project."

Problem Area 15: Lack of Unified and Consistent Treatment in the Literature

The literature on capital expenditure analysis is far from being infallible. Many problems are still unresolved, and many are highly controversial. It is not uncommon to find disagreement among writers about what method should be used for evaluating capital expenditure proposals.

A good example of this lack of agreement is the selection of the discounted cash flow rate of return method versus net present value. One debated issue is whether the first method implies the assumption of reinvesting the returns or not. There are, as indicated earlier, two different views: the first is that there is such an assumption, and the second is that such an assumption does not exist.

Many schools of engineering, business, and economics provide inadequate training of students in the theory of capital expenditure analysis and its application.

The director of resource planning and analysis of a large food and beverages manufacturer maintains that the available literature on capital expenditure analysis is, for the most part, totally unrealistic. It does not take into consideration the actualities of the decision-making process. He believes that he would have a hard time trying to find a book on capital expenditure analysis to recommend to an analyst, and he observed that there are several misuses of statistics and mathematics in this area. Because of his engineering background, he is familiar with the mathematical concepts used. However, as he sees it, the real problem is not one of finding a precise mathematical tool, but of translating the mathematics into a real-life situation.

The Problem in Practice. For major projects, lack of unified and consistent treatment of the topic in the literature is a major problem in 18 responding firms, a minor problem in 51 firms, and no problem in 91 firms. Therefore, it is considered a problem in 69 (43 percent) of the 160 responding firms.

For "all other projects," it is considered a major problem in 13 firms, a minor problem in 48, and no problem in 86. Thus, it is considered a problem in 61 (41 percent) of the 147 responding firms.

Lack of unified and consistent treatment of the topic in the literature fails to qualify as a common problem in the responding firms.

Problem Area 16: Top Management's Shortage of Time

Top management in this time and age has tremendous responsibilities. Paperwork and other duties impose heavy demands on the time of top executives. The fact that articles and books on capital expenditures and their evaluation run into the hundreds of titles and more written material in that area is constantly available, combined with other pressing demands on the time of the executives, often prevents them from keeping up with new developments in the field.

The Problem in Practice. For major projects, shortage of spare time of top management is a major problem in 25 responding firms, a minor problem in 58, and no problem in 74. Therefore, it is a problem in 83 (53 percent) of the 157 responding firms.

For "all other projects," shortage of spare time of top management is a major problem in 17 responding firms, a minor problem in 51 firms, and no problem in 72 firms. Thus, it is a problem in 68 (49 percent) of the 140 responding firms.

The shortage of time on the part of top management to keep up with the developments in the field is a common problem for major projects but not for "all other projects." The index of importance ranks it the eleventh and last common problem for major projects.

Summary of Major Problems

A study of the responses to the evaluation questionnaire indicates that, for major projects, the top five *major* problems in the evaluation of capital expenditure proposals are:

Problem	*No. of Firms*
1. Forecasting in general	80
2. Disclosure of alternatives	52
3. Inability of accounting department at later date to confirm or disprove accuracy of cash flows in the original capital expenditure projection	51
4. Qualitative information not subject to quantitative analysis	47
5. Overestimation of benefits	43

The top five major problems in the evaluation of capital expenditure proposals for "all other projects" are:

Problem	*No. of Firms*
1. Forecasting in general	48
2. Inability of accounting department at later date to confirm or disprove accuracy of cash flows in the original capital expenditure projection	39
3. Disclosure of alternatives	38
4. Qualitative information not subject to quantitative analysis	30
5. Lack of standardization in methods and assumptions used by analysts and evaluators	28

The top four major problems are the same for both major projects and "all other projects" (forecasting in general, inability of the accounting department at a later date to confirm or disprove the accuracy of cash flows in the original capital expenditure projection, disclosure of alternatives, and qualitative information not subject to quantitative analysis). The data indicate that forecasting in general is a major problem for both major projects and "all other projects." Despite all the achievements in the quantitative area and the development of what is called the science of decision making, forecasting is still a major problem.

The following problem areas are of least importance as major problems for both major projects and "all other projects":

1. Overestimation of costs.
2. Underestimation of benefits.
3. Background and interests of top management.
4. Background and interests of the board of directors.
5. Lack of unified and consistent treatment of the topic in the literature.
6. Shortage of time on the part of top management to keep up with the developments in the field.

Problem Areas: Interview Data

Several interviews were conducted during the preliminary stages of the study and near its completion. One main objective of the latter interviews was to see if the conclusions based on questionnaire data were correct and to uncover additional problem areas. These interviews confirmed the conclusions reached from the questionnaire data.

The vice-president of a large food manufacturer stated that in his company the major problem is people. Since capital expenditure proposals are originated, justified, evaluated, approved, executed, and postaudited by individuals, the human element plays a major and dominant role. Company politics—who has the most influence, who is close to the president, who has the most profitable division, and who is the best salesman—will, in the final analysis, determine which projects will be accepted. People, their resistance to change, job security, favoritism, and nepotism play a major role (an informal role, if you will) in capital expenditure analysis.

The manager of capital investment planning of a large electronics manufacturer indicated that one of his major problems lies in the inability of individuals, particularly operating personnel, to understand and correctly follow the directions on capital expenditure analysis.

The vice-president and treasurer of a large mining company maintained that there are two main problems with the capital expenditure analysis program in his firm. The first and biggest problem, as he sees it, is to get the individuals who make the final decisions to stay away from purely subjective methods and to have firmly established minimum criteria for evaluating proposals, such as minimum acceptable returns.

The second problem is to find a way to assure that projects are evaluated on the same basic terms and assumptions. After all the work of the analysis is done, top management usually looks at one or two figures and treats them as whole truths, without regard for other factors that are equally important. These other factors should be considered if proposals are to be compared on the same basis. Examples of these factors include the underlying assumptions and whether they are optimistic, pessimistic, or realistic; sensitivity of the profitability to changes in key elements; and the probability of achieving expected results.

A production supervisor of a plant of a large chemical company specified the two main problems in evaluating capital expenditures as (1) underestimation of costs (such as maintenance and labor costs) required for solving problems of output and quality, and (2) unavailability of adequate or proper records of investments, particularly when previous managers have left the company.

The controller of a large paper manufacturing plant indicated that he has two main problems. The first is the length of time it takes to get the required capital expenditure approval from the corporate office. It is not uncommon for an approval, especially for a major capital expenditure, to take as long as six months. Of course, the longer the delay, the more opportunity losses incurred. His second problem is the inability to express the qualitative benefits of capital expenditures in terms of profitability. As an example, the building in which the plant is located is very old, and a new building is desperately needed. However, each time a proposal to build a new building is submitted, it is rejected. The reason, as he sees it, is that no tangible returns are expected. All intangibles, such as improvement of employee morale, better working conditions, fewer hazards, improvement of plant appearance, and less noise, are considered of zero value by top management.

The main problem, as seen by the controller of a manufacturer of trade and custom design machinery, is the tendency of operating individuals to push pet projects even when alternatives that are more beneficial to the corporation are available.

Conclusions

The following conclusions are reached:

- The selected sixteen problem areas are in fact problems for large firms.
- Each of the problems assumes a different role in the different firms.
- Forecasting is the number-one major and common problem. A possible explanation is that achievements in forecasting theory and techniques in the last decade have failed to solve the forecasting problem.
- Despite frequent complaints about the lack of unified and consistent treatment of the analysis of capital investments in the literature, the lack is not ranked high as a problem.
- Underestimation of costs is a greater problem than overestimation. This may be due to difficulties in foreseeing all possible expenditures in advance.
- Overestimation of benefits is a greater problem than underestimation of benefits.

NOTES

1. Elly Vassilatou-Thanopoulos, *Financial Analysis Techniques for Equipment Replacement Decisions,* N.A.A. Research Monograph 1 (New York: National Association of Accountants, 1965), p. 7.
2. Fred J. Weston and Eugene F. Brigham, *Essentials of Managerial Finance* (New York: Holt, Rinehart & Winston, 1968), p. 130.
3. Eldon S. Hendriksen, *Accounting Theory* (Homewood, Ill.: Richard D. Irwin, 1965), pp. 166–167.
4. For a more detailed coverage, see Harold Bierman, Jr., and Seymour Smidt, *The Capital Budgeting Decision,* 3rd ed. (New York: Macmillan, 1971), Chapter 15.
5. John W. Coughlan, "Profit and Probability," *Advanced Management Journal,* Vol. 33, No. 2 (April 1968), pp. 67–68.

11 / Capital Expenditure Analysis: Another Look

GOOD administrative procedures are essential to the effective management of capital expenditures. This chapter describes selected administrative aspects and offers some observations based on a review of many procedures manuals.*

Selected Administrative Aspects

Complete coverage of administrative aspects of capital expenditure analysis is beyond the scope of this book. Administration usually differs from one company to another and from one time to another within the same company. What is good for one company is not necessarily good for another. Each company has its own unique characteristics of size, number of employees and their backgrounds and training, type of industry, and development stage. These differences justify the wide variance in practices with respect to the administrative procedures. Therefore, procedures should be tailored to the particular company.

The following administrative aspects are selected for discussion because of their importance: minimum amounts, classification, postaudits, training, and written policies. Finally, a description of items often found in company capital expenditure analysis manuals (commonly known as procedures manuals) is provided.

Minimum Amounts

Some firms establish minimum costs for classifying items as capital expenditures. Such minimums eliminate subjecting trivial expenditures to extensive and costly analysis. One minimum may be established for all types of investments, or a number of minimums may be established, one for each type of investment.

*For additional forms and related procedures, see Ernest H. Weinwurm and George F. Weinwurm, *Long-Term Profit Planning* (AMA, 1971), pp. 64–75, 221–227.

Minimum Amounts in Practice. Respondents were asked if their firm specifies a minimum cost for an item to be considered a capital expenditure and, if so, to indicate the amount. Of 198 firms, 161 (81 percent) require that an item cost a minimum amount before it is considered a capital expenditure. Only 37 (19 percent) do not specify such a minimum. Two of the 200 responding firms did not answer the question.

The stated amounts varied. Also, some firms use different minimums for different types of investment. Of the amounts reported, $100 is required by 54 firms, $500 by 25 firms, $200 by 20 firms, $250 by 19 firms, and $1,000 by 18 firms. Various minimums are required by 37 firms. (The total number of firms is more than 161 because some respondents stated more than one minimum.) Size of the firm seems to have little influence on the required minimum.

Classification

The classification of capital expenditures is the process of grouping similar capital expenditure proposals into separate categories or classes.

Such classification helps in identifying projects, particularly when those reviewing the proposals are not familiar with them. It helps in summarizing budget totals for similar projects, and may indicate the type of analysis required for each category.

The ideal classification of capital expenditures does not exist. Each firm must tailor its classification to its own needs. Classifications of capital expenditures differ according to their purpose and according to who is doing the classifying.

Dean classifies capital expenditures as: (1) replacement investments (either like-for-like or obsolescence), (2) expansion investments (to expand the capacity to produce and sell existing products), (3) product-line investments (improvements in existing products and additions to the product line), and (4) strategic investments (defensive, aggressive, and welfare).[1]

One writer, after studying the capital expenditures policies and procedures of a dozen firms, found a simple and interesting classification of capital expenditures. He classified capital expenditures as either increasing the earning power of the firm or not adding to that earning power.[2]

Capital expenditure proposals may be classified as independent or dependent. Independent proposals are those that do not affect decisions on other proposals. Dependent proposals are either mutually exclusive (the selection of one proposal means the rejection of others) or complementary (the undertaking of one project requires or encourages undertaking the other).

Capital expenditures can be classified simply as major expenditures and minor expenditures. Generally, all other classifications could be looked upon as subdivisions of the major and minor categories.

Classification in Practice. Respondents were asked to indicate whether their firm specifies classifications of capital expenditures and, if so, to list these classifications. Of the 200 companies, 152 (76 percent) specify classifications of capital expenditure proposals, and 48 (24 percent) do not. Of the 152 firms that specify classifications, 145 listed them. A study of these lists endorses Dean's conclusion that capital expenditure classifications differ considerably from one company to another.[3]

The classifications of capital expenditures reported by the responding firms disclose that some categories are used more often than others. One or more of the following were included frequently in the classifications reported: replacement, expansion, income improving, income maintaining, cost reduction or cost-saving, necessity, new products.

Examples of the classifications of capital expenditures reported by the respondents from selected industries are listed below:

- Mining: replacement, cost reduction, plant improvement, quality improvement, working conditions, increased production, other.
- Petroleum, crude oil, and natural gas: new, replacement, upgrading.
- Tobacco: replacement, expansion.
- Food and beverage: replacement, expansion, risk hedging, strategic.
- Textiles: replacement, profit maintenance, profit expansion, necessity.
- Paper and allied products: basic upkeep, improvements, savings, sales expansion, sales retention, drawings and patterns, customers' equipment.
- Chemicals: small tools, rebuilding and replacement, safety and health, general plant improvement, cost reduction, quality improvement, expansion, new product.
- Pharmaceuticals: replacement, expansion, cost reduction, personnel welfare, community responsibility.
- Soap and cosmetics: capacity, new products, quality improvement or package changes, savings, plant maintenance and replacement required by law or community relations, plant safety and protection, personnel.
- Petroleum refining: standard projects, growth projects, venture projects, operating necessities.
- Rubber: increase capacity, cost savings, safety, quality control, replacements, research and development.

- Stone, clay, glass, and concrete products: new business, expansion of existing business, improved performance, defensive, acquisitions of going concerns, other.
- Metal manufacturing: normal, trade demands, cost reduction, environmental control, acquisition, expansion, raw materials, international.
- Metal products: expansion, cost reduction, profit maintaining, mandatory, profit improvement.
- Farm and industrial machinery: new product, product improvement, marketing and distribution, facility expansion, cost reduction, business systems, research, maintenance, unclassified.
- Appliances, electronics: new product, capacity increase, cost reduction, quality/reliability, safety/legal, replacement, employee welfare, development.
- Motor vehicles and trucks: new model and new products, expansion, maintenance and replacement, corporate and dealer identity, profit improvement, research and development and quality improvements, other.
- Aircraft: modernization (including replacement) expansion, new skills and technology development, strategic.
- Measuring, scientific, and photographic: new product, cost reduction, additional capacity, replacement, acquisition, non-income generating, make/buy, lease/buy.
- Office machines and other miscellaneous machines: cost reduction, revenue producing, strategic investments, essential replacements.

Postaudits

Another administrative aspect of utmost importance to the completion of any capital expenditure analysis program is that of postauditing investments.

A postaudit is a comparative study of the estimated and the actual results of a capital expenditure project. Thus, postaudit studies refer to: (1) collecting data on the actual results of the projects, (2) comparing actual results with those estimated in the proposals and determining the differences between actual and forecast results, and (3) studying those differences. (See Appendix C.)

Postaudits are also known as follow-up studies, make-good studies, performance audits, post-completion studies, and post mortems.

Reasons for Postaudits. Reasons for performing postaudits include:

1. Knowledge gained from past projects provides a necessary feedback that helps to improve future decisions. The postaudit serves as a training technique

so that mistakes made in the past can be avoided in the future, and mistakes made in one department of a firm can be avoided in other departments.

2. Postaudits have a psychological effect that encourages proponents of proposals to submit realistic estimates. More than 15 years ago, L. E. Grimes, then assistant controller at E. I. du Pont de Nemours & Company, described this psychological effect in the following manner:

> Not many are likely to sponsor capital projects on the basis of vague information and casual study if they fully realize that their predictions on a specific facility will eventually be matched against actual results and that they may have to stand up, utterly embarrassed to explain how they could have been so greatly mistaken.[4]

3. When projects are to be audited, an incentive is provided for operating management to meet the goals established in proposals. When operating management knows that results will be revealed, the goals of proposals serve as a challenge for everyone concerned to achieve them.

4. Postaudits serve in evaluating the performance of operating management. Performance is evaluated on the basis of how well the assumptions and estimates used in the original proposal were realized. Performance evaluations are thus based on objective information, with both good and bad incidents included.

5. Audits help to identify good estimators and decision makers. This information is useful when candidates are being considered for promotion.

6. Postaudits serve in detecting personal bias. If the bias is unalterable, a method of allowing for it can be developed.

7. Postaudits can pinpoint trouble areas and warn the decision maker when corrective action is needed.

8. There are other advantages of postaudits, one of which is that they may reveal other investment opportunities.

A Word of Caution. Although postaudits are very useful, they have weaknesses. Some of these are:

1. If carried to an extreme, postaudits may encourage submitting only fully realizable proposals, which can result in the loss of valuable opportunities.

2. Postaudits are expensive and should be used only when the expected results justify the cost.

3. Postaudits could be viewed by some managements as a substitute for the complete analysis of projects before they are accepted. In such a case, the purpose of postaudits is self-defeating.

4. Postaudits can be subject to manipulation by those authorizing them. The N.A.A. study states: "Our research indicates that companies' procedures for postaudit are heavily influenced by their managements' choice as to which purposes are dominant."[5]

5. A human relations problem may exist with the introduction of postaudits. The fear of using the results for punishment can hinder the success of any postauditing program. A healthy spirit of mutual trust may be weakened by the existence of postaudits.

6. Serious difficulties are faced when trying to use accounting data for postaudits. Accounting books and records in their normal form are not suited to providing information required for postaudits.

7. Difficulty may arise regarding responsibility for postaudits. An objective review is more likely to be assured when postauditing responsibility is assigned to individuals outside the involved department. However, the operating personnel working on a project are more familiar with that project and, if they so desire, can provide accurate information in a shorter time.

Two Related Questions. Two questions about postaudits need a more detailed discussion. First, when should a postaudit be performed?

Postaudits should be performed as soon as possible; as soon as a project is completed and operational its performance should be reviewed. In many cases this would be at the end of the first or second year of the project. Too early an audit may not show the actual benefits from the project. On the other hand, a postaudit that is delayed for several years is meaningless. In the latter case, the lesson-learning would be less effective, it would not deter individuals from "playing the budget game," and many of those connected with the project may have moved to other positions. Postaudits of major projects might be conducted more than once (this is not common practice, however); for example, once at the end of the first year of operation, and again at the end of the third year of operation.

The second question is: Who should do the postaudit? Viewpoints and practices vary regarding who should perform the postaudit—the department in charge of the project or other individuals. It is easier for those executing the project to postaudit it. However, to assure a more objective review, responsibility for postauditing should be assigned to an individual outside the operating department. The operating department may help with the postauditing or provide some inputs to the analysis, but it should not be in charge of the postaudit. Using an outsider does not constitute an act of distrust or lack of confidence, but is merely an accepted principle of internal control.

Postaudits in Practice. Respondents were asked to check the percentage of postaudits of completed projects performed in their firms, both for major projects and for "all other projects." Only 14 responding firms perform no postaudit of their major projects, whereas 37 companies perform no postaudit of "all other projects."

Some sort of postauditing is reported with respect to major projects by 172 (92.5 percent) of the 186 responding firms, and with respect to "all other projects" by 138 (78.9 percent) of the 175 responding firms.

Postauditing of some sort is conducted on about 96 to 100 percent of their major projects by the majority of responding firms, but on less than 25 percent of "all other projects." Additional research is needed, however, to determine more precisely the extent and nature of these postaudits.

The rationale of postaudits (sometimes called performance evaluations) is explicitly stated in the following quotation from a policy statement:

> The investment analysis function maintains a system of post-completion project appropriation reviews. Generally, these reviews are required on all financially justified project appropriations and on any non-financial project deemed necessary at the discretion of management.
>
> The Project Performance Evaluation compares the plan and estimates included in the approved project appropriation with the actual accomplishments, project expenditures and operating results in order to: (1) determine if planned objectives have been attained, (2) determine corrective action required, (3) provide a motivation to improve future project planning and estimates, (4) provide a means for extending benefits gained at one location to other locations with similar operations, (5) improve future decisions.

One correspondent explained why postaudits are valuable to his firm:

> All completed projects are reappraised [postaudited] on an average of two years after the date of completion. This reappraisal is designed for "lesson learning." The information obtained provides (a) a basis for reconsideration and possible alteration of spending plans on similar items being considered for other affiliates, (b) a means to assist in initiating action for improvement in existing units, and (c) specific findings about our investment decision-making process which enables us to make improvements in this process and therefore make better use of our shareholders' capital.

Training

Analysis of capital expenditures in the setting of twentieth-century technology and economics is a difficult matter. Projects are more sophisticated than ever before, the theory of investment analysis is becoming more complicated, competition is becoming more acute, and practices of business firms are watched more closely by the stockholders, the government, unions, and the public. In this environment, business firms cannot afford to leave employees on their own to learn the theory and practice of efficient investment analysis through the slow process of self-development and trial and error. Therefore, systematic and formal programs for the training and development of employees in the theory and practice of economic evaluation of capital expenditure proposals are essential for any progressive firm.

Dean considers the need for training in capital productivity measurement one of three administrative requirements that apply to all types of investments. The other two requirements are postaudits and the need for different stages of refinement in earnings estimates.[6]

Although some writers differentiate between the terms "training" and "development," for the purposes of this study these terms are used synonymously.

Training in capital expenditure analysis is useful for the following reasons:

- Training can help maintain consistency and accuracy in the application of policies and principles of measurement of capital expenditures.
- Training is needed not only to learn new methods and techniques, but also to help *unlearn* and abandon inefficient practices.
- Training helps to inform the trainees of new developments in investment analysis.
- The training program forces busy personnel to take time out to study the decision-making process and the tools available for capital expenditure evaluation.

The treasurer of a large pharmaceuticals company indicated that training operating managers in capital expenditure analysis has paid off in the form of improvement in relationships between the operating managers and the finance department; the finance department has come to be regarded as a source of help rather than a hindrance.

Training in Practice. Respondents were asked if their firm has a formal program for the training and development of employees in the theory and practice of economic evaluation of capital expenditure proposals. Of the 200 respondents, only 48 (24 percent) have such a program. No such program was reported by 145 (72.5 percent) of the respondents, and the remaining 7 did not answer the question.

Of the 48 firms that have formal training and development programs, in 32 (66.7 percent) these programs take place within the organization, and 16 firms (33.3 percent) have programs both within and outside the organization.

None of the responding firms have programs that take place entirely outside the organization.

When asked to check each category that is descriptive of the participants in the training program, the 48 respondents gave the answers shown in Table 37.

Table 37. Description of participants in training programs.

Type of Participant	*No. of Firms*
Analysts and reviewers	38
Middle management (or department heads or division heads)	35
Top management personnel	19
First-line supervisors	16
Operating personnel	13
Miscellaneous	4
No answer	1
Total	126*

*The total is more than 48 because some firms checked more than one category.

At a time when training and development programs in a variety of areas are well known and generally accepted, it is surprising to find that only 24 percent of the responding firms have such a program for capital expenditure analysis.

Three possible explanations can be offered for the low percentage of formal training and development programs. The first is that some companies consider such programs to have limited value. Second, some firms depend on informal on-the-job training for this purpose. Finally, the need for such training and development is often not recognized by top management.

Written Policies

Policies are general guidelines of company philosophy and purpose. In such an important area as capital investments, the value of policies cannot be overestimated. (See Appendix C.) For policies to be effective they should be in written form, for a variety of reasons:

1. The writing of statements of policy helps to avoid issuing ambiguous and ill-thought-through policies, because policies are usually well defined before they are issued if they are written.

2. Written policies may be regarded as positive commitments. They constitute a declaration by top management that it means what it says.

3. Policies are apt to be applied more consistently, especially in large corporations, when they are available in written form, thus relieving reviewers, analysts, and decision makers of dependence upon the "grapevine" and informal interpretations and suggestions.

4. Written policies can help in the orientation and training of newcomers.

5. Written policies are more susceptible to continuing study for updating and improvement than are unwritten policies.

6. Written policies can save valuable time for busy executives by reducing repetitious questions. They allow the practice of management by exception.

Written policies should be general enough to allow for the creative thinking and initiative of those who execute them, and also flexible enough to allow for exceptions.

Written Policies in Practice. Respondents were asked if their corporation has a written policy on the capital expenditure decision-making process. Of 198 responding firms, 186 (94 percent) indicate that their corporation has such a written policy, and only 12 (6 percent) indicated that they have no such written policy. Two firms did not reply.

Capital Expenditures Manuals

A majority of business firms seem to have written statements to describe their policies and procedures for the planning and control of capital expenditures. The objective here is to present some observations based on the review of policies and procedures of over 100 large industrial corporations.

Policy Statements Versus Procedures

Written statements covering capital expenditures may be divided into policy statements and procedures. Policy statements are usually very general and reflect a company's philosophy and purpose with regard to capital expenditures. Following are some examples of what is included in policy statements.

1. Specification of the primary objective of the capital expenditures program. Profitability is the most common objective, supplemented at times by such other considerations as employee safety and social responsibility.

2. Designation of the type of capital expenditure that the president and the company's board of directors must review and approve (for example, major lease commitments, real estate transactions, and major projects above certain dollar amounts).

3. A broad guideline with respect to the delegation of authority to commit capital expenditures. Some policy statements specify who may sign on behalf of the corporation to commit funds for capital expenditure projects.

4. Specification of the capital expenditure evaluation committee's role in the review and evaluation of capital expenditures.

5. Emphasis that budget approval does not constitute authorization for expenditure. (Before funds are committed, a capital expenditure appropriation request must be approved.)

6. A statement that all appropriation requests must include supporting papers.

7. A statement that sufficient analysis must be made of proposed expenditures to determine their economic worth.

8. In some cases, designation of the method of evaluation to be used. Some firms specify that whenever it is applicable, the discounted cash flow method is to be used in evaluating capital expenditure proposals.

9. Specification of the responsibilities of operating units and other key individuals involved with capital expenditures.

10. Specification of the role of the capital expenditures manual and other procedures manuals, and the relationship between them.

Practices vary with respect to the location of policy statements on capital expenditure. In some firms, capital expenditures policy is included in the company's general policy manual; in others, it is found at the beginning of the capital expenditures manual.

Instead of a separate statement of policy as a whole, in some firms each policy statement made is followed by the procedures necessary to implement it. For example, a policy statement may specify that major projects be postaudited as soon as possible. Then, the procedures necessary to implement this policy are described—what is considered a major project, when the postaudit should be conducted, who should conduct the postaudit, what type of information is to be collected, related forms and reports to be prepared, and distribution to be made of the reports.

Procedures are detailed statements designed to implement the capital expenditures policy. They are more specific and detailed than policy statements, but the amount of detail varies from one firm to another. Some company procedures are limited to a few pages; others are 100 pages or more. The majority of companies establish capital expenditure procedures to assure achieving company goals.

Separate Versus Composite Manual

In recognition of the importance of capital expenditures, some firms have found it advantageous to designate a separate manual to capital expenditures. This manual is known by many different names: capital expenditures manual, capital investment manual, capital programming manual, capital budgeting decision, facilities expenditures planning and control, corporate guideline for capital control system, capital expenditure procedure, request for capital appropriations procedure, policy and procedure for the approval and post-completion of capital transactions, evaluation and control of capital and lease expenditures, project authorization request preparation manual, handbook on appropriation requests, appropriations procedure, capital expenditure program, capital purchase approval procedure, capital project request procedure, business investment procedure, capital asset manual, and capital planning and control manual.

Capital expenditure procedures are often part of other manuals or statements of procedure. They may be part of the controller's procedures, corporate policy and standard practice, corporate finance policy, corporate financial procedure, executive orders, accounting policy, policy and procedure, controller's policy bulletins, standing instructions, standard practice instructions, financial handbook, corporate accounting and finance policy, manufacturing engineering operations manual, corporate finance bulletins, organization and policy manual, corporate standard procedure, or management guide.

The degree of completeness and the quality of the capital expenditure procedures vary with the size of the company. Larger corporations usually have more comprehensive procedures than smaller corporations. It is logical that larger corporations depend on manuals more than the smaller corporations because of the larger dollar amounts involved and because of the large scale of operations. Top management of a large corporation cannot be as familiar with the specific details of all projects as is possible in a small company.

Regardless of whether capital expenditure procedures are a separate manual or part of another manual, they have common features, which will be described below.

Subjects Treated by Manuals of Capital Expenditure Procedures

The question to be raised now is, What do capital expenditure procedures include? On the basis of a review of what others are doing, some broad categories have been determined and are described briefly here. To prepare a capital expenditures manual, the categories presented here may be used and others added if needed. The order of presentation of these categories does not necessarily reflect their relative standing. Also, while some companies place such things as forms used in the text of the manual, other companies place them in an appendix.

The language used and the level of sophistication of capital expenditures manuals should be easily understood by the average operating manager. Highly technical terms should be either avoided or defined.

Introduction. Some capital expenditures manuals start with introductory statements related to the scope of application and the purpose of the system. Scope of application may state those areas in which divisions and subsidiaries are free to maintain their own procedures, and those areas and types of expenditures to which the manual is applicable.

The purpose of capital expenditure analysis planning and control is frequently stated in the introduction. Some firms specify that the purpose is to keep management informed of the need for proposed capital expenditures, and when the funds are needed, to assure proper control of funds and full utilization of opportunities for investment.

Definitions. The majority of capital expenditures procedures include a section on definitions. (See Appendix C.) Terms that are used frequently but may not be familiar to some employees are defined.

Examples of terms that are defined are: capital expenditure, project, major project, minor project, program, proposal, investment, supporting facilities, cash flow, working capital, inventory, receivables, payables, incremental cost, salvage value, risk, capital plan, budget proposal, research and development, capital budget, budget supplements, appropriation request, idle property, retirements, division, postaudits, profit center, overrun, underrun, transfer, economic justification, and cost of capital.

Project Classifications or Categories. A usual topic in procedures manuals is project classification, which is concerned with the capital expenditure categories specified by the corporation. (See Appendix B.) It is common practice to describe what is included in these categories; for example, replacement, cost reduction, expansion, and upkeep. An "other" category is frequently added to cover items that do not warrant a separate classification or those that fall into more than one classification. Some firms use a blanket appropriation category to cover miscellaneous items and to provide for emergency expenditures.

Capital Budget. The capital budget section relates to procedures for including items in the capital budget and for preparation, revision, and approval of this budget. It is customary to request that departments and divisions prepare their capital budget six months to a year in advance. For long-term planning purposes, capital budgets may be asked for as far ahead as three to five years. Because conditions change, and it is often impossible to provide accurate data for needs very far in the future, the inclusion of a certain proposal in the capital budget represents approval in principle only. Before actual spending, an appropriation request must be submitted and approved to commit the funds, and it is customary to conduct a more detailed evaluation and analysis of the expenditure at that time.

The two types of capital budgets are known as *financing budgets* and *rationing budgets.*

When a financing budget is used, all proposals that meet the minimum requirements will be approved. If the needed funds exceed the internally generated amount, the excess is financed either by borrowing or by raising more equity. For example, if a 20 percent minimum DCFR is required, all proposals that earn 20 percent or more are approved, and arrangements are made to finance them.

A rationing budget is used when, for one reason or another, a given total dollar value is established as a ceiling for capital expenditures and all proposals that are made compete for funds. In this case, some method of establishing priorities is used. Usually, the more profitable investments are chosen before the less profitable.

When a rationing budget is employed, methods of evaluating capital expenditures *should be selected with care.* A study should be made of the types of projects proposed and the suitability of the primary method for selecting from among them. Evaluation is a greater problem when choosing between mutually exclusive projects (that is, one project or the other can be selected, but not both, such as building a factory of one-million-unit capacity versus two-million-unit capacity), or between projects of unequal lives.

Several of the corporate executives interviewed indicated that they usually use rationing budgets. Internally generated funds, supplemented sometimes by a small amount of long-term debt, determine the capital expenditure budget ceiling. In some firms, particularly very large corporations, internally generated funds were deemed sufficient to cover all capital expenditure proposals that satisfy the criteria established for their approval.

One reason cited for limiting the total capital expenditures to a certain amount is to reduce excessive demands on top management's time. It is argued that even if more profitable investments could be financed, each approved project would require more attention from top management for execution and follow-up, and if there were no set limits, top management would not be able to handle all the projects. The result would be a less profitable situation. The financing budget required for each project would entail incurring additional long-term debt, frequently frowned upon by top management.

Some firms use a combination of rationing and financing budgets. A total capital expenditures ceiling is established, but exceptions are made for especially profitable investments. When internal funds are not available to finance them, the firm makes arrangements to acquire the necessary funds externally.

Appropriation Requests. Another common procedure is that of appropriation requests. (See Appendix A.) These requests are also known as requests for capital appropriation (RCA) and authorization for expenditure (AFE).

An appropriation request (also known as an AR) is, in essence, a petition to top management to authorize the expenditure of funds for a capital project. The project concept is often used in this regard; all expenditures related to a specific objective are submitted as one proposal to avoid duplication of effort and bypassing of authorization levels.

Specific forms are usually used for appropriation requests. These forms may differ according to the type of project and whether a quantitative or qualitative capital expenditure analysis is needed.

Various supporting papers are usually submitted along with the appropriation request.

Who May Prepare a Capital Expenditure Request? Some procedures specify who may prepare a capital expenditure request. Although it is common practice to require that appropriation requests be approved at high managerial levels, there is little restriction on the level at which the initiation of a capital expenditure request may be made. (Remember, this is not an *approved* request.)

Authorization Levels. Another topic usually included in a capital expenditure procedures manual is that of authorization levels. (See Appendix A.) They indicate the levels of approval necessary for various types of capital expenditures. These levels are usually related to the dollar amounts involved; the higher the amount, the higher the level of approval required.

Approval levels differ from one company to another, and may even differ from time to time in the same company. However, the following appropriation approval levels for capital expenditures in a large conglomerate corporation, as provided by an interviewee, may be considered typical.

Amount	*Required Approval*
Up to $20,000	Division manager
$20,001–30,000	Group vice-president
$30,001–50,000	Executive vice-president
$50,001–100,000	President
$100,001–300,000	Executive committee
Over $300,000	Board of directors

Authorization Period. The period between authorization for expenditure and the time the authorization will expire is known as the authorization period. To assure the adequacy of capital expenditures and their proper timing, some firms specify that unless part of the authorized expenditure is committed within a given period, the authorization is expired and a new authorization is needed to commit funds for the project. This period is usually about six months and may extend to a year.

Forms Used. Capital expenditure procedures usually include copies of the forms used for capital expenditure analysis and an explanation of each item on these forms. (See Appendixes A and C.) Forms differ from one company to another in size, content (items listed), and type of directions. A capital budget request form may contain the item number, a description of the requested item, the amount, and the justification. The capital appropriation request form may include a description of the proposed investment and its use, the justification, detailed cash flows, a summary, measures of the economic worth of the project, and approvals.

For a major project, the appropriation request form serves as a summary form or cover sheet, supplemented by various income projections, detailed estimates of cash flows, and such other details as engineering or economic studies.

The authorization for expenditure forms include, basically, three types of information: (1) quantitative data related to the proposed project, (2) descriptive data on the project, (3) signatures and approvals needed.

Numbering System, Routing, Review, Filing, and Advice of Completion of Project. The procedures specify the routine related to the capital expenditure system of numbering and reviewing appropriation requests, routing forms, filing copies, and reporting on completed projects. Some procedures also clearly state who is responsible for maintaining company appropriation request files.

Project Justification. For a project to be approved, justification for the investment is needed. Procedures often describe the type of justification required—technical, economic, qualitative, or a combination of these—and examples are frequently described in the procedures. (See Appendix A.)

Quantitative Versus Qualitative Analysis. Some procedures acknowledge clearly that quantitative analysis, although a must when applicable, is not the only prerequisite for approval of capital expenditure proposals. Nonquantitative analysis may be used for proposals that do not qualify for quantitative analysis or to supplement the quantitative analysis.

Who Performs the Economic Analysis? Some company procedures specify who is to compute the return on investment, or the economic analysis, of capital expenditures. For major projects the sponsor or initiator may leave the analysis to the corporate office. Often, financial analysts are available to provide help with the analysis when requested by the sponsor of a project. The controller's office may provide help when needed.

For projects to be approved by the corporate office, it is customary for the analysis to be performed by individuals from that office. When the computations have already been performed by the operating department, they are usually double-checked by the corporate office to assure that the assumptions and methods used are realistic.

Evaluation Method. The evaluation method or methods to be used, such as payback or discounted cash flow, are usually specified in the procedures manual. Each method may be explained in detail, the philosophy behind using the method cited, and examples offered to explain how to use it. It is quite apparent from the procedures reviewed that the discounted cash flow rate of return method is emphasized as the primary method, with payback as a supplementary method.

Capitalization of Assets. Some capital expenditure procedures include statements regarding which expenditures are to be capitalized and which are to be expensed. These statements are generally in agreement with tax regulations.

Depreciation Method. Some procedures manuals specify the method of depreciation to be used for capital expenditure analysis purposes. In theory, the actual depreciation method used for tax purposes should be used in the evaluation. However, in practice, for convenience and for conservatism, the straight-line depreciation method is often designated for capital expenditure evaluation.

Corporate Tax Rate. To facilitate the analysis of capital expenditures, some firms specify in their procedures the corporate tax rate to be applied in the computations. This figure includes the total of federal and other taxes. The figure most often used is 50 percent. Differences in the results from using a more accurate rate do not justify the extra costs involved.

Emergency Requests. To allow for emergencies, the procedures usually include information about obtaining immediate approval for a capital expenditure. Emergency situations are usually specified and described in the procedures.

In some companies, when company interests or the safety of its employees or customers is endangered and the expenditure has to be made in a short time, verbal approval may be obtained from designated officers (for example, executive vice-presidents) before submitting a capital expenditure appropriation request. Then, immediately after (within one to three days, for example), an appropriation request must be submitted.

Risk Analysis. Reference to capital expenditure analysis techniques in capital expenditure procedures is a new practice. The review of more than 100 manuals shows that risk analysis and other techniques are not commonly found in capital expenditures manuals, although some executives have stated that revised versions of their manuals will include a section on risk analysis. Of all the techniques referred to earlier, risk analysis seems to be the most popular. At present, most of the references are to risk analysis done in a simplified manner. However, some companies have rather sophisticated approaches.

Risk is usually defined as the expected distribution of cash flows. A project with a narrow variation in cash flows is considered less risky than one with a greater variation. Some of the simplified ways of dealing with risk that are found in manuals are:

1. To describe verbally the degree of risk associated with each project. Some firms require that the appropriation request contain information about the type of risk involved in the project with regard to costs of raw materials, labor, and capital; the reliability of the equipment; and marketing factors. An interesting method classifies projects into three risk classes: low risk, medium risk, and high risk. The first class is associated with a 90 to 100 percent probability of obtaining the estimated returns; the second class, 60 to less than 90 percent; and the last class, less than 60 percent. Another interesting way is to state each determinable factor related to a project in terms of best probable, worst probable, and most likely probable.

2. To group proposals into different risk groups and apply different cutoff points or discount rates to these groups when computing the economic worth of the projects.

3. To use probability factors and compute a conditional probability measure (the expected cash flow times the probability of realizing these flows).

Computers. Computers have a place in capital expenditure analysis; they are indispensable to large corporations. Therefore, company procedures with respect to capital expenditure analysis frequently refer to computer utilization and rules governing such use, divisions with access to time-sharing facilities or with computers of their own, programs available and how to obtain them, how to get access to computer facilities, related forms, examples of printouts, and how the computer can make additional computations using several methods of evaluation or a single method, at a nominal or no additional cost.

Status of Proposals. The sponsor of a capital expenditure proposal has an interest in knowing the status of his request. Therefore, some procedures specify how and when the sponsor of a proposal should be informed of its approval or rejection.

Rejected Proposals. Some procedures include reference to what is to be done with rejected proposals. While in some cases rejection means the end of a proposal, some firms maintain a file of rejected projects for a second look a year later, or when conditions have changed enough to make previously rejected proposals attractive.

Postaudits and Progress Reports. Capital expenditure procedures usually contain a specification for and description of progress reports for the projects, appropriations spent and outstanding, and postaudits. Progress reports (or capital projects status reports) summarize the progress of projects and show differences between approved appropriations and actual amounts spent. They help to reveal trouble areas.

Post-completion audits are performed after the project is completed and operational. The procedure usually specifies what type of project is audited, who is responsible for maintaining records on the performance of the project, and the roles played by the operating division and corporate headquarters. (See Appendix C.)

Project Overruns, Underruns, and Cancellations. A procedure is usually specified for handling project overruns. If actual expenditures exceed the initially authorized appropriations by a stated amount, a supplementary appropriation request must be made before committing the funds. In many firms, an excess of 10 percent or more over the authorized appropriation requires such action. Other firms set the amounts, for example, at 10 percent or $5,000, whichever is smaller; 10 percent or $1,000, whichever is greater; 10 percent or $1,000, whichever is greater, up to $20,000; or 10 percent or $25,000, whichever is smaller. Usually, the supplemental request is required to follow the same approval route as the initial appropriation request.

On the other hand, underrun amounts of appropriations are not usually allowed to be spent on other projects. Appropriations for canceled projects cannot be used for any other purpose.

Accounting and Internal Control. Some procedures specify the accounting and internal control measures to be applied to capital expenditures.

Capital Asset Identification. To safeguard the assets of the corporation, some manuals specify procedures for identifying the assets and for maintaining needed records and lists of assets by location.

Legal Review. Reference is made in some procedures manuals to the requirement that all capital expenditure contracts and certain related company commitments be reviewed by the legal department.

Life Guidelines. To help those involved with capital expenditure analysis, some procedures include a life guideline for selected assets that are commonly acquired by the firm.

Leases and Special Investments. Some firms specify procedures for long-term leases, real estate projects, and purchases or leases of electronic data processing equipment.

Excess and Obsolete Facilities. Procedures for the disposal of excess and obsolete facilities are frequently included for the purpose of assuring a sufficient study of such facilities and making excess facilities available to other segments of the organization to accomplish the most economical transfer or disposition.

Excerpts from Related Manuals. Some firms include excerpts from other manuals or references to other manuals for more detailed coverage of certain procedures applicable also to capital expenditures.

Dates and Deadlines. As a convenience for the operating managers and other individuals using the manual, some procedures include a listing of dates and deadlines applicable to the capital budget and approval of proposals.

Flow Charts. To simplify the capital expenditures procedure, some manuals include a flow chart that portrays the flow of a capital expenditure proposal from initiation to approval.

Decision Tables. Decision tables may be included to help in identifying types of actions needed under certain set conditions. Table 38 is an example of a simple decision table. The first part of the decision table helps to

Table 38. Sample decision table.

	Rule			
Condition	*1*	*2*	*3*	*4*
Is it under $10,000?	Y	Y	N	N
Is it $10,000 or more?	N	N	Y	Y
Is it a new venture?	Y	N	Y	N

	Rule			
Action	*1*	*2*	*3*	*4*
Within local authority		√		
Requires approval of the corporate office	√		√	√
Submit form AA		√		√
Submit form BB	√		√	
Use risk analysis			√	

identify the type of expenditure (Y = Yes; N = No). The second part specifies the action needed. For example, if the expenditure is under $10,000 and it is a new venture, condition 1 applies. The action for condition 1 indicates that it requires the approval of the corporate office and that form BB should be used.

Condition 2 applies when the expenditure is under $10,000 and is not a new venture. The action indicator shows that approval is within the local authority and that form AA should be used.

Condition 3 applies when the expenditure is $10,000 or more and is a new venture. The required action is to obtain approval of the corporate office, submit form BB, and use risk analysis.

Condition 4 applies when the expenditure of $10,000 or more is not a new venture. The required action is approval of the corporate office and submission of form AA.

Discount Tables. Since discounted cash flow methods are currently used by many firms, some procedures include discount tables. These discount tables are usually designed to suit the needs of the manual user.

NOTES

1. Joel Dean, *Capital Budgeting* (New York: Columbia University Press, 1951), pp. 86–87.
2. John B. Matthews, Jr., "How to Administer Capital Spending," in *Capital Investment Series* (Boston: Harvard Graduate School of Business Administration, 1964), p. 11.
3. Dean, op. cit., pp. 84–85.
4. L. E. Grimes, "A Comprehensive System of Performance Reports," in *Tested Approaches to Capital Equipment Replacement,* AMA Special Report 1 (New York: AMA, 1954), p. 86.
5. *Financial Analysis to Guide Capital Expenditure Decisions,* N.A.A. Research Report 43 (New York: National Association of Accountants, 1967), p. 85.
6. Dean, op. cit., p. 32.

12 / Other Applications

THE usual practice is to limit the application of capital expenditure analysis methods and techniques to the evaluation of fixed assets. The purpose of this chapter is to extend this analysis beyond the confines of fixed assets, to cite some examples of areas in which capital expenditure analysis methods and techniques could be used, and to provide information about current practices in this regard.

Items Evaluated as Capital Expenditures

Two requirements are essential for using the methods and techniques of capital expenditure analysis to evaluate an expenditure proposal. First, the cost of the expenditure must be above an established minimum amount. Second, the life expectancy of the benefits from such an expenditure must exceed one year. Therefore, any item that qualifies as a capital expenditure must have both the dollar dimension and the time dimension. Any other requirements are unnecessary restrictions. For example, an expenditure does not have to result in an increase in a fixed asset account to be evaluated as a capital expenditure.

The question of whether an expenditure should be evaluated as a capital expenditure is different from the question of whether it should be capitalized. The accounting treatment of an expenditure (that is, whether it is capitalized or expensed) has no bearing on the discussion at hand. Capital expenditure analysis methods and techniques may be regarded as decision-making tools. These tools have a variety of applications, and they can assist in the decision-making process, regardless of accounting conventions.

Hundreds of books and articles have been written on the use of capital expenditure analysis tools for evaluating fixed-asset proposals, but relatively few deal with other applications of these tools. Let us look at what are considered capital expenditure items for decision-making purposes by the responding firms.

Capital Expenditure Items in Practice

Recent studies of company practices have shown some deviation from the classical approach of subjecting to capital expenditure analysis only those expenditures that result in an increase in the fixed asset account. Some companies include marketing programs and research and development in their capital budgets, even though there is little association with an increase in fixed assets.

Each respondent was asked to check, from a list of ten, each item that his company considers a capital expenditure. Of the 200 respondents, 2 did not answer the question, and 198 checked the items shown in Table 39 (ranked in order of magnitude). A summary of the number of items checked and the number of firms that checked these items is given in Table 40. The most common combinations of items considered capital expenditures are summarized in Table 41. (The 7- and 8-item combinations do not warrant listing because too few responses are found in these categories.) As would be expected, the investment in fixed assets is common to all combinations of items considered capital expenditures by the respondents.

Table 39. Types of capital expenditures.

Item	*No. of Firms*
1. An expenditure that results in an increase in the fixed asset account	198
2. An expenditure required by authority (for example, air and water pollution)	99
3. Commitment on a long-term lease	90
4. Investments in partially owned subsidiaries	90
5. Permanent addition to working capital	44
6. Commitment of a long-term nature	39
7. Research and development project	38
8. Long-term advertising costs	5
9. Training or development programs	4
10. Miscellaneous	7
	614*

*The total is more than 198 because some firms checked more than one item.

Table 40. Number of capital expenditure items checked.

No. of Items Checked	*No. of Firms*
1	38
2	46
3	45
4	25
5	22
6	16
7	5
8	1
Total	198

Table 41. Combinations of items considered capital expenditures.

	Most Common Combination (No. of Items) in Each Category					
Item	*1*	*2*	*3*	*4*	*5*	*6*
One that results in an increase in the fixed asset account	√	√	√	√	√	√
One that is required by authority (e.g., air and water pollution)		√	√	√	√	√
Investments in partially owned subsidiaries			√	√	√	√
A commitment on a long-term lease				√	√	√
A commitment of a long-term nature					√	√
A permanent addition to working capital						√

Concepts of Capital Expenditure. The results of this survey differ from those reported by Istvan in his 1959 study. Istvan found that 35 of the 48 firms he studied defined a capital expenditure as one that resulted in an increase in the fixed asset account. He found that 7 companies broadened that definition slightly to include extraordinary repairs or some special expenses directly related to a fixed asset. Only 6 firms (13 percent) used a broader definition of capital expenditure.[1] These firms deviated enough from the narrow concept to include such items as future commitments on long-term leases, research and development programs, and advertising expenditures.

Istvan suggested that, in view of the limited number of firms that used the broader definition, two conclusions were possible: first, that the concept did not go beyond the narrow definition, and second that traditional accounting training was responsible for such practices. Istvan was of the opinion that the latter conclusion was the more representative of the actual situation.[2]

The writer tends to agree with Istvan's conclusion. The present survey shows that more firms are now accepting some broad definitions. Of 198 responding firms, 160 (81 percent) use liberal concepts of capital expenditure. Only 38 firms (19 percent) limit capital expenditures to increases in the fixed asset accounts. Therefore, a conclusion that the concept of capital expenditure cannot go beyond the traditional definition is not justified.

When the total number of selected items is divided by the number of respondents, the average is about three items per firm. This average indicates that, although a majority of responding firms report using a broad definition, the practice is far from full recognition of the broad concept; it is only a small deviation from the conventional definition.

Although the survey indicates what items are considered capital expenditures, it does not reveal the methods used in evaluation. Recognition of an item as a capital expenditure item is the initial step required, but this does not necessarily mean that it is fully treated as a capital expenditure. For example, it is quite possible for a manager to admit that a major training and development program is a capital expenditure and yet apply some rule-of-thumb method and insufficient analysis to it.

Some observations are worthy of mention in this respect. In the companies interviewed, it was evident that application of capital expenditure analysis tools is usually limited to proposals that result in acquiring fixed assets.

Some departure from the classical definition of capital expenditures was noted in regard to working capital, long-term leases, and research and development expenditures. When a project requires an additional investment in working capital (cash, accounts receivable, and inventory), the additional investment is usually treated as part of the initial cash outflow. Long-term leases frequently have to be budgeted for according to the same procedure that is used for fixed assets.

Funds required for research and development are often included in the capital budget. Inclusion in the capital budget usually means that an appropriation request procedure must be followed to get approval before funds are committed. Although an expenditure may be included in the capital budget, the analysis often does not include the use of capital expenditure analysis tools. None of the companies that were interviewed evaluate their expenditures for training and development or advertising as capital expenditures.

A review of several capital expenditures manuals confirmed the above observations. These may be summarized as follows:

1. Capital expenditure analysis tools are applied mainly to fixed assets proposals.
2. The concept of capital expenditures usually covers permanent additions to working capital when they are part of a new facility, even though they are not capitalized by the accountant.
3. Expenditures for long-term leases are frequently included in the capital budget.
4. Research and development expenditures are frequently governed by the same (or similar) appropriations procedures that apply to capital expenditures.
5. Indications are that capital expenditure analysis tools would be applied extensively if satisfactory answers could be found to some questions about their effectiveness.

Maximization of Company Objectives. One question that has been raised is, How can the advanced discounted cash flow methods of capital expenditure analysis be made to maximize the correct objective of the firm? It is argued that the familiar net present value method does not adequately consider the important objective of maintaining a desirable rate of growth in earnings of common stock. Accordingly, selection of proposals with the highest net present value may lead to wide fluctuation in the market price of the stock, thereby maximizing the long run at the expense of the short run.

Top management, in its selection of capital expenditure projects, cannot ignore consideration of the desirable growth in earnings. Lerner and Rappaport recommend using the net present value method with an earnings growth requirement for evaluating capital expenditures. Selection of the proper planning horizon for capital expenditure analysis, they state, is a related problem that needs further study.[3]

Another argument is that advanced methods of capital expenditure analysis, usually stated in terms of individual projects, do not lend themselves to selecting the best set of capital expenditure proposals.

Obviously, all the answers to capital expenditure analysis have not yet been found. More research is needed to provide some answers regarding the proper and realistic objective (or objectives) of capital expenditures, the proper planning horizon for capital expenditure analysis, and the best mix of projects under conditions of capital rationing.

These and similar unanswered questions may slow the rate of use of capital expenditure analysis tools. However, the fact that some problems relative to capital expenditure analysis are not fully resolved should not prevent the recognition of situations in which the use of capital expenditure analysis tools would be profitable. It is logical to pursue the two fronts simultaneously—attempt to find solutions to the problems at hand, and explore other possible areas of application of capital expenditure analysis tools. The common practice of using combinations of methods for evaluating capital expenditures helps to reveal the different aspects of a proposal and their effect on the objectives of the firm.

Applications of a Broader Capital Expenditure Concept

Several benefits may accrue from a broader definition of capital expenditures. First, by recognizing as capital expenditures the costs of such things as advertising campaigns and training and development programs, a more realistic treatment may result. Such recognition will help to assure that equal treatment is given to all requests for long-term funds, regardless of their form, and may promote better and more efficient allocation of resources.

Second, such recognition may help to reduce the dependency on such arbitrary methods of allocating funds as spending as much as competitors. Third, such recognition may help to overcome the problem of indiscriminately cutting budgets for these expenditures under tight money conditions.

Following are some selected examples of possible applications of capital expenditure analysis tools.

Research and Development

The majority of expenditures for research and development (R&D) programs are in fact capital expenditures. The funds are spent now with the intention of gaining benefits in years to come. Recognizing R&D as a capital expenditure has many beneficial implications.

Frequently, researchers tend to continue working on a problem until a solution is found, regardless of economic considerations. Capital expenditure treatment implies that, for a business concern working for profit, the expected gains should exceed the costs. If a given product in a developmental stage is not expected when finally developed to produce sufficient revenue to cover its R&D expenditure, then development of that product should be discontinued. Such treatment will avoid spending effort and funds on marginal and unworthy projects. This, of course, does not mean that all support of pure research should be discontinued; it means only that if the objective of a certain research program is to produce profits, that program should be treated accordingly.

Capital expenditure analysis methods and techniques should be modified to apply to R&D expenditures. Much uncertainty surrounds R&D projects: costs are frequently underestimated, and the particular characteristics of the scientific and professional people working on R&D projects affect decisions in that area. However, the after-tax cost of an R&D project is less than the face value of the expenditure, if it is deducted for tax purposes. For example, for a firm taxed at 52 percent, a $10,000 expensed investment costs the company an after-tax amount of $4,800 ($10,000 multiplied by [1 - tax rate]). The analysis should be done after taxes so as to include the favorable tax treatment of R&D expenditures.

Advertising

Most major advertising campaigns are, in effect, capital expenditures. The expenditures made now are expected to be compensated for by benefits (increase in sales) extending over a number of years to come. In other words, a $2 million expenditure on an advertising campaign should be treated as a capital expenditure in the same manner as an investment in a new plant. Naturally, since advertising expenditures are usually immediately deductible for tax purposes, this $2 million expenditure does not represent the same burden as an equivalent amount invested in fixed assets. For a firm taxed at 52 percent, the $2 million expensed immediately costs only $960,000.

Although the cash outlay can easily be estimated, the benefits from an advertising campaign and their timing are extremely difficult to estimate. Even when advertising is recognized as a capital expenditure, the determination of the amount to invest in advertising is indeed a difficult problem, which cannot be fully resolved until a satisfactory answer is found to many other related questions. These questions include advertising alternatives, measurement of advertising productivity, and the role to be played by rate of return and cost of capital.

Despite all the difficulties associated with determining the amount to spend on advertising and of measuring the benefits, some capital expenditure analysis concepts—alternatives, futurity, increments, and cash flows—may be useful.[4] When analyzing a proposed advertising expenditure, it is beneficial to recognize it as a capital expenditure, to study it in view of other alternatives, to consider only future costs and future benefits, to determine the additional (incremental) costs and benefits, and to express all figures in terms of cash flows.

Although much uncertainty is associated with estimates related to an advertising investment, the treatment of advertising as a capital expenditure could increase the effectiveness of dollars spent on advertising. Furthermore, such treatment may direct efforts toward the development of better methods of measuring advertising productivity.

An approach that may be useful in analyzing advertising proposals is to ask, How much additional annual net cash flow do we have to receive over the life of the benefits to recover the advertising expenditure? For example, a $3,791 investment should result in annual cash flows of $1,000 for 5 years if the cost of capital is 10 percent and the advertising effect is assumed to last for 5 years. (One dollar received annually at 10 percent for 5 years has a present value of $3.791*; therefore, $3,791 would result from $1,000 annual cash flow.)

Training and Development

Except for minor short-term training efforts, expenditures for training and development of a firm's employees are in effect capital expenditures. The reason is simply that the expenditures (time taken from work, and other training costs) are paid now with the expectation of benefits from better performance for a number of years to come.

Having recognized that major training and development expenditures are in effect capital expenditures, the immediate problem of measuring the benefits is bound to exist since, so far, limited progress has been achieved in measuring such returns.

Because of not recognizing training and development expenditures as capital expenditures, and because of the difficulty of measuring the returns, some absurd practices are found among business firms. When a company is in good financial condition and the economy is expanding, expenditures for training and development are frequently made without careful analysis of their advisability, whereas, at the downswing of the economic cycle, expenditures for training and development–needed most at that time–are usually among the budget items cut. Perhaps if an acceptable way is found to measure the return on the training and development investment, more rational decisions will be made. Two things should be considered here. First, expenditures for training and development are usually deducted immediately for tax purposes,

*Derived from Table 12, p. 75.

which reduces the after-tax cost of the program. Second, the risk involved–that the employee might not stay with the company after he acquires the additional training–should be considered.

Working Capital

Working capital may refer to current assets (basically cash, accounts receivable, and inventory). Some projects require permanent increases in the company's working capital. As would be expected, some short-term credit may be extended when a capital expenditure proposal is accepted. The excess of current assets over current liabilities (also called net working capital) should be considered a capital expenditure and should be included in the cost of the investment.

This permanent addition to working capital is considered a capital expenditure because it is above a certain minimum, it is tied up for the life of the projects, and the returns (through sales, for example) are expected to be obtained over a number of years to come.

Working capital is usually expected to be recovered at the end of the life of a project. Therefore, it is not subject to depreciation, and no deduction of working capital is allowed for tax purposes. Also, the working capital released at the end of the project's life should be added to the cash flows in the last year.

Long-Term Leases

Long-term leases are popular with many firms. Unlike a regular lease that can be canceled within a short time (for example, an apartment lease could be canceled if proper notice is given prior to the annual renewal date), long-term leases for periods of 20 to 30 years are not cancelable or can be canceled only at a very high cost. Leases are popular because of many often-cited advantages. These include increased flexibility, inexpensive maintenance, reduced risk of obsolescence, allowance for 100 percent financing of an asset, off-the-balance-sheet financing, favorable tax treatment, avoidance of an after-acquired mortgage clause in a bond indenture, and avoidance of budgetary restrictions. A careful examination of these advantages reveals that, for the most part, they are illusory. However, three advantages are of substantive value:

1. Leases allow the financing of an asset without showing the asset and the related debt on the balance sheet of the lessee, since, from a legal view, he does not own the asset. If the funds are borrowed and the asset is subsequently purchased, both the debt and the asset will appear on the balance sheet. (Of course, the inclusion of more debt on the balance sheet may show

a less favorable financial position.) This advantage is only temporary, since both the investors and the accounting profession are increasingly advocating and requesting disclosure of long-term lease commitments.

2. Some budgetary restrictions may be avoided by leasing instead of purchasing an asset. This is also a temporary advantage, since many companies are restating their procedures to treat long-term leases as capital expenditures and to consider the required appropriation for the whole life of the lease. For example, a 20-year lease with \$100,000 rent requires an approved appropriation of \$2,000,000 (20 × \$100,000).

3. Leasing may be the only possible way of acquiring an asset.

Regardless of the advantages or disadvantages of long-term leases, if they are used they should be evaluated as capital expenditures. The decision to lease or buy an asset (for example, a building) is a capital expenditure decision. Leasing represents a long-term commitment from which the benefits (the use of the building) accrue over a number of years to come, and once the decision is made it is irreversible or it is reversible at a high cost.

To help reach the decision to lease or buy an asset, the net present value method could be used to determine the alternative with the least cost. Cash flows will be affected by the fact that rent and other expenses incurred by the lessee under a lease agreement are tax deductible, whereas, under purchase, only depreciation on depreciable items (for example, land could not be depreciated), maintenance costs, and other expenses are deductible for tax purposes.

Other Possible Applications

Capital expenditure analysis tools may be applied to various other situations. Examples of these situations are cited below.

Retirement of debt. At times, a corporation finds it advantageous to retire its long-term debt in advance of the maturity date. If funds are available and an outstanding bond issue has a higher interest rate, it might be beneficial to retire the debt. This is a capital expenditure decision since it involves paying now for future benefits (reduction of interest burden).

Refunding of debt. Refunding means replacing a long-term issue with a new long-term issue. When a corporation with a 6 percent bond issue outstanding sells a new 5 percent bond issue and retires the old one, the associated costs should be regarded as a capital expenditure. The decision involves expenditure now (overlapping interest payment, and retirement premium) in return for reduction of interest payments in years to come. Expenses resulting from the refunding of debt are usually tax deductible.

Miscellaneous. Other applications of capital expenditure analysis tools include: long-term purchase agreements, office rearrangement expenditures, projects required by an authority (air and water pollution controls), long-term investments in securities, abandonment or liquidation of assets, acquisitions or mergers, pricing, asset valuation, and dividend policy.

Conclusion

Capital expenditure analysis methods and techniques may be regarded as useful decision-making tools with a variety of applications. More research is needed to discover additional applications and to provide satisfactory answers to such questions as: What is the objective of the firm? What is the proper span of the planning horizon for capital expenditure analysis? What is the best way of selecting from among competing proposals under capital rationing conditions?

NOTES

1. Donald F. Istvan, "The Capital-Expenditure Decision-Making Process in Forty-eight Large Corporations" (D.B.A. dissertation, Indiana University School of Business, 1959), pp. 32–35.
2. Ibid., p. 35.
3. Eugene M. Lerner and Alfred Rappaport, "Limit DCF in Capital Budgeting," in *Capital Investment Series,* Part II (a bound set of reprints from the *Harvard Business Review*) (Boston: Harvard Graduate School of Business Administration, 1969), p. 6.
4. Joel Dean, "Does Advertising Belong in the Capital Budget?" *Journal of Marketing,* Vol. 30 (October 1966), p. 19.

APPENDIX A

Excerpts from
the Facilities Expenditures Planning
and Control Manual of the
Westinghouse Electric Corporation

Reproduced by courtesy of the Westinghouse Electric Corporation

SECTION I - PROJECT CONCEPTION

A. Definition

Facilities Expenditures include all expenditures resulting from projects involving the construction, purchase, rearrangement, or lease of land, buildings, machinery or equipment. "Expense" outlays of $10,000 or more for rearrangement or alterations to buildings or equipment are to be included, even if no capital expenditures are involved in the project.

B. Description

A project should include all expenditures associated with the objective to be accomplished. The scope of the project should therefore be broad enough to evaluate the total effect on the Division, Product Line, or the individual part to be produced. Decisions made on too narrow a scope may "lock-in" methods or flow to a point that subsequent projects cannot be economically justified. Furthermore, projects conceived too narrowly may necessitate future Appropriation Requests to obtain related items or services not considered originally.

Divisions, having established and outlined the full scope and size of projects, may choose to request funds in several stages until the project is completed. A series of checkpoints may aid in controlling expenditures, or reevaluating elements of risk as knowledge is developed. Indeed, checkpoints may be appropriate from time to time to insure that the strategic program is still needed.

When a project affects another Westinghouse Division's operations, either utilizing the second Division as a supplier or ceasing Interunit purchases (and conversely when the first Division intends to become a supplier or cease to be one), it is necessary that the project be evaluated on a Corporate rather than a Divisional basis. In these cases, the proper approach is for the Division initiating the project to solicit the required information from the affected Division to make valid comparisons and decisions. The Headquarters Manufacturing Staff will provide information and guidance in this area upon request.

C. Classification

Projects are segregated into two general categories: MAJOR projects in which the total of capital expenditure, appropriation expense and the total lease commitment is $1,000,000 or more; and ANNUAL projects involving total expenditures of less than $1,000,000. ALL projects are further classified according to the primary objective to be accomplished as follows:

Class 1

Volume Improvement -- Projects intended to increase capacity, or to manufacture new products, or to enter new businesses.

These projects will be a direct outgrowth of the Division's Business Planning and will require a complete financial analysis of sales, profits, and return-on-investment. In most cases, supporting information for ANNUAL Volume Improvement projects will be similar to that requested for MAJOR projects (See Section III).

Class 2

Product Improvement -- Projects intended to improve saleability of the product through quality improvement, line-broadening, or improvement in product performance, efficiency, or reliability.

These should be tied to the Division development programs and supported with engineering and marketing opinions regarding product deficiency, competitive standing and the advantages expected from the project.

Product Improvement projects may contain elements of Cost or Volume Improvement, or they may prevent decreases in volume or price. Engineering Development Labs should normally be included in this class.

Class 3

Cost Improvement -- Projects intended to reduce costs or expenses.

In tabulating savings, all reductions in labor, material, inventory, factory expense, managed costs, etc., should be included and the return-on-investment calculated accordingly. Also, consideration should be given to other hard-to-quantify advantages such as floor space savings, reduced need for critical skills, capacity margins in capacity-limited operations, or other significant benefits. Tabulations of savings should be clearly outlined for presentation if requested.

Divisions are encouraged to place heavy emphasis on Cost Improvement Projects in their annual programs.

Class 4

Other -- These projects to some extent must be appraised by evaluation of intangible factors. However, the financial advantages should be indicated when they exist. This class includes:

Service facilities such as offices, furniture, power plants, substations, water supply, and similar supporting services when the expenditure is not directly or primarily associated with expansion, product improvement, or cost reduction projects.

Facilities required for plant security and protection, improved working conditions, employe relations or welfare, or new facilities required by law such as those for control of smoke, fumes or steam pollution.

Forced replacements or restorations resulting from accidents, floods, and other insured casualties. Losses covered by insurance require no appropriation.

REPLACEMENT OF EQUIPMENT, FOR REASONS OTHER THAN LISTED IN CLASS 4 ABOVE, WHICH HAS MEASURABLE OPERATING COSTS ARE NOT TO BE INCLUDED IN CLASS 4, BUT RATHER SHOULD BE ENTERED AS CLASS 1, 2 OR 3 PROJECTS WITH WHATEVER RETURN THEY SHOW.

Class 5

Government-Owned Facilities -- Projects reimbursed by, and title vested with, the Government.

D. Considerations for Evaluating Projects

When evaluating a project, Divisions are urged to search out all possible areas of benefits, including direct and indirect labor, materials, factory expense, managed costs and reduced freight.

When a project results in the reduced amounts of inventory required, these reductions serve to offset the cash outflow. In effect a $20,000 inventory reduction on a $100,000 project means that only the $80,000 outlay needs be justified. There is a similar effect when present equipment is sold or traded in, further reducing the outlay to be justified. (See Appendix E, Example Form 34835).

The full manufacturing system should be carefully analyzed. The additional benefits of Cost Improvements are added capacity and reduced manufacturing cycle, and especially in growth businesses, these should be quantified and claimed as benefits.

On projects which involve additional and essentially duplicate facilities, the possibility of displacing present work from existing facilities (by subcontracting, routing to other less productive equipment, re-design of parts, or even line-pruning of low activity items) should be thoroughly examined.

The scope of the project should finally be determined by selecting the one of several alternatives which shows the most promise. (See Alternatives Appendix D.) All benefits (contrasted with minimum acceptable or conservative estimates) should then be specified on the Appropriation Request so that, at project completion, the savings and benefits realized can be compared against those originally documented.

E. General

1. Each Division, if it elects to do so, may include an annual project covering miscellaneous expenditures which may arise during the year but which are not foreseen at the time the Facilities Expenditure Plan is submitted. The dollar amount is not to exceed $25,000 for a Division. This miscellaneous expenditures project should be listed under Class 4 - Other, but may be substituted for projects in any class upon the Division Manager's approval.

2. Requirements for office furniture and equipment which are associated specifically with the project listed in Classes 1 through 5 should be included as part of the project. Routine additions and replacements for this type of facility are to be handled as a single project covering all requirements for the Division or Product Line, and shown as Class 4 - Other.

3. Leases are to be listed in the appropriate class (1 through 5) (See Section IV).

SECTION III - APPROPRIATION PROCEDURES

A. Development of Appropriation Requests

After Board approval of the Facilities Investment Plan, expenditures must be authorized by an approved Appropriation Request. Facilities expenditures requiring Executive Vice President's approval will be submitted on Appropriation Request Form 29067, along with supporting information as outlined in SECTION III, Part B.

In determining the facilities to be specified, Headquarters staff services should be utilized to the extent necessary. In matters involving land, buildings or real estate leases, the Real Estate Department must be contacted prior to forwarding an Appropriation Request. (Reference Management Guides MG-D25, MG-R20, MG-S20).

The Appropriation Request Form 29067 (page 1) serves as the routing sheet for the required approvals and contains basically the financial information from Form 3 along with a brief statement of the actions to be taken. If the project is not included on the Facilities Investment Plan, assign a new project number, following the last in the series on Form 3, even if the project is a substitution for an existing project.

The Appropriation Request Form 29067 (pages 2 and 3) serves as support information in addition to the financial data on the Strategic Project Evaluation Sheets. The Present Situation, details of Expenditures, Alternatives, Personnel Effects, and Basis of Confidence are to be explained in detail so as to preclude formal presentations to the Capital Expenditures Committee of most Appropriations in the $100,000 – $999,999 range. (Request for MAJOR projects are to be made by formal presentation in all cases.)

The Appropriation Detail – Form 29068 – serves to list each item in a manner to simplify subsequent E-Order preparation.

Evaluation of all projects, regardless of class, is to be performed using the following forms:
34835 - Strategic Project Evaluation Sheet
34836 - Strategic Project Evaluation - Worksheet A
34837 - Strategic Project Evaluation - Worksheet B
36163 - Computer Input Data Worksheet (instead of Worksheet B)

These are to accompany the Appropriation Request as outlined in SECTION III, Part B.

Incremental cash flows, both outlays and receipts, which are anticipated as a direct result of the project are listed on the forms in the years in which they occur. These flows are then used to calculate a discounted rate of return over the economic life of the project.

The minimum after tax rate of return, including Terminal Value for MAJOR projects, but excluding Terminal Value for all others, is 15%. However, Divisions are urged to concentrate on projects which have returns significantly larger than the minimum. Some Divisions have set self-imposed minimums of 20%, 25%, or even higher to pull their Division ROI above the 15% Corporate objective in the shortest possible time.

Detailed instructions for the completion of Forms involved in preparation of Appropriations are shown in Appendix B.

B. Submission & Approval (except for Substitutions, see Sec. III C.1.)

1. For Projects up to $50,000 (Not including Land)

Routing: Division General Manager

Data Required: Appropriation Request Form 29067
Appropriation Detail 29068
NOTE: Division may elect to authorize by E-Order only, in which case Form 29067 (Page 1) and Form 29068 may be eliminated. In this case, Form 29067 (pages 2 and 3) is still recommended.
Strategic Project Evaluation Sheet (SPES) Form 34835

Timing: Due dates established by Division General Manager

2. For Projects $50,000 to $99,999 (Not including Land)

Routing: Approvals required by Division General Manager, Executive Vice President and Vice President, Manufacturing.

Data Required: Six (6) copies each of:
Appropriation Request 29067
Appropriation Detail 29068
S.P.E.S. 34835

Timing: As required by Executive Vice President

Approval: Executive Vice President returns one signed copy to Division General Manager.

3. For Projects $100,000 to $999,999 (Not including Land)

Routing: Approvals required by Division General Manager, Executive Vice President, Vice President-Manufacturing, and, after review by Capital Expenditures Committee, by President.
NOTE: Capital Expenditures Committee consists of Vice Chairman, Planning (Committee Chm.); Vice President, Manufacturing (Committee Sec'y.); Vice President, Marketing; Vice President, Engineering; Vice President, Industrial Relations; Vice President & Treasurer.

Data Required: Six (6) copies each of:
Appropriation Request 29067
Appropriation Detail 29068
S.P.E.S. 34835

On occasion, Division General Manager may be invited to make a presentation to the Capital Expenditures Committee.

Timing: Six (6) weeks prior to the monthly Capital Expenditures Committee meeting date at which appropriation is to be reviewed, Divisions are requested to forward one PRELIMINARY unsigned copy of Appropriation Form 29067 (Page 1 only) to the Secretary, Capital Expenditures Committee.

Final data is to be furnished to the Executive Vice President in time to secure his approval and be forwarded to the Capital Expenditures Committee <u>two weeks</u> in advance of the meeting at which action is expected.

Approval: Capital Expenditures Committee reviews primarily the information on Appropriation Request Form 29067 (Pages 2 and 3). If Committee is in agreement, the Secretary transmits the Appropriation Request to the Company President. Notification of final approval is made by Secretary to Executive Vice President to the Division.

4. <u>For MAJOR Projects ($1,000,000 and over)</u>

Routing: Approval is required by Division General Manager, Executive Vice President, Vice President-Manufacturing, Capital Expenditures Committee, President, and Board of Directors.

Data Required: Twenty (20) copies of a brochure which include:
Title Page
Contents
Appropriation Request 29067
Appropriation Detail 29068
S.P.E.S. Forms 34835 and (if applicable) 34836
Market & Volume Projections
Price Realization & Market Penetration Objectives
Relation to on-going and future projects
Description of implementation and schedule of events
Organization Charts, manning schedule
Plant Layout
Other pertinent information

Divisions will be required to make both a preliminary and a formal presentation of MAJOR Projects to the Capital Expenditures Committee.

Timing: PRELIMINARY PRESENTATION is to be made to the Capital Expenditures Committee <u>three to six</u> months prior to formal submittal of MAJOR Projects. The purpose is to afford the Capital Expenditures Committee the opportunity to examine and discuss the basis on which the project is being planned.

This PRELIMINARY PRESENTATION will normally be accompanied with an Appropriation Request covering such critical items as Site options, long-lead-time equipment ordering, construction materials procurement, and other planning expenditures. Such a preliminary review is especially important where real estate purchases, expiration of leases, or acquisition of major data processing equipment is involved.

The final data (brochure) is to be furnished to the Executive Vice President in time to be approved and forwarded to the Capital Expenditures Committee two weeks prior to the monthly meeting in which the FORMAL PRESENTATION is to be made.

Approval: Following this FORMAL PRESENTATION, the Capital Expenditures Committee approval of the Appropriation Request is forwarded to the President, then to the Board of Directors.

Notification of final approval is given to the Secretary, Capital Expenditures Committee, who advises the Executive Vice President by letter (copies to President, and Vice President & Controller).

The original signed copy of the approved Appropriation is forwarded to the Division by the Executive Vice President and a copy of the approval is forwarded to the office of the Vice President & Controller.

5. For ANNUAL Projects involving Land (up to $1,000,000)

Routing: Approval is required by Division General Manager, Executive Vice President, Vice President-Manufacturing, Capital Expenditures Committee, President and Board of Directors.

Data Required: Twenty (20) copies each of:
Appropriation Request 29067
Appropriation Detail 29068
S.P.E.S. 34835
Such other information (similar to that for a MAJOR) as is applicable.

Timing: Six (6) weeks prior to the monthly Capital Expenditures Committee meeting date at which the Appropriation is to be presented, Divisions are to forward one PRELIMINARY unsigned copy of Appropriation Form 29067 (Page 1 only) to the Secretary, Capital Expenditures Committee. The Description of Project (or in lieu of this, a cover letter) should state briefly the real estate aspects (land or buildings to be purchased or leased) and the situation regarding hiring of people-in-place. This will enable Headquarters Real Estate and Industrial Relations Departments to complete their part of the negotiation before the Appropriation is included on the Capital Expenditures Committee agenda.

Final data related to the Appropriation is to be submitted to the Executive Vice President in time to secure his approval and be forwarded to the Capital Expenditures Committee two weeks prior to the meeting at which final approval is expected.

Approval: Following the review and approval by the Capital Expenditures Committee, the Appropriation Request is forwarded to the President, then to the Board of Directors.

Notification of final approval is given to the Secretary, Capital Expenditures Committee, who advises the Executive Vice President by letter (copies to President, and Vice President & Controller.)

The original signed copy of the approved Appropriation is forwarded to the Division by the Executive Vice President and a copy of the approval is forwarded to the office of the Vice President & Controller.

6. Procedures for Foreign Subsidiaries

Majority owned Foreign Subsidiaries will establish local facilities-expenditures procedures to be approved by the (W) Company President, and the Capital Expenditures Committee.

7. Acquisition of Going Businesses

Acquisition of Going Businesses in any amount must be authorized by the Executive Vice President, the Capital Expenditures Committee, President, and by the Board of Directors. Final approval is by resolution of the Board of Directors. Prior approval must be obtained from the Vice Chairman, Planning, before approaching a potential acquisition candidate. To assist line management in the discharge of their responsibilities and to coordinate the review of acquisition proposals, the Director, Corporate Development, will appoint a member of his staff to act as coordinator of material for Capital Expenditures Committee review. This will normally require notification to the office of the Vice President, Manufacturing, of the existence of agenda items two weeks before the Capital Expenditures Committee meeting, and distribution of supporting information to each member of the Committee one week before the Capital Expenditures Committee meeting.

8. Projects involving Acquisition of Assets & Concurrent Hiring of Personnel

On occasion Division seeks to improve operations by purchasing or leasing significant assets and the concurrent hiring of significant numbers of personnel from another company, but the seller continues to function as an autonomous company.

Projects of this nature will be the subject of a FORMAL PRESENTATION to the Capital Expenditures Committee. Documentation and Routing should follow the pattern in Part 5 above.

9. Manufacturing Operations in Puerto Rico

When a Division is considering the manufacture of some of its product in Puerto Rico, the Strategic Project Evaluation Sheet should be prepared the same as for a domestic venture, including taxes at the U.S. Rate. Puerto Rican projects will be evaluated on this basis against the corporate target of 15% return on investment.

If the Puerto Rican venture, when implemented, would have a significant effect on the work load or financial performance of the U.S. Division, an analysis should be presented which shows the consolidated effect on the Division statements as part of the justification of the project.

C. General

1. Substitutions

It is recognized that conditions may arise which make it desirable to substitute new projects for those described in the Facilities Investment Plan.

"Substitution for projects within protected funds" does not apply to MAJORS since the Board of Directors does not extend its authorizations beyond ANNUAL programs during its year-end consideration of Facilities Investment Plans.

ANNUAL projects may be substituted for each other by combining smaller projects or dividing larger ones within the funds protected by the approved Plan and the Mid-Year Review. The dollar amount on the Facilities Investment Plan or the dollar amount on the substitute project being requested, whichever is larger, will establish the approvals required.

For certain substitutions additional approvals beyond usual requirements must be obtained as follows:

a. President's approval required for appropriation requests in the range $50,000 - $99,999 substituted for projects which were originally $100,000 to $999,999.

b. Executive Vice President and Vice President-Manufacturing, approval required for projects less than $50,000 which are substituted for projects of a different class, or for projects originally $100,000 to $999,999.

2. Unforeseen Projects

Projects for which funds were NOT included on the Facilities Investment Plan, and for which funds cannot be obtained by substitution, will be routed to the Executive Vice President and the Vice President-Manufacturing for appropriate action.

3. Review of Open MAJOR Projects

Approximately once per year, Divisions will be invited to a Capital Expenditures Committee Meeting to review status of open MAJOR Appropriations. The purpose of these reviews is to keep the Committee abreast of progress and developments which may affect funds flow or have potential cross-influences with other Divisions' Major Projects.

4. Appropriation Revisions

Changes in scope or expenditures on current or prior years appropriations will require an Appropriation Revision for:

a. Over-runs - when increases of 5% or $1,000,000, whichever is less, are anticipated. The revised dollar amount will determine the approvals required in line with SECTION III (B).

b. Under-runs - when the project is substantially decreased or cancelled. The dollar amount preceding the revision will determine the approvals required in line with SECTION III (B).

c. Changes in scope - where the scope of the project changes materially, even though the expenditures do not.

5. Appropriation Closings and Extensions

Appropriations should be closed promptly by the Division upon completion of the project.

In the local administration of appropriations, procedures will be established to assure that no commitments will be made against an appropriation that cannot be completed by the closing date.

No expenditures can be applied to an appropriation after the closing date, unless extension of closing date has been authorized as follows:

a. Division Manager may authorize an extension in any appropriation where the extended date is not more than two (2) years from final authorization date of the original appropriation.

b. Executive Vice President approval is required to extend closing dates where the extended date is more than two (2) years from the final authorization date of the original appropriation. Requests for such extensions are to be made by letter, with a copy to the Division Controller and the Secretary, Capital Expenditures Committee.

6. E-Orders

Expenditure (E) Orders are used to commit expenditures under the authority of an approved Appropriation. See the Controllers Manual for detailed instructions. (See Appendix C).

EVALUATION OF INVESTMENT PROPOSALS
(Excerpt from Controllers Manual 3-5-1.2)

1. General

A. The basic criterion for evaluation of investment proposals - particularly those involving facilities expenditures - is the net financial impact upon the Corporation. Thus, such evaluations should include analyses of estimated cash expenditures and cash receipts resulting from the proposal.

B. The pertinent expression of financial results is Return on Investment, over the total life of the project. Return on Investment, in the context of project evaluation, is the rate of interest (productivity of money) as developed using the Discounted Cash Flow (DCF) technique.

C. The corporate "minimum" for project acceptance is 15% - after federal income taxes.

D. This manual subject is intended to provide instructions for the preparation of financial analyses and evaluation of investment projects.

2. Framework for Analysis

A. Cash Flows

The relevant data for consideration of the financial impact are the incremental cash flows resulting from the project. Cash flows are the projected cash receipts and outlays made, and may differ from revenues and expenses expressed on financial statements, which are prepared on an "accrual" basis in order to properly reflect earnings or profits. Thus, incremental cash flows are those which occur (or do not occur) as a direct result of a particular project or course of action.

B. Project Life

The life, or duration, of a project is its economic life. Such life begins with the basic decision to make an expenditure. In practice, this decision is considered to be made at the time the appropriation request is to be approved. The economic life continues until:

1. The project will be superseded by changes in end-use markets, product design, or methods of manufacture.

2. The projected life is so far into the future that uncertainty precludes the use of discrete financial data.

Economic life, for evaluation of facilities projects, is limited to ten full years, with recognition of remaining or future benefits through calculation of "Terminal Value."

C. Terminal Value

The "terminal" value of a project is the remaining potential value at the end of the economic life, or ten years, whichever is less.

The basis for actual calculation of terminal value is the projected cash flows that occur upon termination of the project. The procedure for determining these cash flows is dependent upon the economic life of the project. Specifically:

1. Where the economic life is <u>less than</u> ten years:

Terminal Value = A. The value of any working capital which will be liquidated at the end of the project.

plus

B. The current tax rate times the undepreciated cost of capital assets employed in the project. (This represents the remaining "tax-shield" resulting from either depreciating or retiring such capital equipment.)

2. Where the economic life is <u>greater than</u> ten years:

Terminal Value = A. Tenth-year after-tax earnings before depreciation (Strategic Project Evaluation Sheet - Line 27 minus Line 28 - See page 31a), times 5.4,

minus

B. The cost of replacing all machinery and equipment, times .4.

The above decimal factors reflect the "value" as would be determined by a potential purchaser, based upon discounted cash flows, at 15% for ten years. The factors give recognition to both the tax-shield from depreciating existing and new equipment, as well as the fact that replacement occurs at a <u>future</u> date.

3. Strategic Project Evaluation Sheet - Form 34835 (See page 31a)

A. General

The strategic Project Evaluation Sheet (SPES) is designed to present the pertinent financial data for use in evaluating strategic projects. Submission of this form is required in support of appropriation requests for $50,000 or more. <u>Use</u> of the form, however, is anticipated to include evaluation of alternatives such as "make-or-buy" and projects where the investment is of an "expense" nature, and submission, therefore, is not required.

The SPES is designed to present both the Incremental Cash Flows that are expected to occur as a direct result of a project, for use in evaluation purposes, as well as the net effect upon financial statements for each year of the project.

B. Form Preparation

1. Indicate the nature of the project by placing X's in the appropriate squares, and completing the descriptive information. "Product Line" refers to the product line(s) affected by the project. The appropriation and project numbers must agree with those shown on the Appropriation Request - Form 29067 and the Facilities Investment Plan - Form 3.

2. "Prior To" column should reflect all cash flows which have occurred prior to the year in which the Appropriation Request is expected to be approved.

3. "Total Project" column reflects the total, for each line, of columns 1 through 10 plus the "Prior To" column.

4. Line Definitions:

Lines 1-9 — Strategic expenses, as related to investment projects, are of two types and should be considered independently. These are:

1. Those required to initiate the project (non-recurring expenses) - such as initial product and manufacturing development, major rearrangement, introductory advertising campaigns, etc. (Such items may or may not be part of Schedule D shown on the Appropriation Request.) These items are to be reflected on Lines 1-5. Lines 6-8 may be used to reflect expenses which may not appear on the Profit Center's Statement #6, but are required in support of the project. (R&D contracts, additional field sales personnel, etc.) Lines 6-8 may also be used as a memo to expenses included in Lines 1-5.

2. Those required to sustain the project, after initiation, including such items as product and cost improvement programs, normal advertising programs, etc. These recurring strategic expenses should be reflected in the Incremental IBT, shown on Line 25.

Lines 10-13 — Record the capital portion of the Appropriation Request, segregated to the appropriate lines. Use Line 13 for office equipment, etc. Show actual expenditures for each year. (The timing of expenditures and capitalizations may differ.)

Line 14 — Indicate the salvage value of any present equipment which will be available as a result of the project. (Show amount in the year of disposition.)

Line 15 — Extra line - may be used for memo purposes.

Line 16 — Sum of Lines 10-13, less Line 14.

Lines 17-19 — Indicate incremental increases in "non-capital" assets which are a direct result of the project. Show incremental increases (changes), for each year. Decreases are to be shown on Line 32 as return of working capital.

Line 20 — Record incremental increases in trade payables and product warranties (Acct. 2230, 2640) resulting from the project.

Line 21 — Sum of Lines 17-19, less Line 20.

Line 22 Indicate the difference, if any, between the purchase price and book value of any going business acquired (Goodwill). Record the book values of capital equipment and working capital on the appropriate lines above.

Line 23 Sum of Lines 9, 16, 21 and 22.

Line 24 Record Incremental Sales Billed from Worksheet A - Form 34836, Line 7.

Line 25 Record Incremental IBT from Worksheet A, Line 26.

Line 26 Record Net Cost Improvement amounts from Worksheet A, Line 27.

Line 27 Income Before Taxes (before Depr.) equals Line 25 plus Line 26. This line represents the incremental "cash flow earnings" in contrast to IBT on a #6 Statement basis, which reflects both the additional expenses shown on Line 9 and straight-line depreciation.

Line 28 Calculate the incremental federal income taxes applicable to the IBT reported on Line 27. Use tax rate in effect at time of preparation for all years.

Line 29 The Strategic Expense Tax Adjustment reflects the reduction in tax liability arising from strategic expenses reported on Line 9. Calculate by multiplying the current tax rate times Line 9 for each year.

Line 30 Accelerated Depreciation Tax Adjustment reflects the reduction of tax liability based on the accelerated depreciation method even though straight-line depreciation is used for "Book" purposes. Calculate the annual depreciation amount per Controllers Manual subject 3-16-1.1. The following decimal factors may be applied to the capitalized cost of equipment to determine annual depreciation tax adjustment amount on the double-declining balance basis.

Years	Commercial Divisions	Electronics Divisions
1	.083 x Tax Rate	.125 x Tax Rate
2	.153 x Tax Rate	.219 x Tax Rate
3	.127 x Tax Rate	.164 x Tax Rate
4	.106 x Tax Rate	.123 x Tax Rate
5	.088 x Tax Rate	.092 x Tax Rate
6	.074 x Tax Rate	.069 x Tax Rate
7	.062 x Tax Rate	.052 x Tax Rate
8	.051 x Tax Rate	.039 x Tax Rate
9	.043 x Tax Rate	
10	.036 x Tax Rate	
11	.030 x Tax Rate	
12	.024 x Tax Rate	

Factors for calculating the accelerated depreciation tax adjustment amounts for buildings with 45 year depreciable life are as follows:

Year	Factor
1	.022 x Tax Rate
2	.043 x Tax Rate
3	.042 x Tax Rate
4	.040 x Tax Rate
5	.038 x Tax Rate
6	.036 x Tax Rate
7	.035 x Tax Rate
8	.033 x Tax Rate
9	.032 x Tax Rate
10	.030 x Tax Rate

Line 31 Investment Credit, per Controllers Manual 3-16-3.1, shall be shown in the year each capital item is capitalized.

Line 32 Return of Working Capital and/or Terminal Value. Report any reduction in Working Capital (current assets minus current liabilities) in the year of occurrence. Report Terminal Value (see page 22) in tenth year, or last year of economic life.

Line 33 Cash Flow - Receipts may be defined as the after-tax "operating benefits" plus any tax reductions due to depreciation charges, strategic expenses, and investment credit, plus return or liquidation of working capital items. Calculation equals Line 27 minus Line 28, plus Lines 29, 30, 31 and 32.

Line 34 Net Cash Flows are the net of Line 23 - Cash Flow - Expenditures and Line 33 - Cash Flow - Receipts, and therefore may be negative in the first year(s) (net cash outflows) and positive in later years (net cash inflows). These Net Cash Flows are the amounts to be discounted to determine the rate of return of the project.

Line 35 Memo: Straight Line Depreciation reflects the depreciation amounts that will appear on Statement #6 as a result of the project, and will therefore be used in determining I.A.T. - net cash flows.

Line 36 Project I.A.T. reflects the impact of the project, by year, upon the division's I.A.T. (Statement #6 basis). Calculation equals Line 27 less Lines 9 and 35, times (1 - Current Tax Rate) plus Line 31 - Investment Credit.

Line 37 Corporate Investment (balance sheet basis) represents the impact of the project upon the division's Corporate Investment (Statement #4 basis). This effect is calculated by accumulating projected changes in assets and liabilities as itemized above, plus changes in other items not detailed, such as Cash - Oper. Reqm't, Accrued Payrolls, etc.

Line 38 Percent Return on Investment. This is calculated by dividing the I.A.T. reported on Line 36 by the Corporate Investment - Line 37 for each year.

Line 39 Indicate total I.A.T. of the product line(s) affected by the project (including the effect of the project). Show in Prior Year column the I.A.T. of the affected product line(s) for the calendar year preceding the Appropriation Request.

Line 40 When the project is the acquisition of a going business, indicate in the Description column the number of shares (or equivalent - see Note below) used in the acquisition. Report earnings per share for each year (I.A.T. ÷ No. of Shares).

Line 41 Line 39 ÷ Total Sales of Product Line - including effect of project.

Line 42 Return on Investment (Statement #6 basis) Line 39 divided by the Corp. Investment for the product line. This line is optional, and may be omitted if data is not readily available.

Line 43 Percent Return on Investment (Discounted Cash Flow Method - Excluding Terminal Value). Record the percentage developed from Worksheet B - Form 34837, or from Message Reply received from the Tele-Computer Center.

Line 44 Same as Line 43 - including terminal value.

NOTE: When cash is used in the acquisition of a going business, determine the "equivalent" number of shares by dividing the purchase price by the current market price-per-share of Westinghouse common stock at the time of preparation.

4. Worksheet A (Strategic Project Evaluation) - Form 34836A (See page 27b)

A. General

Worksheet A is provided for the development of the operating data recorded on the SPES. Submission of Worksheet A is recommended in support of the SPES.

The basic approach, in preparing Worksheet A, is to identify:

1. The projected sales, costs and resultant IAT that would occur if the project were not undertaken.
2. The benefits anticipated from the project - in terms of additional or "protected" sales, reduced cost levels, and resultant IAT and cash flows.
3. The projected sales, costs and resultant IAT that will occur if the project is undertaken.

B. Form Preparation

1. Sales Data

Line 1 Base Sales are the projected sales of the product line(s) affected by the project - at current price levels. This is intended to reflect anticipated changes in physical volume (without the project), after considering changes in market size and competitive factors influencing Westinghouse penetration of the market.

Line 2 Anticipated price changes (in dollars) applicable to Line 1. This represents the effect of projected price-level changes upon the base volume, excluding any changes expected to result from the project. Show reductions in price levels as contra (*).

Line 3 Total Base Sales are the projected total dollars of sales of the product line - excluding any benefits from the project. (Line 1 plus or minus Line 2).

Line 4 Incremental Project Sales are the sales which result directly from the project - at constant price levels (current price, or price in first year of sale). This line will reflect the projected volume levels of the sales. Incremental sales for volume improvement projects are resultant sales in excess of the current manufacturing capacity of the product line. Incremental sales for product improvement projects are those in excess of the base sales, shown on Line 1. For cost improvement projects, incremental sales will be zero - unless the cost improvement is expected to have an impact upon price and/or volume levels. In the latter case, only the volume impact should be reflected on Line 4. Price changes are reported on Lines 5 and 6, as explained below.

Line 5 Resulting price changes - project sales are forecasted price changes (in dollars), applicable to Line 4, resulting from the project. Show reductions as contra (*).

Line 6 Resulting price changes - total base sales is the effect, upon the total base sales on Line 3, of price changes resulting from the project. Show reductions as contra (*).

Line 7 Total incremental sales (Line 4 ± Lines 5 and 6) represents the total additions to the total base sales on Line 3. This represents (1) added volume, and (2) price appreciation or depreciation on both the added volume and the total base sales, which occur as a direct result of the project.

Line 8 Total sales (Line 3 plus Line 7) represents the projected total sales of the product line(s) including the effect of the project.

Line 9 Base product costs are the anticipated costs of producing the base volume indicated on Line 1. The base product costs shall include the effects of anticipated cost "creep" as well as "routine" net cost improvements. Exclude, however, any changes resulting from the project.

Line 10 Reduction in base product costs - direct labor reflects net cost improvements, in the direct labor portion of base product costs on Line 9, which are a direct result of the project. Indicate amount as contra (*).

Line 11 Reduction in base product costs - direct material is as Line 10, net cost improvements in the direct material portion of Line 9, resulting from the project.

Line 12 Reduction in base product costs - other. Same as Lines 10 and 11 for all other product costs.

Line 13 Incremental project product costs are the increases in product costs, associated with the incremental project sales, on Line 4. Calculate and record costs at levels which include net cost reductions resulting from the project, as well as projected "creep" in the "reduced" costs.

Line 14 Total product costs (Line 9, plus Lines 10, 11, 12 and 13). Record the total product costs of the product line(s) - including the effect of the project. Total is algebraic sum, reflecting the base cost, less improvements in the base, plus increases (at new cost levels) associated with any incremental volume (Line 4).

Line 15 Base committed and managed costs (Division Control), is the projected total of all managed and committed costs required to achieve the base sales volume (Line 1). Projections should include both the effect of "creep" and "routine" net cost improvements - excluding any cost changes which are the result of the project. Non-divisional costs (group and corporate) shall be omitted from this line.

Line 16 Reduction in base costs - due to project is the projected net cost improvement in any of the committed and managed costs on Line 15, resulting directly from the project. Show only the net cost change in the base level of costs. Increases (if any) associated with the project will be shown on Lines 16 through 19. Show net reductions as contra (*).

Line 17 Non-recurring strategic expense - due to project, represents those expenses, of a non-recurring nature (see paragraph 3.B.4., page 23) required to initiate the project.

Line 18 Depreciation (S.L. basis) - project facilities, is the straight-line depreciation on all capital assets acquired as a result of the project.

Line 19 Incremental project recurring committed and managed costs, represents increases in both operating and strategic costs - of a recurring nature - required to sustain the project. Non-divisional costs shall be omitted from this line.

Line 20 Non-divisional control costs. Calculate these costs as outlined in the current Planning Procedures Book. Where the project is to create a new division, or the acquisition of a going business, the Controller for the appropriate Executive

Vice-President will assist in developing this data. This calculation is used to develop projected #6 Statement results, and is omitted in developing cash-flow data.

Line 21 Total committed and managed costs. (Line 15 minus Line 16, plus Lines 17 through 20). Calculation is basically the same as for Line 14. Total is the algebraic sum of Lines 15 through 20, and represents the projected total of committed and managed costs - including the effect of the project.

Line 22 Total IBT of product line. (Line 8 minus 14 and 21). Calculation represents the IBT that will appear on financial statements during each of the years of the project life.

Line 23 Federal income taxes. Calculate for each year as Line 22 times current tax rate.

Line 24 Investment credit. Reflect appropriate investment credit (Controllers Manual 3-16-3.1) applicable to capital assets acquired as a direct result of the project.

Line 25 Total IAT of product line (Line 22, minus Line 23, plus Line 24). This is the IAT for the total product line(s), including the effect of the project, as will appear on Statement #6.

Line 26 Incremental IBT of project. (Line 7 minus Lines 13 and 19). This calculation represents the incremental recurring benefits resulting from the project, and therefore excludes non-recurring strategic expenses and depreciation charges, which are considered separately.

Line 27 Net cost improvement from project. (Lines 10, 11, 12 and 16). Represents reductions in base product, committed, and managed costs, resulting from the project.

Line 28 Total IBT of project (Line 26 plus 27, minus Lines 17 and 18). Represents total change in IBT (as reported on Statement #6) resulting from the project.

Line 29 Federal income taxes. (Line 28 times current tax rate)

Line 30 Investment credit. Same as Line 24.

Line 31 Total IAT of project. (Line 28 minus Line 29, plus Line 30).

Line 32 Memo: Accelerated depreciation on project facilities. This is provided to facilitate calculation of annual accelerated depreciation amounts, for cash flow analysis, on capital assets acquired as a result of the project. (See 3-16-1.1 and 3-5-1.2, par. 3.B.4.)

5. Worksheet B (Strategic Project Evaluation) Form 34837 (See page 31c)

A. General

Worksheet B is provided for use in determining the rate of return of the project on a Discounted Cash Flow (DCF) basis. The basic technique is to "discount" each year's net cash flows by application of the decimal factors on the form. This process of discounting gives recognition to the "time-value" of money, attaching greatest importance to cash flows which occur in the earlier years of project life.

B. Rate of Return

The sum of the discounted cash flows, at a specified interest rate is the "Present Value" of such flows. The Net Present Value of a project is the excess of the Present Value of Receipts over the Present Value of Expenditures at a specified interest rate.

The rate of return on a project may be defined and calculated in either of two ways:

1. That rate of interest, at which, upon application of the discount factors, results in a Net Present Value of zero.

2. That rate of interest, at which the Present Value of the receipts is equal to the Present Value of the expenditures.

The above definitions are synonomous.

Worksheet B is designed so that calculation of the rate of return may be accomplished using either definition. Use of the form may be circumvented through Computer Input-Form 36163 (see below) which may be transmitted to Tele-Computer Center for calculation.

C. Form Preparation

1. Calculation based upon Net Present Value

Record the Net Cash Flows, with appropriate sign, from Line 34 Years 1-10 of the Strategic Project Evaluation Sheet, in either the Actual Expenditures or Actual Receipts column. (Factors are the same).

Multiply these Net Cash Flows by the discount factors shown in the percentage column selected as the approximate rate of return, (see paragraph 5.C.2. below) entering the products in the value column, with appropriate sign.

The rate of return for the project is the rate where the sum of the extended (discounted) Net Cash Flows equals zero. If the sum is either positive or negative, the correct rate may be calculated by interpolation to zero. (See example of interpolation - paragraph 5.D.)

2. Calculation based upon Equal Present Values

Record Cash Flow-Expenditures (Line 23-SPES) and Cash-Flow-Receipts (Line 33-SPES) in the Actual Expenditures and Receipts columns. Calculate totals A, B, and C.

Calculate A/B and A/C ratios, and enter in blocks provided.

The approximate rate to use for discounting may be determined as follows:

a. Divide amount in total (c) by ten years or the economic life, whichever is less.

b. Divide the result, above, by the total (a). This decimal amount will be the approximate rate, which may be used as a starting point for discounting.

After discounting Actual Expenditures and Receipts, (at the same rate) calculate the A/B and A/C ratios, and enter in the blocks provided. The correct rate is the one where the ratio is equal to 1.00. If the ratio developed is greater than 1.00, repeat the extension at a lower rate. If the ratio developed is less than 1.00, repeat at a higher rate. Perform these calculations until the ratio is both over and under 1.00 for both the A/B and A/C ratios - then interpolate to find the rate of return. (See below.)

D. Interpolation for Calculating Rate of Return

The following is an illustration of interpolation, to be used after A/B and A/C ratios have been calculated.

	Discount Rate	A/B Ratio
1. Ratio greater than 1.00	20	1.07
2. Ratio less than 1.00	15	.91
3. Difference	5	.16
4. 1.00 minus ratio (Line 2)		.09
5. Line 4 divided by Line 3		.56 (.09 ÷ .16)
6. Line 5 times difference in discount rates (Line 3)		2.80 (.56 x 5.0)
7. Rate of Return Lower rate of discount (Line 2) plus Line 6		17.80 (15.0 + 2.80)

6. Computer Input Data Worksheet - Form 36163 (See page 31d)

A. General

Manual calculation of rate of return can be eliminated by transmitting cash flow data to the Tele-Computer Center. This transmission can be sent from any standard Westinghouse teletype station. The computer program will calculate the rate to the nearest tenth of one percent. Priority is such that no more than five minutes delay should occur.

B. Computer Input Data Instructions

Form 36163 uses Net Cash Flows - Line 34 of the Strategic Project Evaluation Sheet. Computer input instructions are printed on page 33 of this manual.

WESTINGHOUSE FORM 34835 B

STRATEGIC PROJECT EVALUATION SHEET

(DOLLARS IN THOUSANDS)

DATE

FACILITIES ☐ DEVELOPMENT ☐	OTHER ☐	MAJOR ACQUISITION ☐	COST IMPROVEMENT ☐ REPLACEMENT ☐	VOLUME IMPROVEMENT ☐ PRODUCT IMPROVEMENT ☐	DIVISION	PRODUCT LINE	APPROPRIATION NO.	PROJECT NO.

LINE NO.	DESCRIPTION OF EXPENDITURES	PRIOR TO 19	TOTAL PROJECT	(1) 19	(2) 19	(3) 19	(4) 19	(5) 19	(6) 19	(7) 19	(8) 19	(9) 19	(10) 19
1	APPROPRIATION EXPENSE												
2	MANUFACTURING - OTHER												
3	ENGINEERING												
4	MARKETING												
5	ADMINISTRATION												
6	OTHER												
7													
8													
9	**TOTAL DIV. - STRATEGIC EXPENSE**												
10	LAND												
11	BUILDING												
12	MACHINERY & EQUIPMENT												
13	OTHER (SPECIFY)												
14	LESS - SALVAGE VALUE PRESENT EQUIP.												
15													
16	**NET CAPITAL EXPENDITURES**												
17	ADDITIONAL ACCTS. RECEIVABLE												
18	INCREASED INVENTORY REQ.												
19	OTHER (SPECIFY)												
20	LESS: TRADE PAYABLES OR PROD. GUAR.												
21	**NET WORKING CAPITAL**												
22	PURCHASE PRICE OF GOING BUSINESS												
23	**CASH FLOW - EXPENDITURES**												

LINE NO.	DESCRIPTION OF RECEIPTS	PRIOR TO 19	TOTAL PROJECT	(1) 19	(2) 19	(3) 19	(4) 19	(5) 19	(6) 19	(7) 19	(8) 19	(9) 19	(10) 19
24	INCREMENTAL SALES BILLED												
25	INCREMENTAL I.B.T. (BEFORE DEPR.)												
26	NET COST IMPROVEMENT (BEFORE DEPR.)												
27	INCOME BEFORE TAXES (BEFORE DEPR.)												
28	FEDERAL INCOME TAXES												
29	STRATEGIC EXPENSE TAX ADJ.												
30	ACC DEPREC. TAX ADJ.												
31	INVESTMENT CREDIT												
32	RET. OF WORKING CAP. AND/OR T.V.												
33	**CASH FLOW - RECEIPTS**												
34	**NET CASH FLOWS**												
35	MEMO: STRAIGHT LINE DEPREC.												
36	PROJECT I.A.T. (S.L. BASIS)												
37	CORP. INVESTMENT (BALANCE SHEET BASIS)		X										
38	PERCENT RETURN ON INVESTMENT		X										
39	TOTAL I.A.T. OF PRODUCT LINE (S.L. BASIS)		X										
40	EPS (ACQUISITIONS) SHARES		X										
41	PERCENT OF SALES BILLED		X										
42	PERCENT RETURN ON INVESTMENT		X										
43	PERCENT RETURN ON INVESTMENT - (DISCOUNTED CASH FLOW METHOD - EXCLUDING TERMINAL VALUE - A/B)	X		X	X	X	X	X	X	X	X	X	X
44	PERCENT RETURN ON INVESTMENT - (DISCOUNTED CASH FLOW METHOD - INCLUDING TERMINAL VALUE - A/C)	X		X	X	X	X	X	X	X	X	X	X

WESTINGHOUSE FORM 34836A

STRATEGIC PROJECT EVALUATION
(DOLLARS IN THOUSANDS)

WORKSHEET A

LINE NO. (L)	DESCRIPTION	PRIOR TO 19	TOTAL PROJECT	(1) 19	(2) 19
1	Base Sales (Excl. Project at Current Prices)				
2	Anticipated Price Changes				
3	Total Base Sales (L1 + L2)				
4	Incremental Project Sales (At Current Prices)				
5	Resulting Price Changes - Project Sales				
6	- Total Base Sales				
7	Total Incremental Sales (L4 + or — L5 & L6)				
8	TOTAL SALES (L3 + L7)				
9	Base Product Costs				
10	Reduction in Base Product Costs - Direct Labor				
11	- Direct Material				
12	- Other				
13	Incremental Project Product Costs				
14	TOTAL PRODUCT COSTS (L9 — L10 thru 12 + L13)				
15	Base Committed and Managed Costs (Div. Control)				
16	Reduction in Base Costs - Due to Project				
17	Non-Recurring Strategic Expense - Due to Project				
18	Depreciation (S.L. Basis) - Project Facilities				
19	Incremental Project Recurring Comm. & Mgd. Costs				
20	Non-Divisional - Control Costs				
21	TOTAL COMM. & MGD. COSTS (L15 — L16 + L17 thru 20)				
22	Total IBT of Product Line (L8 — L14 and L21)				
23	Federal Income Taxes (L22 Times Current Tax Rate)				
24	Investment Credit (Project Facilities)				
25	TOTAL I.A.T. OF PRODUCT LINE (L22 — L23 + L24)				
26	Incremental IBT of Project (L7 — L13 and L19)				
27	Net Cost Improvement From Project (Sum of L10, 11, 12 & 16)				
28	Total IBT of Project (L26 + L27 — L17 & L18)				
29	Federal Income Taxes (L28 Times Current Tax Rate)				
30	Investment Credit (Project Facilities)				
31	TOTAL I.A.T. OF PROJECT (L28 — L29 + L30)				
32	MEMO: Accelerated Depreciation on Project Facilities				

(3) 19	(4) 19	(5) 19	(6) 19	(7) 19	(8) 19	(9) 19	(10) 19

WESTINGHOUSE FORM 34837 A

STRATEGIC PROJECT EVALUATION

WORKSHEET B

(DOLLARS IN THOUSANDS)

PERIOD	ACTUAL EXPENDITURES	@ 10%		@ 15%		@ 18%		@ 20%	
		FACTOR	VALUE	FACTOR	VALUE	FACTOR	VALUE	FACTOR	VALUE
1ST YEAR		.95		.93		.92		.91	
2ND YEAR		.86		.81		.78		.76	
3RD YEAR		.79		.70		.66		.63	
4TH YEAR		.71		.61		.56		.53	
5TH YEAR		.65		.53		.47		.44	
6TH YEAR		.59		.46		.40		.37	
7TH YEAR		.54		.40		.34		.30	
8TH YEAR		.49		.35		.29		.25	
9TH YEAR		.44		.30		.24		.21	
10TH YEAR		.40		.26		.21		.18	
TOTAL (A)		X X X		X X X		X X X		X X X	

PERIOD	ACTUAL RECEIPTS	@ 10%		@ 15%		@ 18%		@ 20%	
		FACTOR	VALUE	FACTOR	VALUE	FACTOR	VALUE	FACTOR	VALUE
1ST YEAR		.95		.93		.92		.91	
2ND YEAR		.86		.81		.78		.76	
3RD YEAR		.79		.70		.66		.63	
4TH YEAR		.71		.61		.56		.53	
5TH YEAR		.65		.53		.47		.44	
6TH YEAR		.59		.46		.40		.37	
7TH YEAR		.54		.40		.34		.30	
8TH YEAR		.49		.35		.29		.25	
9TH YEAR		.44		.30		.24		.21	
10TH YEAR		.40		.26		.21		.18	
TOTAL (B)		X X X		X X X		X X X		X X X	
TERMINAL VALUE		.40		.26		.21		.18	
TOTAL (C)		X X X		X X X		X X X		X X X	
RATIO	A/B	☐		☐		☐		☐	☐
RATIO (WITH T.V.)	A/C	☐		☐		☐		☐	☐

@ 25%		@ 30%		@ 35%		@ 40%		@ 45%		@ 50%	
FACTOR	VALUE	FACTOR	VALUE	FACTOR	VALUE	FACTOR	VALUE	FACTOR	VALUE	FACTOR	VALUE
.89		.87		.85		.84		.82		.81	
.71		.67		.63		.60		.57		.54	
.57		.52		.47		.43		.39		.36	
.46		.40		.35		.31		.27		.24	
.36		.31		.26		.22		.19		.16	
.29		.23		.19		.16		.13		.11	
.23		.18		.14		.11		.09		.08	
.19		.14		.10		.08		.06		.05	
.15		.11		.08		.06		.04		.03	
.12		.08		.06		.04		.03		.02	
X X X		X X X		X X X		X X X		X X X		X X X	

@ 25%		@ 30%		@ 35%		@ 40%		@ 45%		@ 50%	
FACTOR	VALUE	FACTOR	VALUE	FACTOR	VALUE	FACTOR	VALUE	FACTOR	VALUE	FACTOR	VALUE
.89		.87		.85		.84		.82		.81	
.71		.67		.63		.60		.57		.54	
.57		.52		.47		.43		.39		.36	
.46		.40		.35		.31		.27		.24	
.36		.31		.26		.22		.19		.16	
.29		.23		.19		.16		.13		.11	
.23		.18		.14		.11		.09		.08	
.19		.14		.10		.08		.06		.05	
.15		.11		.08		.06		.04		.03	
.12		.08		.06		.04		.03		.02	
X X X		X X X		X X X		X X X		X X X		X X X	
.12		.08		.06		.04		.03		.02	
X X X		X X X		X X X		X X X		X X X		X X X	
	☐		☐		☐		☐		☐		☐
	☐		☐		☐		☐		☐		☐

COMPUTER INPUT DATA WORKSHEET
DISCOUNTED CASH FLOW – RETURN ON INVESTMENT CALCULATION
WESTINGHOUSE FORM 36163

TRANSMISSION FORMAT

1 FIGS	2 H	3 LTRS	4 M	5 A	6 LTRS	7 CAR RET	8 LINE FEED	9 M	10 A	11 SPACE	CALL DIRECTING CODE OF SENDING STATION →	12	13
14 CAR RET	15 LINE FEED	16 FIGS	17 M	18 LTRS	19 R	MESSAGE IDENTIFICATION →	20	21	22	23	24 CAR RET	25 LINE FEED	26 FIGS

YEAR		SIGN	NET CASH AMOUNT (LEFT JUSTIFIED)						CARRIAGE RETURN	LINE FEED	YEAR		SIGN	NET CASH AMOUNT (LEFT JUSTIFIED)						CARRIAGE RETURN	LINE FEED
0	1										0	7									
0	2										0	8									
0	3										0	9									
0	4										1	0									
0	5																				
0	6										LTRS		E	N		D		FIGS		H	

TRANSMISSION FORMAT

1 FIGS	2 H	3 LTRS	4 M	5 A	6 LTRS	7 CAR RET	8 LINE FEED	9 M	10 A	11 SPACE	CALL DIRECTING CODE OF SENDING STATION →	12	13
14 CAR RET	15 LINE FEED	16 FIGS	17 M	18 LTRS	19 R	MESSAGE IDENTIFICATION →	20	21	22	23	24 CAR RET	25 LINE FEED	26 FIGS

YEAR		SIGN	NET CASH AMOUNT (LEFT JUSTIFIED)						CARRIAGE RETURN	LINE FEED	YEAR		SIGN	NET CASH AMOUNT (LEFT JUSTIFIED)						CARRIAGE RETURN	LINE FEED
0	1										0	7									
0	2										0	8									
0	3										0	9									
0	4										1	0									
0	5																				
0	6										LTRS		E	N		D		FIGS		H	

TRANSMISSION FORMAT

1 FIGS	2 H	3 LTRS	4 M	5 A	6 LTRS	7 CAR RET	8 LINE FEED	9 M	10 A	11 SPACE	CALL DIRECTING CODE OF SENDING STATION →	12	13
14 CAR RET	15 LINE FEED	16 FIGS	17 M	18 LTRS	19 R	MESSAGE IDENTIFICATION →	20	21	22	23	24 CAR RET	25 LINE FEED	26 FIGS

YEAR		SIGN	NET CASH AMOUNT (LEFT JUSTIFIED)						CARRIAGE RETURN	LINE FEED	YEAR		SIGN	NET CASH AMOUNT (LEFT JUSTIFIED)						CARRIAGE RETURN	LINE FEED
0	1										0	7									
0	2										0	8									
0	3										0	9									
0	4										1	0									
0	5																				
0	6										LTRS		E	N		D		FIGS		H	

INSTRUCTIONS FOR USE OF FORM 36163

General

1. The input information required to obtain the percent return on investment is the net cash expenditures or cash receipts for each year of economic life of the project being evaluated up to a maximum of 10 years.

2. The input information should be transmitted to Tele-Computer by teletype using the format contained on Form 36163. This form provides space for three separate message transmissions.

Specifications

1. The opening format of the message consists of 26 characters. Characters 12 and 13 are to be the call directing code of transmitting teletype station which is the station at which answer message will be received.

   *Characters 20 through 23 are provided for local sender identification (division alpha code, message number, etc.). The use of these characters is optional, they may be omitted from message transmission.

2. The first two characters of message data portion represents the year of project life (01, 02 ... 10). There may be as little as two or as many as ten years used in the message. Lines must be transmitted in numerical order.

3. The third character of each data portion line must be the sign, either cash flow receipts (.) or cash flow expenditures (-).

4. The fourth through ninth characters must be numeric representing dollars. The money field may be from one to six positions. The amount should be "left justified" and it should be followed by the Car. Ret. line feed without additional spaces.

5. The message must end with the characters "end" and Figs H on the last line, as shown on the message format.

6. There must be some net cash flow expenditures or the return will be infinite. Also sum of all cash flows must be positive.

7. If return of investment is wanted including terminal value and excluding terminal value, two completely separate messages must be transmitted. The data portion of the two messages will be identical except for cash flow receipts in the last year.

Message Reply

1. Reply should be received within 5 minutes after message transmission.

2. Rate of return will be calculated to a tenth of one percent.

*Use only alpha designations or leave blank. Do not use "1" or "0."

EXPLANATION OF FORM 29067

Appropriation Request

Page 1

This page is to serve as a routing sheet and as input information to the Tele-Computer records.

Title blocks should agree with information submitted on the Facilities Investment Plan.

Brief Description should serve to elaborate on the Project Title. In many cases it will parallel the description which was submitted with the cover letter accompanying the Facilities Investment Plan earlier.

Return on Investment figures will be those calculated on Strategic Project Evaluation Sheet Form 34835.

Financial Information should tabulate latest estimates of Capital and Expense outlays expected, entered by Schedule under "Original Amount." If these amounts do not agree with the estimates as listed on the Facilities Investment Plan, explain where additional funds are to be obtained, or where excess funds will be applied, in the following section "FUNDS FOR THIS APPROPRIATION . . ."

Lease Commitment is to be shown as a separate line entry, with the total amount over the full term of the lease under "Original Amount." On occasion Lease Agreements are changed during the term of the lease, and when these are tied to other Appropriation Expenditures, these changes are to be shown by an Appropriation Revision. (Where changes in Lease arrangements are independent of Appropriation Expenditures, notification of changes can be made by letter to the Capital Expenditures Committee.)

Timing of Expenditures, current year, next year, and following year, should show latest schedule of outlays of Capital, Expense, and Lease funds.

Source of Funds will normally list the amount (in Thousands of Dollars) which is shown on the approved Facilities Investment Plan. Where this amount differs or where other projects are substituted, the situation is to be explained in the space provided.

Approval Signatures are to be affixed as required by the type or amount of expenditure as discussed in Section III.

Pages 2 & 3

These pages represent expanded information compared with former Appropriation Request instructions to furnish the Capital Expenditures Committee (or Division Management on smaller projects) with a more complete explanation of the nature of the project and the extent of the planning involved in its inception.

Item 1 Expected Benefits - List Annual Sales Billed & Product Cost both Actual and Anticipated with and without the project, for the Product Code(s), or for the Division if the project affects all Products. Repeat the ROI information shown on Page 1.

Item 2 Present Situation - Describe the procedures now being followed and reasons for the proposal. State the problems associated with inventory, defective work, excessive overtime, inadequate test capability, field adjustment, capacity limitations, etc.

Item 3 Facilities - List amount and value of Land and Buildings to be added, along with amount of Durable Equipment to be obtained. Tabulate old items to be released and state what disposition will probably be made of them -- scrap, sell, trade-in, or declare surplus. Knowledge of future disposition items, in some instances, will preclude purchases by other Divisions. If floor space will be made available by this project, the amount should be stated and the probable use made of it, mentioned.

Item 4 Alternatives - State the alternatives considered and the economics of each in cost and ROI where applicable. In most cases it is expected that the alternatives will "bracket" the option being requested -- at least one will be more conservative and another of greater magnitude -- but any of the alternatives should be acceptable to the Division if other Corporate considerations prevail. At least two acceptable alternatives in addition to the one preferred by the Division should be described. For further discussion on Alternatives, see Appendix D.

Item 5 Personnel Effects - The before and after numbers of hourly people with and without the project are to be stated, along with the effect, if any, on salaried personnel. If a change in wage payment plan is involved in the request, this fact should be so stated. Acquisition of significant assets of an outside business may involve the hiring-in-place of people, and although this should be cleared with Industrial Realtions in advance, the arrangements in this regard should be stated in this section.

Item 6 Uncertainties & Basis of Confidence - This is to be a brief discussion on the probability of success of the proposed project. Supplier information, other Westinghouse Divisions' experiences, the position of our principal competitors, or new materials on the market all may have influences on the decision. On Volume or Product Improvement Projects, the price, volume and timing projections should be evaluated as to the risk involved in the venture.

Approvals: Appropriation Request is to be approved by the Division General Manager and, preferably, countersigned by the Manufacturing, Industrial Relations, Engineering and/or Marketing Managers.

APPROPRIATION REQUEST
WESTINGHOUSE FORM 29067F

ORIGINAL ☐ REVISION ☐ APPROPRIATION NO.__________

DIVISION	FACILITIES CLASS NO. & NAME	PRODUCT LINE(S)	CLOSING DATE

PROJECT TITLE

BRIEF DESCRIPTION OF PROJECT IN TERMS OF THE ACTIONS TO BE TAKEN.

RETURN ON INVESTMENT______% WITH TERMINAL VALUE, ______% EXCLUDING TERMINAL VALUE

ESTIMATED COST	ORIGINAL AMOUNT	AMOUNT OF REVISION	REVISED AMOUNT
SCHEDULE A - DURABLE EQUIPMENT			
SCHEDULE C - LAND AND BUILDINGS			
SCHEDULE D - EXPENSE			
APPROPRIATION TOTAL			
______YEAR LEASE COMMITMENT			

		THIS YEAR	NEXT YEAR	FOLLOWING YEAR
ESTIMATED TIMING OF EXPENDITURES	CAPITAL			
	EXPENSE			
	LEASE COST			

THE FUNDS FOR THIS APPROPRIATION ARE ANTICIPATED IN THE FACILITIES INVESTMENT PLAN, SUBMITTED FOR CURRENT YEAR, IN THE AMOUNT (000$)______. ADDITIONAL FUNDING IS BY SUBSTITUTION AS FOLLOWS:

PROJECT #	AMT. IN ORIG. PLAN	TITLE-ORIGINAL PROJECT

DIVISION SIGNATURES		HEADQUARTERS SIGNATURES		
DEPARTMENT HEAD	DATE	REVIEWED BY HEADQUARTERS MANUFACTURING		DATE
REVIEWED BY (DIV. CONTROLLER)	DATE	APPROVALS AS REQUIRED	EXECUTIVE VICE PRESIDENT	DATE
APPROVED BY (DIV. GEN. MGR.)	DATE		FOR CAPITAL EXPENDITURES COMMITTEE	DATE
	DATE		PRESIDENT	DATE
			BOARD OF DIRECTORS SECRETARY	DATE

APPROPRIATION DESCRIPTION

WESTINGHOUSE FORM 29067F

DIVISION ______________ APPROPRIATION NO. ______________

1. EXPECTED BENEFITS FROM PROJECT:

	LATEST YEAR ACTUAL	FIRST YEAR OF NORMAL OPERATION YEAR	
		WITHOUT PROJECT	WITH PROJECT
ANNUAL SALES BILLED (000)	$ ______	$ ______	$ ______
PRODUCT COST (000)	______	______	______

RETURN ON INVESTMENT ______% WITH, ______% WITHOUT TERMINAL VALUE

2. DESCRIPTION OF PRESENT SITUATION WITH REASONS FOR PROPOSAL.

3. FACILITIES EXPENDITURES

BUILDINGS ______ SQ. FT. AT $ ______ PER SQ. FT.

LAND ______ ACRES AT ______ PER ACRE.

DURABLE EQUIPMENT $ ______.

DISPOSITION OF OLD FACILITIES

APPROPRIATION DESCRIPTION
WESTINGHOUSE FORM 29067F

DIVISION ____________ APPROPRIATION NO. ____________

4. STATE PRINCIPAL FEASIBLE ALTERNATIVES

5. PERSONNEL EFFECTS.

6. WHAT ARE THE MAJOR AREAS OF UNCERTAINTY IN THE PROJECT

☐ INDUSTRIAL RELATIONS MANAGER

☐ ENGINEERING MANAGER

☐ MANUFACTURING MANAGER

☐ MARKETING MANAGER

DIVISION MANAGER ____________ DATE ____________

APPROPRIATION DETAIL - FORM 29068 (page 37a)

A. General

This form is used to detail the specific facilities included in the appropriation request.

B. Form Preparation

1. Item

List each item in an order that will lend itself to a clear explanation of the project, and to subsequent preparation of E-Orders.

2. Section

Specify the area where the item will be physically located. (May be left blank, if not applicable.)

3. Description of Item

Brief statement to identify each item.

4. Schedule

Show the letter designation which identifies the type of expenditure as follows:

A = Machinery and Equipment (See 3-16-1.1)
C = Land and Buildings (See 3-16-1.1)
D = Expense - Non-recurring expense, directly associated with the facilities project, such as rearrangement.

5.

List cost estimate for each item described on Appropriation Detail. Show sub-totals for each schedule and a grand total. These totals are reported on the Appropriation Request Form 29067.

PAGE _____ OF _____ PAGES

APPROPRIATION DETAIL
WESTINGHOUSE FORM 29068

DIVISION ______________________________ APPROPRIATION NO. ____________________

ITEM	SECTION	DESCRIPTION OF ITEM	SCHED.	ESTIMATED COST

APPENDIX B

Excerpt from
the Capital Appropriations Manual
of the American Can Company

Reprinted by courtesy of the American Can Company

PROJECT CLASSIFICATION

On the Forms 49, 49C and 49E there are blocks at the top of the form requesting budget reference data. If the project was listed in your Operating Plan Capital Budget specific information relating to the assigned budget number and the budgeted amount should be recorded on the form. This permits cross referencing against the original budgeted figures and the final appropriated requests. Normally the project classification has been handled on the original budget listing. However, in some cases, operations may choose to change the classification after further review has been made, or on a new project, the classification must be determined.

The classification of projects is an important part of both the budget and appropriations system.

Following are the classifications and general descriptions of each. You should be able to properly classify all projects by placing each project in one of the categories as described below:

Class 1 Basic Upkeep

Any project required for basic upkeep of a plant or support department location is to be filed under this category. Typical of the types of items that would be under this category would be major repairs to a building, an addition, such as ventilation of a department.

Required by Law

Typical of the projects under this category would be Air and Water Pollution Control, Noise Abatement Programs, etc.

Industrial Relations

From time to time, Industrial Relations will indicate employee problems that can be alleviated by capital additions. Typical of items in this category would be parking problems, noise abatement, odor problems, locker rooms, cafeteria, etc.

Public Relations

This area might involve improvements to the exterior brought about by area clean ups, company signs, etc. Any project geared to improve the public image falls in this category.

Class 2 Quality Improvement

Any capital addition that is required to bring about a general improvement in the quality of our products or is required to remedy major or minor complaints by our customers falls in this classification.

Frequently there is a fine line drawn between quality improvement and sales expansion or retention, which is Class 4 or Class 5. The determination is usually made when quality is the prime mover for the need of the capital item.

Class 3 Savings

This will include all projects primarily undertaken to obtain a financial saving over our present practices. Additions to an existing line, modification of or replacement by new machinery that will bring about reductions in labor, higher output, greater yields are typical of items in this category.

The resultant saving must be of sufficient value to justify its need. It must be recognized that any savings brought about are subject to Federal taxation. Therefore, the savings justification should be measured on an after-tax basis. The important criterion is, of course, return on investment or the pay-back period.

Class 4 Sales Expansion

Any project undertaken for new business or expansion of existing business will come in this classification. Capital additions are not limited to actual production items, but would also include items such as industrial trucks, additional space, offices, office equipment brought about by the expansion of sales.

Class 5 Sales Retention

This covers investments made to retain or protect existing business. Projects of this type must be reviewed very thoroughly by the operations to ascertain that the additional investment for the retention of business is warranted and continues to keep a decent profit level. If the return on investment or profit level is marginal, the options of continued business or phasing out should be weighed.

Class 6 **Equipment for Lease**

This class includes all expenditures in connection with the construction, purchase or major overhauling of customer equipment for inventory, which will be subsequently leased or sold.

Class 7 **Development**

This class is intended for use primarily by the Research and Development or Engineering and Equipment Development Departments. It may be used on plant projects where those projects are accomplished in conjunction with, or under the direction of, Research & Development or Engineering and Equipment.

Class 8 **Drawings and Patterns**

This category is used primarily by the Engineering Department and covers the capital involved in the engineering time of development projects, as well as the pattern costs for prototype equipment.

NOTE: At times projects are borderline as to one classification versus another. When this occurs judgment should be made as to which classification provides the strongest factor and strengthens the justification of the project. Leasing of equipment or facilities is to be classified in the same manner as if they were purchased.

APPENDIX C

Excerpts from
the TRW Capital Programming Manual

Reproduced by courtesy of TRW Inc.

STANDARD PRACTICE INSTRUCTIONS
TRW INC.

TPFC-1354 REV. 3 PRINTED IN U.S.A.

SUBJECT INDEX	CAPITAL PROGRAMMING		
S.P.I. No. AND DIVISION	01-53-1 Rev. 3		
SUPERSEDES: SPI No. 01-53-1 Rev. 2	PAGE No.	DATED 8-1-68	
EFFECTIVE DATE 3-15-70	PAGE 1		
SUBJECT: Capital Programming - Acquisition, Use, and Disposal of Plant, Property, and Equipment			
OTHER DIVISIONS AFFECTED	TRW Inc.		

1.0 PURPOSE

To establish TRW corporate policy for planning, forecasting, approving, and reporting the acquisition, use and disposal of plant, property, and equipment, including:

a) The establishment of a uniform system of planning, controlling and reporting the expenditures for owned and leased capital facilities, including both chattel property and real estate.

b) The establishment of a consistent format for presentation of data.

c) The establishment of responsibilities for the administration of the system.

d) The presentation of sample forms for guidance in proper completion.

2.0 SCOPE

The provisions of this document apply to all domestic and foreign operating divisions, staff organizations, and subsidiary and affiliate companies, and cover capital expenditures, limited life facilities, and leases. They include additions, replacements and improvements of all classes of property chargeable to fixed asset or deferred expense accounts as defined in Property Accounting Manual, SPI 01-12-1.

3.0 PRINCIPLES

a) It is the corporate policy to invest capital and lease funds to sustain operations, to provide the capability for growth, and to increase the corporate return on investment. Facilities purchased or leased should be of high quality, abreast of competitive technology, and commensurate with long-term objectives and economic plans. Commitment of funds for capital assets should be appropriately timed to minimize the risk involved.

b) Definitions of terms used in this instruction are included in Appendix A.

c) The recommended analytical tool for making economic comparisons between investment alternatives is the discounted cash flow after-tax return on investment method. The economic worth of a planned alternative as compared with the present is expressed as a percentage after-tax return on investment exclusive of the cost of money.

4.0 RESPONSIBILITIES

4.1 Division Manager

a) Establish business and investment objectives with the Group objectives.

b) Plan the acquisition of property, plant, and equipment on a continuous basis.

c) Administer the approved capital budget.

d) Prepare Capital Expenditure Appropriation Requests and supporting material.

e) Forecast capital and lease commitments and expenditures.

f) Maintain records of capital program activity and report status monthly.

g) Monitor facilities utilization and administer surplus and idle property programs.

h) Maintain proper accounting procedures in accordance with Property Accounting Manual, SPI 01-12-1.

i) Solicit proposals and place purchase orders for capital and lease procurements in accordance with Corporate Purchasing Manual 01-70.000 dated September 1, 1960.

j) Prepare post-audit reports on capital appropriations in accordance with the instructions in Appendix F.

[signature]
Vice-President
Manufacturing Services

4.2 Group Vice President or Executive Vice President

a) Establish investment objectives consistent with TRW's Financial and Long-Range Plans.

b) Consolidate the Division capital plans and recommend a Group program in terms of commitment and expenditure.

c) Review and approve Capital Expenditure Appropriation Requests delegated to the Group level.

d) Consolidate the Division forecasts of capital and lease commitments and expenditures, and submit to Corporate Staff Manufacturing Services.

e) Conduct periodic audits of specific major investments and summarize post-audit results for the Group.

f) Maintain capital expenditures within budget and limitations; alternatively, present Staff Manufacturing Services with a well-justified request for additional funds in time to present such a request to the President and Board of Directors, if necessary.

4.3 President

a) Interpret TRW Financial and Long-Range Planning objectives into corporate investment objectives.

b) Consolidate the Group capital plans and recommend an annual budget to Board of Directors.

c) Review and approve Capital Expenditure appropriation requests submitted to the corporate level for approval.

d) Forecast corporate capital and lease commitments and expenditures.

e) Conduct periodic cyclical reviews of Group and Division programs, and undertake specific audit of major investments.

f) Report capital and lease status and activity on monthly basis.

g) Summarize post-audit results on periodic basis for corporation.

5.0 STATEMENTS OF PRACTICE

5.1 Capital Planning

5.1.1 Capital Planning Cycle

Capital Planning is an integral part of business planning and should be performed on a continuous basis. As business plans and objectives change, plans for capital acquisitions should be adjusted.

Funding approval by the Board of Directors will be obtained annually for property, plant, and equipment coordinated with the (-1) business forecast. The corporate capital budget on which the funding is based should represent a consolidated "snapshot" of the Division and Group Capital Plan as of November 15. The requirement for funds may be amended by subsequent Board of Directors action if circumstances warrant. Planning foresight rather than frequent amendment is expected.

Projects uncommitted at the end of a calendar year are automatically considered abandoned. If such projects are still considered valid, they should be included in the Capital Plan for the next year.

5.1.2 Financial Implications of Capital Expenditures

Staff Manufacturing Services evaluates each Division's Capital Plan and the financial ramifications on the organization in the context of the business assumptions and plans they have made for the year. In addition, the total corporate program is evaluated in the light of financial ramifications on the company. These evaluations include the following factors:

TPPC-1354CC Rev. 2 PRINTED IN U.S.A.

S. P. I. No.	EFFECTIVE DATE	SUPERSEDES PAGE No	SUPERSEDES DATE	PAGE
01-53-1 Rev. 3	3-15-70			3

a) Effect of capital expenditures on cash flow projections.

b) Return on investment analysis based on the financial forecast.

c) Comparison and evaluation of capital expenditures with business-level projections.

d) Depreciation impact on the Division and company.

5.1.3 Management Review Criteria

Staff Manufacturing Services conducts a periodic cyclical review of the Divisions during the year. The intent of these reviews is:

a) To establish an acquaintance with approaching plans, programs and projects involving investments in capital for the following forecast year.

b) To obtain an understanding of timing, urgency, alternatives available, and consequences of deferral as basis for establishing priorities.

c) To form a framework for consistent evaluation of projects among the Divisions.

d) To arrive at tentative conclusions on a recommended Capital Plan for each Division around which its final submission should be made.

5.1.4 Numbering of Projects

For ease of recordkeeping and program identification, project numbers designate the following information:

1) The Division IBM Code number.

2) The last two digits of the program year.

3) The respective Works Code number of a Division.

4) The project identification number.

5) The letter suffix, if applicable. See Section 5.5.

6) The individual item number within the project (optional).

The arrangement of the number is as follows:

16	-66	2	09	C	-01
Division IBM Code	Program Year	Works	Project Identification Number	Suffix	Individual Items in Project

The project number is written in the following manner: 16-66209C-01. The project identification numbers are assigned serially, beginning with 00 for Miscellaneous Fund, followed by major project numbers of 01, 02, etc. Insofar as possible, projects are arranged in order of importance under the primary objective groupings with the most important project listed first. Individual items within each project are assigned serially beginning with -01.

5.2 Capital Budget

The approved Capital Plan constitutes the capital budget for the fiscal year. The **Capital Budget** represents the funds allocated to a Division for commitment during the year. Staff Manufacturing Services advises each Group of its Division's annual budget following action by the Board of Directors.

5.3 Project Commitment

The commitment of capital projects is requested on the Capital Expenditure Appropriation format in accordance with the instructions defined in Appendix D. Acquisition of capital equipment should be initiated only after it is clear that the equipment requested or similar equipment is not available within the corporation. Commitment of funds should be appropriately timed to minimize the risk involved.

5.3.1 Commitment Format

Authority to commit is granted on a project basis throughout the year in accordance with Section 5.3.2. All projects are prepared on the Capital Expenditure Appropriation format, as defined in Appendix D. Each request must include the following information:

a) Proper identification.

b) Descriptive title.

c) Items and dollar amounts to be committed.

d) Project objective.

e) Economic justification, with appropriate backup engineering economy study.

f) Alternatives considered.

g) Reason for timing.

Each project submitted for economic gain should be supported by an engineering economy study. Instructions for the preparation of economy studies are contained in Appendix C.

5.3.2 Commitment Approval

5.3.2.1 Policy

It is the general policy to delegate commitment approval of capital projects to Groups each year, with certain exceptions which require approval at corporate headquarters. Such exceptions are defined by the following criteria:

1) Any project with intended expenditures or firm lease commitments in excess of $500,000.

2) Any project involving significant new buildings or land.

3) Any project which, if committed, would cause the Group to exceed the dollar limit of its annual capital budget, as described in Section 5.2.

4) Any project which, in the judgment of an Executive Vice-President, involves any of the following:

   a) A significant new commitment to a new product line.

   b) An unusual risk.

   c) A commitment which should have further corporate review.

Supplements and additions, as described in Sections 5.5.1 and 5.5.2, are also subject to the above criteria.

5.3.2.2 Timing

In order to avoid buying unnecessary capital equipment or cancelling previously granted commitment approvals as business conditions and capital requirements change, commitment approval should be granted as late as practical prior to actual commitment of funds. When a Group desires to allow Divisions to establish project timing, commitment

TPPC-1384CC REV. 2 PRINTED IN U.S.A.

S. P. I. No.	EFFECTIVE DATE	SUPERSEDES PAGE No	SUPERSEDES DATE	PAGE
01-53-1 Rev. 3	3-15-70			5

approval authority should be delegated to the Division, rather than approval being given far in advance. Thus, in the Monthly Summary of Capital Expenditures as described in Appendix E, Section 2.0, the column headed "Commitments, approved for" should not show an entry until final approval is granted, shortly prior to actual commitment of funds.

5.3.3 Purchase Requisitions and Shop Orders

Since Purchase Requisitions and Shop Orders are not submitted to Staff Manufacturing Services for Corporate approval, it is the responsibility of the Division to institute a method of control that insures that no Purchase Requisition or Shop Order for a capital asset is placed until the respective Capital Expenditure Appropriation has received Corporate approval.

5.3.4 Justification

A justification or summary of reasons for purchasing or leasing capital equipment and facilities must be outlined on the Capital Expenditure Appropriation form submitted for each project in accordance with the instructions in Appendix D.

5.3.4.1 Primary Objectives

Each proposed project must designate a primary objective, which should be one of the following:

New Product - Applies to acquisition of assets to be used in addition to present facilities for the fabrication of new products.

Increased Capacity - Applies to the acquisition of assets to be used in addition to present facilities to provide for greater output of existing products.

Replacement - Applies to the acquisition of assets required in order to continue the function of capital facilities being retired from service.

Cost Reduction - Applies to the acquisition of assets intended to reduce costs or expenses by improvement of facilities to achieve reductions in labor, materials, or other expenses.

R & D Technical Capability - Applies to the acquisition of assets required for research and development programs or to provide new technical capability.

Pollution Control - Applies to acquisition of assets for control of environmental pollution.

Other - Applies to the acquisition of assets essential to operations, but not lending to classification in any of the six above classes.

5.3.4.2 Economic Justification

An economic justification is required for all projects within the first four primary objective categories mentioned above. These must include all pertinent operating costs, marketing considerations, economic projections, and forecast of expected return on the proposed investment. A summary of the economic justification should be entered in the space provided on the Capital Expenditure Appropriation as indicated in Appendix D.

The economic factors should be summarized and presented on Engineering Economy Study forms. A more thorough analysis should be prepared for major investments.

Assumptions and estimates made by the analyst such as operating cost data, operating rates, startup costs, capital addition requirements, purchase costs and salvage values should be documented. Where relevant economic factors are unavailable, but are significant in evaluating the project, they should be estimated (Appendix C).

5.3.4.3 Facilities Loading

Each Capital Expenditure appropriation for increased capacity or new products is to be supported with a facilities load analysis of the same type or similar type machines. The Facility Load Chart defined in Appendix C-4 or similar type analysis format can be used for this purpose.

5.3.4.4 Proposal Analysis

TRW Inc. purchasing policy stresses the advantages and importance of soliciting competitive quotations on proposed acquisitions. Each quotation or proposal should be carefully evaluated as to price and technical advantages to maximize the TRW Inc. return on investment.

5.3.5 Machinery Specifications

The purchase of standard machine tools of proven capability entails little risk of failure of the machine to perform its intended function or of misunderstandings between TRW and the vendor. Much of the capital equipment we purchase, however, is of new design or capability where the risk is substantial. In these instances the preparation of machine specifications or "work statements" for proposed acquisitions is encouraged. Such "work statements" or "performance specifications" should accomplish these things:

a) Get the work done.

b) Provide objective criteria so that both TRW and the vendor will know when the work is done and payment is due.

c) Provide a firm base from which future changes can be made and justify the increased price which may be involved.

A work statement is part of a contract which describes the essential activity which the contractor is to accomplish. It should be prepared by the engineer who is planning the work on all major machine procurements.

5.4 Forecasts

A quarterly forecast of commitments and expenditures covering a three-year period is to be prepared at the Division level. This forecast should be keyed to the business forecasting program and represents a continuous appraisal of the resources necessary to achieve the objectives of the business plan. It should take into account all changes in planning which have occurred since the prior forecast. The initial forecast for each year (i.e. -1) is prepared simultaneously with the Capital Plan and should be based on it.

5.5 Changes to the Budget

Changes in business or engineering plans will at times make it necessary to alter the property, plant and equipment requirements. These changes include: supplements, additions, and abandonments.

5.5.1 Supplements

A Supplement is an extension of an approved project, included in concept in the current year program. It may be funded from within the Group budget through offsetting abandonments, and identified by the suffix A in the project number. Alternatively, it may require corporate funds and be identified by the suffix B in the project number.

5.5.2 Additions

An Addition is a project not included in concept in the current year program. It may be funded from within the Group budget through offsetting abandonments and identified by the suffix C in the project number. Alternatively, it may require corporate funds and be identified by the suffix D in the project number.

5.5.3 Abandonments

If it becomes apparent during the year that it will not be necessary to acquire certain capital items for which funds have been budgeted, the funds should be abandoned.

TPPC-1384CC REV. 2 PRINTED IN U.S.A.

S. P. I. No.	EFFECTIVE DATE	SUPERSEDES PAGE No	SUPERSEDES DATE	PAGE
01-53-1 Rev. 3	3-15-70			7

5.6 Reporting

5.6.1 Monthly Summary Capital Expenditure Program

The report "Monthly Summary of Capital Expenditure Program," which is prepared in final form by the Division Controller, is included in SPI 01-17-1, entitled "Corporate Financial Reporting." It is the responsibility of the Division Industrial Engineer to furnish information necessary for completion of this report in an accurate and timely manner. It is the responsibility of the Division Controller to forward a copy to Staff Manufacturing Services. This report is described in detail in paragraph 2.0 of Appendix E.

5.6.2 Monthly Report of Capital Activity

The report "Monthly Report of Capital Activity" is prepared each month by the person responsible for the capital program in each Division, and submitted to Group Headquarters and Staff Manufacturing Services. Reporting responsibility may be delegated to Works. This report is described in detail in paragraph 3.0 of Appendix E.

5.6.3 Staff Reports

Staff Manufacturing Services is to submit to the President monthly and periodic special reports summarizing the Capital Expenditure Program as well as any special reports required by the Board of Directors and Officers of the Corporation.

5.6.4 Carry-over

Some Capital Expenditure projects will not be completed during the year in which they are approved. When preparing the annual capital plan, the projects which will require expenditures in the ensuing year should be carefully reviewed, with the amount remaining to be spent considered as estimated carry-over. All totally uncommitted projects are considered abandoned at the end of the year and, if required, must be resubmitted as new projects. Partially committed projects that will have commitments as well as expenditures in the following year should be presented as such and the total sum included in the estimated carry-over.

The projects comprising the estimated carry-over should be summarized as shown in the example in Appendix B and included in the annual Capital Plan. The approved carry-over is included in the capital budget.

A detailed breakdown of actual carry-over with explanation of significant differences from that estimated is to be submitted to Staff Manufacturing Services for review as soon as the final estimate is available.

5.6.5 Closing Out Projects

All projects must be promptly "closed out" after individual items are installed for operation in order that accounting procedures can commence. Projects should be partially closed out whenever possible.

5.7 Records

Each Division must maintain records of Capital Expenditure Program activity including appropriations, commitments, expenditures, supplements, abandonments, and close-outs. Staff Manufacturing Services maintains current records of Capital Expenditure Program activity with the exception of expenditures and close-outs, which are recorded on a monthly basis and reported on the "Monthly Summary of Capital Expenditure Program."

5.8 Post-Audits

Post-audits of capital projects are an integral part of sound capital expenditure control in order to pinpoint weaknesses in planning and estimating, highlight problem areas in need of correction, and insure that corrective action is promptly taken. While it is recognized that the economic projections used in justification studies are subject to unpredictable changes, and that therefore not all capital decisions will prove out as projected, it is, however, mandatory that mistakes made in the past be analyzed and that their repetition in the future be avoided. Post-audit reports enable Division management to compare planned vs. actual, and to insure more accurate planning, more realistic assumptions, and better selection of alternatives.

TPFC-1984CC REV. 2 PRINTED IN U.S.A.

S. P. I. No.	EFFECTIVE DATE	SUPERSEDES PAGE No	SUPERSEDES DATE	PAGE
01-53-1 Rev. 3	3-15-70			8

All projects over $100,000 and based on economic gain require preparation of post-audit reports in accordance with Appendix F. These post-audit reports are to be reviewed by the Division Manager and submitted to Staff Manufacturing Services on the first working day of the eighteenth month following the project close-out date. Groups may require post-audit reports on capital projects under $100,000 at their discretion.

5.9 Surplus and Idle Property

Capital equipment which is determined by the Division to be excess to its needs is to be reported to Staff Manufacturing Services, in accordance with the instruction defined in Appendix G. All equipment idle for more than 90 days, and with no foreseeable use, should be declared excess for allocation to other Divisions in the corporation.

Any Division interested in acquiring surplus equipment listed on the quarterly Corporate Staff Surplus Letter may direct technical or financial questions to the Industrial Engineer of the Division declaring the item surplus. If the item is needed, a short justification is submitted to Staff Manufacturing Services, stating how the equipment will be used. These are reviewed and allocations made on the basis of need. All interested Divisions are notified of the disposition. No transmittal of move orders, purchase orders, account numbers or other correspondence relative to acquisition of surplus equipment is to be made prior to allocation by Staff Manufacturing Services.

Transfer of surplus equipment is to be made on the basis of arms-length bargaining defined in Appendix G, with the receiving Division paying for shipping and crating charges. Charges or transfers of funds for surplus equipment do not appear on any projects or reports associated with the Capital Expenditure Program.

Equipment declared surplus by a Division to the Corporation and not allocated to another Division is released for disposal in a manner consistent with the best interests of the submitting Division. Divisions must then notify Staff Manufacturing Services of the actual sale of the equipment.

TPPC-1304CC Rev. 2 PRINTED IN U.S.A.

S. P. I. No.	EFFECTIVE DATE	SUPERSEDES PAGE No.	SUPERSEDES DATE	PAGE
01-53-1 Rev. 3	3-15-70			A – 1

DEFINITIONS

1.0 CAPITAL ITEMS

All expenditures for land, land improvements, buildings, building extensions, building equipment, leasehold improvements, new and used machinery and equipment, office equipment, and major modifications and rehabilitations to present machinery and equipment; i.e., any unit of property substantial in nature and cost that can be identified physically and having a useful life in excess of one year and with the cost of the complete identifiable item or unit purchased or constructed of $250 or more. Special machine tools or other equipment purchased for a specific customer's order or for a limited application in research and development work should not be capitalized. For the policies and practices in "Accounting for Tooling Expenditure," see SPI 01-11-2.

Generally, items are to be capitalized where the complete identifiable unit purchased or constructed is $250 or more and the estimated useful life of the item is in excess of one year. Where two or more units of equipment, the individual cost of which is less than $250, are incorporated into one unit whose useful life is greater than one year, and the aggregate cost is $250 or more, the physically identifiable assembled unit is capitalized.

For detailed descriptions and guidelines concerning the uniform and consistent practice in the definition and in the recording of capital expenditures; i.e., capital vs. expense, rehabilitation, leasehold improvements, tooling, useful lives, depreciation, etc.; consult the Property Accounting Manual, SPI 01-12-1. The information and instruction set forth in that manual is the governing policy for TRW property accounting practices, and should be closely considered and adhered to concurrently with the policies and instructions contained in this manual.

2.0 LIMITED LIFE ITEMS

All expenditures for machinery, attachments, storage vessels, or equipment which are of such a specialized nature that, without modification or alteration, the use of which either separately or in an assembly is limited to the production or testing of particular parts or supplies, or the performance of services. These are items which at the time of acquisition are required exclusively for, and their economic useful life is limited to, a specific customer contract or a research and development program. (Consult Property Accounting Manual, SPI 01-12-1.)

3.0 LEASE ITEMS SUBJECT TO CONTROL

Lease items are subject to the same control as if they were purchased. Criteria for corporate review, as described in Policy and Practice section 5.3.2.1, are identical. Additionally, computers and electronic data processing equipment are subject to provisions of SPI 01-08-01 titled, "Computers, Acquisition by Rental, Lease, or Purchase."

4.0 PROJECT

An acquisition or group of acquisitions that will achieve a given objective. Each individual item making up a project should be defined relative to the purpose to be achieved. Projects should be related to the business goals and objectives outlined in the business plan.

5.0 CAPITAL PLAN

The annual request for capital funds. It defines capital, lease, and limited life items which are proposed for acquisition during the coming year. It is, in effect, the expression of the capital resources required to support the business plan in order to achieve the overall goals established by each Division. It is the formal framework within which management expresses its capital expenditure decisions in the form of individual projects.

6.0 CAPITAL BUDGET

The approved funds allocated to each Division in the corporation for the procurement of capital, limited life and lease facilities during the corporate fiscal year. The capital budget is established and approved in December of each year by the Board of Directors.

TPFC-1384CC Rev. 2 PRINTED IN U.S.A.

S. P. I. No.	EFFECTIVE DATE	SUPERSEDES PAGE No.	SUPERSEDES DATE	PAGE
01-53-1 Rev. 3	3-15-70			A – 2

7.0 MONTHLY SUMMARY OF CAPITAL EXPENDITURE PROGRAM

The monthly status report for the Capital Expenditure Program identifying on a cumulative basis the following:

a) Status of the budget appropriation, taking abandonments and supplements into consideration.

b) Status of approvals and commitments.

c) Status of expenditures.

8.0 CAPITAL EXPENDITURE APPROPRIATION

The cover and summary sheet for the presentation of each capital project.

9.0 CAPITAL COMMITMENT

Funds for a capital item committed by TRW in the form of a purchase order, work order, or shop order.

10.0 CAPITAL EXPENDITURE

Funds for capital item spent by TRW.

11.0 SURPLUS PROPERTY

Facilities, machinery, equipment and building space excess to the needs of the Division with no foreseeable use.

12.0 IDLE PROPERTY

Facilities, machinery, equipment and building space idle for more than ninety (90) days.

13.0 CARRY-OVER ITEMS

All expenditures for projects approved for commitment that are not completed and closed out during the calendar year. These projects are carried over to the next year and automatically become a part of that year's capital program.

14.0 DIVISION

For purposes of this policy, applies to all domestic and Canadian operating divisions, staff organizations, and subsidiary and affiliate companies.

15.0 CURRENT YEAR PROGRAM

The current year program is composed of the prior year carry-over (as defined in paragraph 13.0) plus the current year capital budget (as defined in paragraph 6.0).

TPPC-1384CC Rev. 2 PRINTED IN U.S.A.

S. P. I. No.	EFFECTIVE DATE	SUPERSEDES PAGE No	SUPERSEDES DATE	PAGE
01-53-1 Rev. 3	3-15-70			C-3–1

REPLACEMENT/COST REDUCTION

3.0 REPLACEMENT AND COST REDUCTION ENGINEERING ECONOMY STUDIES

3.1 Replacement Proposals

An Engineering Economy Study (EES) analyzing a proposed expenditure for the replacement of a capital asset compares the costs associated with the existing item – either "as is" or rebuilt – to the estimated costs associated with a proposed replacement item. When these cost comparisons are analyzed by the discounted cash flow method, the resulting rate of return provides an index of the replacement proposal's economic soundness. This type of EES is particularly applicable in situations where an existing item of equipment is judged incapable of performing to operation requirements and either rebuild or replacement capital expenditures are proposed as alternative remedies to the situation.

The definitions of specific cost considerations and their treatment relative to the previously mentioned alternatives are covered on the following pages of this section (3.0).

3.2 Cost Reduction Proposals

An Engineering Economy Study (EES) analyzing a proposed capital expenditure for the purpose of achieving a cost reduction compares the costs associated with an existing operating method to the estimated costs associated with a proposed operating method. When this cost comparison is analyzed by the discounted cash flow method, the resulting rate of return provides an index of the cost reduction proposal's economic soundness.

The definition of specific cost considerations and their treatment relative to the previously mentioned alternatives are covered on the following pages of this section (3.0).

Both the Replacement and Cost Reduction types of EES involve the use of a similar analytical approach and data from either type are submitted on the same EES form. **However,** although both types of proposals basically involve a potential reduction in operating costs, those proposals corresponding to the situation described in paragraph 3.1 (above) and/or intended primarily as "Replacement" types should be specifically indentified as such.

3.3 Engineering Economy Study Form: Replacement, Cost Reduction

The form on which a Replacement or Cost Reduction type of Engineering Economy Study (EES) should be submitted is illustrated on the last page of this appendix. The gray shaded areas shown in this black-and-white illustration correspond with areas that are green shaded on the actual form. These shaded areas serve to distinguish information that is submitted for post-audit purposes (see Appendix F) from information that is included for justification of the original project submitted for approval.

The Replacement/Cost Reduction EES consists of the following six major parts:

Heading Information

1 - Present Facility
2 - Proposed Facility
3 - Operational Comparison
4 - Gain from Capital Expenditure
5 - Surplus Availability

Guidelines regarding the information required in each of these parts will be found in subsequent paragraphs.

TPFC-1384CC Rev. 2 PRINTED IN U.S.A.

S. P. I. No.	EFFECTIVE DATE	SUPERSEDES PAGE No.	SUPERSEDES DATE	PAGE
01-53-1 Rev. 3	3-15-70			C-3–2

Heading Information

ENGINEERING ECONOMY STUDY - Replacement, Cost Reduction

Division-Works
Department
Product Line
Project No.
Project Description
Prepared by
Industrial Engineering Manager

While this information is self-explanatory, it should be entered completely and in a manner consistent with that information entered on the Capital Expenditure Appropriation Form.

1 - PRESENT FACILITY

1 - PRESENT FACILITY				
a. DESCRIPTION				
b. MOD/SIZE		g. USAGE		
c. TP OR TRW NO.	d. DATE MFG.			
e. NET VALUE			YEAR	(A) DEPRECIATION
			1st	$
f. CAPITAL ADDITION			2nd	
$ FOR YRS.			3rd	
			4th	
			5th	
			UNAMORTIZED AMOUNT	

Note: When a combination of machines or equipment is indicated, descriptive terms should be used to identify the unit, such as: Heat Treat Facilities or Finish Grinding Line. Information about each item should be included as part of supporting detail.

b. Model/Size - self-explanatory.

c. TP or TRW No. - Property Accounting Number.

d. Date Mfg. - Date facility was manufactured (not acquired).

e. Net Value - The best estimate of that net cash (i.e., less tear-down or related costs) which would be received upon disposal of the present facility. (For this entry, assume that the proposed facility will replace the present facility and that the latter will be disposed of immediately.)

f. Capital Addition - Quotes or engineering estimates of the cost of rehabilitating the equipment if the present facility were to be retained. This capital addition entry should only be completed when service parts are available or rehabilitation of the equipment is feasible in view of obsolescence and operation requirements. When rehabilita ion is feasible, the operating costs estimated for the present facility and presented later in the study should be those fo the rebuilt machine.

g. Usage - Number of days per week - shifts per day equipment is in operation, i.e.: 5-2, 5-3, 6-2, etc.

(A) Depreciation - The total projected annual depreciation for the present facility, including the capital addition (if any). If, for example, the capital addition will extend the facility's useful life for four years, the depreciation and the comparison against the proposed facility can only be for a four-year time period. The comparison of the present with the proposed facility can only be for the estimated life of the present facility (either with or without a capital addition). At the end of this period, a decision as to the future course of action must be made. Depreciation for rebuild or rehabilitation is computed on a straight-line basis.

The Unamortized Amount is the remaining book value of the equipment at the end of the number of years used for the comparison record.

2 - PROPOSED FACILITY

2 - PROPOSED FACILITY	
a. DESCRIPTION	
b. MOD/SIZE	f. INVESTMENT DIFFERENTIAL
c. EST. USEFUL LIFE YEARS	g. USAGE
d. EST. SALVAGE VALUE	
e. INSTALLED COST $	

YEAR	(B) DEPRECIATION
1st	$
2nd	
3rd	
4th	
5th	
UNAMORTIZED AMOUNT	

a. Description - Manufacturer's name and equipment nomenclature.

b. Model/Size - self-explanatory.

c. Estimated Useful Life - The estimated number of years over which the facility will be depreciated. (See Appendix H for guides to establishing useful lives.)

d. Estimated Salvage Value - The estimated dollar salvage value of the proposed facility at the end of its useful life.

e. Installed Cost - The sum of the acquisition, freight and installation costs including the normal complement of tools, motors, tax, cost of foundations, wiring, etc. This figure should be the same as that submitted for approval on the Capital Expenditure Appropriation.

f. Investment Differential - Net investment required. For example, the difference between (2-e) **Installed Cost** of the proposed facility and any (1-d) **Capital Addition** to the present facility (see previous page); or the difference between installed cost and (1-e) **Net Value** received for the old facility; or if no offset, the investment differential is equal to the installed cost.

g. Usage - Number of days per week - shifts per day that the proposed equipment is expected to be in operation.

(B) Depreciation - The projected depreciation of the proposed facility as reported for tax purposes. For guidance, refer to the TRW Property Accounting Manual, SPI 01-12-1. Care should be taken to project the depreciation only for the number of years that you expect the present facility to operate.

The Unamortized Amount is the remaining book value of the equipment at the end of the number of years used for the comparison period.

TPPC-1364CC REV. 2 PRINTED IN U.S.A.

S. P. I. No.	EFFECTIVE DATE	SUPERSEDES PAGE No.	SUPERSEDES DATE	PAGE
01-53-1 Rev. 3	3-15-70			C-3—4

3 - OPERATIONAL COMPARISON

3 - OPERATIONAL COMPARISON

OPERATING COSTS	PRESENT		PROPOSED	
DIRECT LABOR	$	$		$
INDIRECT LABOR				
SET UP				
MATERIAL				
MAINTENANCE				
TOOLS EXP ITEMS				
POWER CONSUMPTION				
FLOOR SPACE				
PROPERTY TAX				
REWORK SCRAP				
DOWNTIME				
DELETE ADD. OPER				
FRINGE BENEFITS				
SUB CONTRACT COSTS				
OTHERS				
INCOME LOSS				
TOTAL	$	$	$	$

(C) EXCESS OPERATING COST OF PRESENT FACILITY (PRESENT MINUS PROPOSED) $ ______ $

(D) ONE TIME ASSOCIATED EXPENSE $ ______ $

Direct Labor - The estimated actual dollar cost of labor to be expended in performing the operations as identified in the standard factory routing, including overtime and shift premiums.

Indirect Labor - Use estimated actual costs. Percentage allocations of indirect labor costs should only be used when the operations being studied will affect all costs included in the Indirect Labor Set-up Accounts.

Set-up - Include only set-up costs accumulated in Indirect Labor Set-up Accounts.

Material - Costs due to changes in quantity or price of material required by present or proposed facility.

Maintenance - Consider both material and labor costs. Data on maintenance of existing equipment should be obtained from machine records. Routinely scheduled maintenance should also be considered. In some instances, new equipment may require greater maintenance care than the old because of critical operating features. **Rehabilitation costs should not be included.**

Tools/Expense Items - Annual "expense" costs for such nondurable items as cutting tools, forming tools, grinding wheels, lubricants and general supplies.

Power Consumption - Electric, compressed air, water and gas costs. Use rated horsepower for electric motor (Horsepower x 0.75 = Kilowatts). Note, however, that electrically powered equipment is seldom operated at 100% rated power output on a continuous basis.

Floor Space - Only released space that can be utilized should be considered.

Property Tax - Use Tax rate and calculation basis applicable to the specific Division or Works.

Rework/Scrap - Cost of scrap and/or repairs to product directly due to equipment inadequacies. A reasonable decrease in scrap cost may be expected with the installation of new equipment.

TPPC-1384CC Rev. 2 PRINTED IN U.S.A.

S. P. I. No.	EFFECTIVE DATE	SUPERSEDES PAGE No.	SUPERSEDES DATE	PAGE
01-53-1 Rev. 3	3-15-70			C-3–5

Downtime - Include "waiting time" labor charges for operators unable to carry on their assigned tasks because of machine breakdown; also, any extra straight time, premium time and/or set-up charges necessary to make up production lost because of machine breakdown.

Delete/Add Operation - Include the cost of any operation – not considered elsewhere – that will be deleted or added if the proposed facility is acquired.

Fringe Benefits - Obtain fringe benefits cost per labor-hour figure from the Division's Accounting Department. Apply this rate to number of hours involved in such labor-related operating cost items as Direct Labor, Indirect Labor, Set-up, Rework/Scrap, Downtime, and Delete/Add Operation.

Subcontract Costs Total costs of subcontract work which would be eliminated or added by installation of the proposed facility

Others - Miscellaneous costs not accounted for in the foregoing operating costs (figures should be supported with explanatory comments).

Income Loss - When lack of capacity is the sole reason for refusing profitable sales, the income which would be derived may be included. Data must be attached to substantiate that:

1) The sales dollars are definite and not estimates of probable sales available.

2) The required capacity cannot be attained by employing more efficient methods on existing equipment or by subcontracting.

(C) Excess Operating Cost of Present Facility - Operating cost of present facility minus operating cost of proposed facility.

(D) One-Time Associated Expense - The sum of those costs expected to occur only for "expense" (not capitalized) items; e.g., tooling, rearrangement, training, start-up expense, etc. These costs must be directly associated with the given capital proposal.

4 - GAIN FROM CAPITAL EXPENDITURE

4 - GAIN FROM CAPITAL EXPENDITURE

YEAR	OPERATING SAVINGS (C - D)	DEPRECIATION (B - A)	NET OPERATING SAVINGS	AFTER TAX SAVINGS	DEPRECIATION (B - A)	INVESTMENT CREDIT	AFTER TAX CASH FLOW	PRESENT VALUE AT %
1st	$	$	$	$	$	$	$	$
2nd								
3rd								
4th								
5th								
				EST RESIDUAL VALUE				
				TOTAL				

DISCOUNTED CASH FLOW RATE OF RETURN ON INVESTMENT (AFTER TAX) ______ %

PAYBACK PERIOD (A T) YRS ______ YRS.

Note - This part of the economy study involves the use of numbers that were encountered and discussed in previous parts of the study. As they arise, these numbers will be referred to by the numerical-alphabetical designation of the space in which they were originally entered on the study form.

Operation Savings - For the "1st year" entry, use the difference 3-(C) minus 3-(D). This difference accounts for the "One-Time Associated Expense" item which is, by definition, expected to be incurred in the first year only. Enter 3-(C) for each of the remaining years of the study period if the Operating Savings is expected to remain constant. If, however, this figure is expected to change in a future year (or years) and this change can be substantiated, adjust and enter figure 3-(C) accordingly.

Depreciation - The difference 2-(B) minus 1-(A), computed for each year of the study period.

TPPC-1384CC Rev. 2 PRINTED IN U.S.A.

S. P. I. No.	EFFECTIVE DATE	SUPERSEDES		PAGE
		PAGE No.	DATE	
01-53-1 Rev. 3	3-15-70			C-3–6

Net Operating Savings - The difference (Operating Savings minus Depreciation) computed for each year of the study period.

After-Tax Savings - As an approximation, to assure uniformity of calculations, apply an assumed tax rate of 50%, yielding an annual After-Tax Savings equal to 50% of the Net Operating Savings. Note: It is not uncommon to encounter a negative Net Operating Savings figure, particularly on the first year of the economy study. The 50% tax rate should be applied, in this case representing a credit against taxes paid on other corporate earnings. Thus, the negative figure for After-Tax Savings should be equal to 50% of the negative figure for Net Operating Savings.

Depreciation - As before, the difference 2-(B) minus 1-(A), computed for each year of the study.

Investment Credit - Tax or other credit, as applicable. For current information on the subject, refer to the TRW Property Accounting Manual (SPI 01-12-1).

After-Tax Cash Flow - The total of After-Tax Savings (or loss) plus Depreciation plus any applicable Investment Credit computed for each year of the study period. Consider the net residual value of the equipment as a cash inflow at the termination of the study, which occurs at the end of the last year in the study period. The Est. Residual Value, entered on the line so designated, is the difference between the (Unamortized Amount + Est. Salvage Value) of the proposed facility and that of the present facility.

Present Value at__% - The discounted (i.e. present) value of each year's after-tax cash flow (calculated as described in Appendix C-2). When the correct discount (i.e., present value factors have been applied, the sum of the year's Present Values will equal the known value of the investment base being analyzed. If the study involves a Capital Addition (1-d), the base is the Investment Differential (2-f); if no capital addition, the base is equal to the Installed Cost (2-e).

Discounted Cash Flow Rate of Return on Investment (After-Tax) - The percentage corresponding with the present value factors used to discount each year's cash flow.

Payback Period (After-Tax) - The number of years required for the cumulative cash flow dollars to equal the investment base dollars (calculated as described in Appendix C-2).

5 - SUPLUS AVAILABILITY - Self-explanatory

5 - SURPLUS AVAILABILITY		
CAN THE PRESENT FACILITY BE CONSIDERED SURPLUS WITH THE INSTALLATION OF THE PROPOSED FACILITY? IF NO EXPLAIN	YES	NO

ENGINEERING ECONOMY STUDY - Replacement, Cost Reduction C-3-7

TPPC-1159 REV. 2 (5/69) PRINTED IN U.S.A.

DIVISION - WORKS	DEPARTMENT	PRODUCT LINE	PROJECT NO.
PROJECT DESCRIPTION	PREPARED BY DATE	DATE	INDUSTRIAL ENGINEERING MANAGER

1 - PRESENT FACILITY

a. DESCRIPTION

b. MOD/SIZE

g. USAGE

c. TP OR TRW NO.

d. DATE MFG.

e. NET VALUE

f. CAPITAL ADDITION

$ FOR YRS.

YEAR	(A) DEPRECIATION
1st	$
2nd	
3rd	
4th	
5th	
UNAMORTIZED AMOUNT	

2 - PROPOSED FACILITY

a. DESCRIPTION

b. MOD/SIZE

f. INVESTMENT DIFFERENTIAL

c. EST. USEFUL LIFE YEARS

g. USAGE

d. EST. SALVAGE VALUE

e. INSTALLED COST

$

YEAR	(B) DEPRECIATION
1st	$
2nd	
3rd	
4th	
5th	
UNAMORTIZED AMOUNT	

3 - OPERATIONAL COMPARISON

OPERATING COSTS		PRESENT		PROPOSED
DIRECT LABOR	$	$		$
INDIRECT LABOR				
SET-UP				
MATERIAL				
MAINTENANCE				
TOOLS/EXP. ITEMS				
POWER CONSUMPTION				
FLOOR SPACE				
PROPERTY TAX				
REWORK/SCRAP				
DOWNTIME				
DELETE/ADD. OPER.				
FRINGE BENEFITS				
SUB CONTRACT COSTS				
OTHERS				
INCOME LOSS				
TOTAL	$	$	$	$

(C) EXCESS OPERATING COST OF PRESENT FACILITY (PRESENT MINUS PROPOSED) $ $

(D) ONE TIME ASSOCIATED EXPENSE $ $

4 - GAIN FROM CAPITAL EXPENDITURE

YEAR	OPERATING SAVINGS (C) - (D)	DEPRECIATION (B) - (A)	NET OPERATING SAVINGS	AFTER TAX SAVINGS	DEPRECIATION (B) - (A)	INVESTMENT CREDIT	AFTER TAX CASH FLOW	PRESENT VALUE AT %
1st	$	$	$	$	$	$	$	$
2nd								
3rd								
4th								
5th								
				EST. RESIDUAL VALUE				
				TOTAL				

DISCOUNTED CASH FLOW RATE OF RETURN ON INVESTMENT (AFTER TAX) % %

PAYBACK PERIOD (A/T) YRS. YRS.

1st	$	$	$	$	$	$	$	$
2nd								
3rd								
4th								
5th								
				EST. RESIDUAL VALUE				
				TOTAL				

5 - SURPLUS AVAILABILITY

CAN THE PRESENT FACILITY BE CONSIDERED SURPLUS WITH THE INSTALLATION OF THE PROPOSED FACILITY? IF NO: EXPLAIN YES ☐ NO ☐

POST-AUDIT REPORTS

1.0 POST-AUDIT REPORTS

Post-Audit Reports are prepared for all capital expenditure appropriations over $100,000 which are submitted in any of the following engineering economy study objective categories:

Replacement, except for replacement of nonproductive equipment (e.g., boilers, roof, air conditioners)
Cost Reduction
New Product
Increased Capacity
R & D Technical Capability

The purpose of the Post-Audit Report is to compare and evaluate the results actually obtained from a project with those factors defined and estimated in the project when originated and submitted for approval. It should normally report a representative 12-month period following shakedown. Post-Audit Reports are due Staff Manufacturing Services the first working day of the eighteenth month following the project close-out date,with exceptions made on an individual basis.

A complete Post-Audit Report package consists of the following three parts:

Face Sheet Summary Form: Capital Expenditure Program - Post-Audit Report (form TPFC-1929 Rev. 2).

Engineering Economy Study Form: Depending upon the major objective category of the project, either a Replacement/Cost Reduction, New Product/Increased Capacity or R & D Technical Capability form.

Backup Data Sheets: As required.

Guidelines for the completion of these parts are included on subsequent pages of this appendix.

1.1 Face Sheet Form

A sample Capital Expenditure Program - Post-Audit Report is included at the end of this appendix. It is composed of the five following information blocks:

1. Summary of Project: A concise statement describing the salient features of the project. Included should be a brief description of the situation existing prior to the project and the major changes and advantages resulting from its completion, covering such points as the effect on operations, production, costs, quality, personnel productivity, etc. Comments should be made regarding problems encountered and solved as well as those still requiring additional work or improvement. An explanation of any significant difference between the total dollars approved for commitment and the total dollar figure at which the project was closed out should be given, as well as an explanation of any significant difference between actual dollar savings (or income from sales) and those originally estimated (or forecast). If a supplemental appropriation was submitted for additional funds, such causes as price increases, engineering changes, modifications of requirements, incomplete estimates or outright errors should be noted. Moreover, such external factors as market conditions, price changes, new contracts, and contract revisions and/or cancellations which affect the performance of the project should be described.

2. Application

A. State the acquired asset's intended use as described in the original project and also its actual application. If different, include an explanation of the specific conditions necessitating the change of application.

B. If one or more existing assets were replaced by one or more acquired in the project under audit,describe whether the replaced assets were transferred to another Division, retained as spare facilities, sold, scrapped or disposed of in some other manner. Any difference between the intended disposition stated in the original project and the actual disposition should be explained.

TPPC-1384CC Rev. 2 PRINTED IN U.S.A.

S. P. I. No.	EFFECTIVE DATE	SUPERSEDES PAGE No.	SUPERSEDES DATE	PAGE
01-53-1 Rev. 3	3-15-70			F–2

3. Performance: Note and explain any significant differences between the indicated performance factors as originally estimated and those actually attained. Where applicable, "Comments" should include the status and cost of any completed or pending modifications initiated to decrease the variance between originally estimated and actual performance.

4. Other Remarks: This space is reserved for additional comments regarding any of the foregoing questions and/or discussion of any specifics not covered elsewhere on the form.

5. Approvals: The completed Post-Audit Report should be approved by the Industrial Engineering, Works and Division Managers and signed in the spaces provided.

1.2 Engineering Economy Study Form

Post-Audit data should be submitted on the same type of Engineering Economy Study (EES) form used in the original project justification and submitted with the Capital Expenditure Appropriation form for approval. Post-Audits presented in this manner permit a direct comparison between estimated (or forecast) and actual performance.

Replacement/Cost Reduction EES forms provide green shaded spaces for the inclusion of Post-Audit data and submission of originally estimated and actual audited figures may be accomplished on a single form.

New Product/Increased Capacity EES forms should be prepared with actual audited figures entered for data covering the first year of the study period. The remaining years of the study period used in the original EES should be re-estimated to reflect the effects of revisions in sales forecasts, selling prices, market conditions, manufacturing costs and the like. A copy of the original EES should be included for submission with the audited EES.

R & D Technical Capability EES forms should be included for submission in the Post-Audit Report whenever any significant departure from the project's originally described goals, methodology or application has occurred. These departures should be specified in the text of the EES form.

1.3 Backup Data Sheets

Information, explanations or remarks which exceed the space provided on the Capital Expenditure Program - Post-Audit Report form should be continued on attached, cross-referenced backup sheets.

CAPITAL EXPENDITURE PROGRAM - POST AUDIT REPORT

TPFC 1929 REV. 2 PRINTED IN U.S.A.

DIVISION - WORKS	DEPARTMENT	PRODUCT LINE	PROJECT NO.

PROJECT DESCRIPTION	ORIGINAL APPROP.	SUPP. APPROP.	TOTAL APPROP.	CLOSE-OUT AMT.	CLOSE-OUT DATE
	$	$	$	$	

1. SUMMARY OF PROJECT

STATE EFFECT ON OPERATIONS, PRODUCTION, QUALITY, COSTS, PERSONNEL, ETC.; ALSO, EXPLAIN ANY SIGNIFICANT DIFFERENCE BETWEEN ORIGINAL APPROPRIATION AND CLOSE-OUT AMOUNT.

2. APPLICATION

A. 1. ORIGINAL INTENDED USE:

2. ACTUAL APPLICATION:

3. REASON FOR CHANGE:

B. 1. DISPOSITION OF REPLACED ITEM:

2. DATE: 3. NET SELLING PRICE $

3. PERFORMANCE

A. UTILIZATION

1. ORIGINAL FORECAST ____ HRS/SHIFT ____ SHIFTS/DAY 2. ACTUAL ____ HRS/SHIFT ____ SHIFTS/DAY
3. ORIG. ESTIMATE OF LIFE OF JOB ____ YEARS (MONTHS) 4. REVISED ESTIMATE OF LIFE OF JOB ____ YEARS (MONTHS)
5. PRODUCTIVITY: ORIGINAL ESTIMATE ____ PCS/HR. 6. ACTUAL EXPERIENCE ____ PCS/HR.

COMMENTS

4. OTHER REMARKS

5. APPROVALS

PREPARED BY	DATE	INDUSTRIAL ENGINEERING MANAGER	DATE
WORKS MANAGER	DATE	DIVISION MANAGER	DATE

Selected Reading List

Chapters to which each reference is particularly applicable are given in brackets.

Bierman, Harold, Jr., and Seymour Smidt. *The Capital Budgeting Decision.* 3rd ed. New York: Macmillan, 1971. [Chapters 6, 9, 10]

Capital Investment Series. Parts I and II. (Bound sets of reprints from the *Harvard Business Review.*) Boston: Harvard Graduate School of Business Administration, 1964, 1969. [Chapters 5, 6, 8, 9, 10, 11]

Dean, Joel. *Capital Budgeting.* New York: Columbia University Press, 1951. [Chapters 1, 2, 8]

_____. "Does Advertising Belong in the Capital Budget?" *Journal of Marketing,* Vol. 30 (October 1966), pp. 15–21. [Chapter 12]

Financial Analysis to Guide Capital Expenditure Decisions. N.A.A. Research Report 43. New York: National Association of Accountants, 1967. [Chapters 9, 11, 12]

House, William C., Jr. *Sensitivity Analysis in Making Capital Investment Decisions.* N.A.A. Research Monograph 3. New York: National Association of Accountants, 1968. [Chapter 9]

Johnson, Robert W. *Capital Budgeting.* Belmont, Calif.: Wadsworth, 1970. [Chapters 6, 9]

Lerner, Eugene M. *Managerial Finance: A Systems Approach.* New York: Harcourt Brace Jovanovich, 1971. [Chapter 1]

Miller, Ernest C. *Advanced Techniques for Strategic Planning.* AMA Research Study 104. AMA, 1971. [Chapter 9]

Murdick, Robert G., and Donald D. Deming. *The Management of Capital Expenditures.* New York: McGraw-Hill, 1968. [Chapters 8, 9]

Pflomm, Norman E. *Managing Capital Expenditures.* Studies in Business Policy 107. New York: National Industrial Conference Board, 1963. [Chapter 11]

Quirin, G. David. *The Capital Expenditure Decision.* Homewood, Ill.: Richard D. Irwin, 1967. [Chapters 2, 4, 5]

Return on Capital as a Guide to Managerial Decisions. N.A.A. Research Report 35. New York: National Association of Accountants, 1959. [Chapter 4]

Shuckett, Donald H., Harlan J. Brown, and Edward J. Mock. *Financing for Growth: Internal Expansion and Merger Techniques.* AMA, 1971. [Chapters, 9, 11]

Shuckett, Donald H., and Edward J. Mock. *Decision Strategies in Financial Management.* AMA, 1973. [Chapters 1, 9]

Solomon, Ezra, ed. *The Management of Corporate Capital.* Chicago: The Free Press of Glencoe, 1959. [Chapter 6]

Terborgh, George. *Business Investment Management.* Washington, D.C.: Machinery and Allied Products Institute and Council for Technological Advancement, 1967. [Chapter 7]

Vassilatou-Thanopoulos, Elly. *Financial Analysis Techniques for Equipment Replacement Decisions.* N.A.A. Research Monograph 1. New York: National Association of Accountants, 1965. [Chapters 3, 4, 8]

Wright, M. G. *Discounted Cash Flow.* London: McGraw-Hill, 1967. [Chapters 5, 6]

Index